JEWISH ETHICS IN A
POST-MADOFF WORLD

Jewish Ethics in a Post-Madoff World

A Case for Optimism

Moses Pava

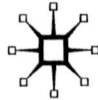

JEWISH ETHICS IN A POST-MADOFF WORLD
Copyright © Moses Pava, 2011.

All rights reserved.

First published in 2011 by
PALGRAVE MACMILLAN®
in the United States—a division of St. Martin's Press LLC,
175 Fifth Avenue, New York, NY 10010.

Where this book is distributed in the UK, Europe and the rest of the world, this is by Palgrave Macmillan, a division of Macmillan Publishers Limited, registered in England, company number 785998, of Houndmills, Basingstoke, Hampshire RG21 6XS.

Palgrave Macmillan is the global academic imprint of the above companies and has companies and representatives throughout the world.

Palgrave® and Macmillan® are registered trademarks in the United States, the United Kingdom, Europe and other countries.

ISBN: 978–0–230–11819–5

Library of Congress Cataloging-in-Publication Data

Pava, Moses L.
   Jewish ethics in a post-Madoff world : a case for optimism / Moses Pava.
     p. cm.
   ISBN 978–0–230–11819–5 (hardback)
   1. Jewish ethics. 2. Jewish way of life. I. Title.
BJ1285.2.P383 2011
296.3'6—dc23
                                                      2011016871

A catalogue record of the book is available from the British Library.

Design by Newgen Imaging Systems (P) Ltd., Chennai, India.

First edition: October 2011

10 9 8 7 6 5 4 3 2 1

Printed in the United States of America.

Contents

Part 1 Overview

Introduction: The "Castle is on Fire" — ix

1. Jewish Ethics in a New Key — 1
2. Temptations of Tradition — 27
3. Sacred Compromise — 47
4. Renewing Jewish Ethics — 67

Part 2 On the Ground

5. Learning to Speak about the Elephant in the Room — 85
6. The Art of Moral Criticism — 91
7. Deal Breaker and the Money-Laundering Rabbis — 105
8. Loving the Stranger and the Fall of Agriprocessors — 119
9. The Problem with Income and Wealth Inequalities — 137

Part 3 Frontiers

10. "The Exaltation of the Possible": Ethics and Play — 149
11. An Optimistic Case for the Future of Jewish Ethics In a Post-Madoff World — 163

Index — 201

PART 1

OVERVIEW

Introduction: The "Castle is on Fire"

> Play is entirely untrivial. God's world depends upon it.
>
> Avivah Zornberg.

This book seeks to fill a gap in the literature on religious ethics. It is written for those of us who recognize that we live in a time marked by ethical crisis, including financial thievery on an unprecedented and unfathomable level, political lobbyists who worship nothing but the dollar, kosher meat producers engaging in an orgy of unkosher activities, sexual abuse scandals, cover-ups, and cover-ups of the cover-ups. Today, the language of ethics is often cynically and purposely exploited to hide wrongdoings and to conceal misdeeds. Such abuse of our inherited ethical language destroys trust and makes it almost impossible to engage in real ethical dialogues. And, without these kinds of dialogues, ethical progress is stunted. In short, the "castle is on fire," to borrow a rabbinic phrase to which we will return in a few moments.

The intended audience for this book is those readers who are willing to examine unflinchingly, and with an open mind, the precise contours of today's ethical failures, even when such failures raise deep questions about the status of one's community and one's own taken-for-granted values. The examination called for in this book demands a kind of courageous toleration, a willingness to patiently stand still, to look and to see, listen and to hear, even when the object of our perceiving causes excruciating anxiety and challenges our very identities.

More than this, though, this book is written for those of us who intuit that it is not just those few others out there who bear responsibility for today's ethical crisis, but it is we too who must begin to acknowledge our own direct and indirect roles in creating and shaping our society and its failing mores. One of the most basic concepts in Jewish ethics is the aspiration of *kol Yisrael arevim zeh bazeh*—all Israel is responsible for one another. While we almost always pay lip service to this value at our public celebrations, when it comes to today's ethics failures, we are more inclined to point fingers at others than to own up to our own responsibilities. Are we willing, though, to avow and to acknowledge the actions of our failed leaders and to accept some level of personal and communal responsibility? Or, do we always limit responsibility to the relatively small number of specific individuals who are finally caught, charged with crimes, and found guilty in a court of law?

For some, today's ethical crisis is pushing them deeper and deeper into a parochial and nostalgic worldview. Every new disclosure proves to the fundamentalists among us how right we always, already were. If it is a financial failure, it demonstrates once again that the Jewish people are not spending enough time studying Torah and observing the ritual commandments. If it is an accusation of sexual abuse, it proves how the sexual ethos of the non-Jews has slipped into the Jewish world, even among those who have put up the highest walls. Finally, if it is a slew of accusations against the world's largest producer of kosher beef, it can only mean one thing. Anti-Semitism is rearing its ugly face once again.

For others among us, at the other extreme, the ethical crisis also proves what it is that we always, already knew. Religion and religious values are the sources of today's ills. For these people, religion evolved in a premodern context, and its values and aspirations are completely out of sync with how the world works today. Religious values are backward-looking, anachronistic, and devoid of contemporary significance. Accordingly, invoking ancient beliefs and attitudes in a completely altered environment must necessarily end in failure.

HOLDING ONTO TRADITION WITH A LIGHTER TOUCH

This book rejects both of these extreme views. It is built upon the assumption that Jewish ethics and Jewish literacy is more necessary now than ever before in Jewish history. There is a paradox here, however, that this book examines in nearly every chapter. The tighter we hold onto the inherited tradition, the less valuable it becomes as a tool to help us lead ethical and meaningful lives, in community, in real time.

We must ease up on our grip without letting go of the reins, if we are to proceed forward. Thus, the primary insight of Jewish ethics in a new key (see Chapter 1) is that we must not kill tradition by embracing it too tightly, nor must we jettison it by trying to forget it altogether. This book is most centrally about learning new and more complex ways of relating to an inherited ethical tradition grounded in religion. In my case, this is the Jewish tradition, but the hope is that the insights and lessons gleaned here will be of interest and practical use to everyone who grapples with his or her own religious tradition or traditions, in one way or another.

The new relational modes called for in this book ask us to see and to contemplate aspects of the world that we might prefer to bracket off and ignore all together. It asks us to tolerate, for a moment in time, that which we may initially code as intolerable. Apologists for the status quo assert that we already know everything we are supposed to do, but we just cannot muster the strength or the will to do it. But, there are occasions, when we are truly baffled as to how to proceed. The call for new relational modes challenges us not to change the subject when the subject itself is challenging. It suggests that much of what we think we already know about tradition may be false and illusory.

Finally, the call for new relational modes goes even deeper than this. At the extreme, it asks us to engage in a process of continuous self-reflection and self-criticism that can potentially lead to a transformation and to a self-transcendence. As we loosen our grip on tradition, we may also loosen the very way we define ourselves and conceive of our own identities. Maimonides, the great Jewish philosopher of the middle ages, noted that in true and complete *teshuva* (repentance) we become a new person, with a new identity, and even a new name. Such transformations may be rare in actual practice, but we are promised that they are not impossible.

A crisis is a moment in time when the risk of failure is high. At the same time, a crisis is an opportunity for growth and development. One should never let a good crisis go to waste. The contemporary ethical crisis in the Jewish community is an opportunity for the community and its members to reevaluate our activities, priorities, and values. Instead of trying to do what we always do, only better and more efficiently, it may be time to seriously reconsider the intelligence of what it is that we always do.

There is a famous and ancient rabbinic story about how the patriarch Abraham first "discovered" God:

> Said Rabbi Isaac, This [God's seemingly arbitrary choice of Abraham] may be compared to a man who was traveling from place to place when he saw a castle on fire. He said, "Would you say that the castle is without a lord?" The lord of the castle glanced out at him and said, "I am the lord of the castle." Similarly, because Abraham our father said, "Would you say that the world is without a master," God glanced out at him and said, "I am the master of the world." (*Bereshit Rabbah* 39:1)

This is a strange story. Why is it that the man who was traveling from place to place in this parable deduces the existence of the lord of the castle, when he sees that the castle is on fire? Might it not make more sense to conclude that, in response to the chaos and destruction of the fire, the lord of the castle has run away and abandoned his property? The point here, though, is that Abraham is given a glimpse of the possibility of order and meaning *only* because he courageously stopped to contemplate and to wonder about the significance of the chaos and destruction in front of him. Abraham's insight, at least according to my reading of this rabbinic embellishment, is that the plain reality of chaos and destruction makes sense only against a backdrop of a preexisting order and meaning. Even disorder requires a conception of order to make sense. The destructive fire, rather than leading to an attitude of pessimism and nihilism, as it easily might have, is interpreted by Abraham as a sign of life and as proof of a transcendent concern and care. "God glanced out at him and said, 'I am the master of the world.'"

The number and magnitude of the ethics failures reported on a nearly daily basis in newspapers and on the blogs are seemingly unprecedented in Jewish history. The "castle is on fire" and the question each one of us is faced with is what does all of this mean? And, is there anything we can do about it? To the extent that our reaction includes an informed, appropriate, and measured indignation, we may catch a glimpse of our own deeply felt sense of justice and fairness, order and meaning, even as it is being violated. A fiery anger in the face of gross ethics violations is a sign of life and hope for better things to come. It is precisely this felt sense of justice and fairness that we need to identify publicly, nurture, and to articulate openly through conversation and dialogue, in order to begin to take baby steps out of our shared predicament.

My suggestion in this book is that it is, in part, through a deep immersion in Jewish texts and concepts, and by exploring new and alternative ways of relating to these texts and concepts, that we will find and invent a vocabulary—nuanced, flexible, and sufficiently sensitive—to conduct such ethical dialogues, both within and between communities, in productive and useful ways. As each of the chapters in this book demonstrate, this new vocabulary will include ancient terms and concepts, borrowed from a rich and varied culture, and tweaked appropriately, to meet the needs of the present moment.

OUTLINE OF THE BOOK

Tradition, from the perspective adopted here, is neither our master nor our slave. It can be approached playfully, provocatively, patiently, mindfully, and even romantically, as argued in Chapter 1, where the major themes of this book, summarized by the phrase "Jewish ethics in a new key" are first introduced and discussed. Chapter 2 extends the overview of what is meant by this "new key" by identifying tradition's own temptations such as nostalgia, certainty, exclusivity, messianism, and several others. As in all of the chapters here, many examples from contemporary Jewish life illustrate and help to explain the major points. It turns out that many of today's Jewish ethics failures may be the result of too literal an application of the tradition rather than mere ignorance of it. Chapter 3 extends the overview by challenging the well-accepted idea that when it comes to religious ethics, compromise is impossible. In fact, the chapter argues for the existence of sacred compromise, a phrase which may seem like an oxymoron to some readers, but, surprisingly, represents a relatively common and extremely important practice in Jewish history, and is fundamental to the contemporary application of Jewish ethics to today's ethics failures. Chapter 4 concludes the overview with a clear call for the need to distinguish Jewish law and Jewish ethics. These are two related, but highly distinct perspectives, and only when joined together do they begin to give us a glimpse of our highest aspirations and deepest responsibilities. From the perspective of Jewish ethics in a new key, it is time to reinvigorate and reenergize Jewish ethics as a unique discipline.

Chapters 5–9 examine specific applications of Jewish ethics of special importance in today's environment. Instead of talking about Jewish ethics in a new key, each of these chapters attempts to engage in the practice of Jewish ethics in a new key. They are designed to provide a view from the ground up rather than from the top down. Chapter 5 challenges the popular wisdom concerning the central importance of *lashon hara* or slander in Jewish thought and practice. While the prohibition on slander certainly has a role to play in building an ethical community, it is often wrongly used by those in power as a device to stifle legitimate and useful dialogue. Chapter 6 continues the discussion on acceptable and unacceptable speech by exploring the contemporary value of rebuke or moral criticism in Jewish ethics. As the rabbis of the Talmud put it many centuries ago:

> Anyone for whom it is possible to protest the wrongdoing of a member of his or her household and does not protest, is held accountable for the wrongdoing of the members of his household. So too in relation to the members of his city; so too in relation to the whole world. (Shabbat 54b)

Chapters 7 and 8 describe the details of two notorious ethics failures in the Jewish community. Chapter 7 outlines the sad story of money-laundering rabbis in New Jersey, and the even sadder story of the strange and fantastical reactions of some in the Jewish community on hearing this news when it was first publicized. Chapter 8 explores what goes wrong when a business, in this case the largest producer of kosher beef in the world, sets aside its biblical obligation to love the stranger, in favor of maximizing profits. Chapter 9 raises the issue of the role of religion in informing questions of public policy. Specifically, this chapter examines income and wealth inequalities, and how a religiously-grounded ethics can usefully and appropriately participate and contribute to the back and forth discussions on this issue.

The last two chapters of this book explore the frontiers of Jewish ethics in a new key. Chapter 10 returns to the theme of ethics and play. It is through play that we evolve. New and challenging ways of interpreting and making meaning in the world are adopted. Perceptions are widened. New connections are made, and old ones are seen as obsolete. It is through play that we learn to suspend judgments, tolerate ambiguity, and experiment with new values. As the great Jewish philosopher and theologian Martin Buber aptly stated, "play is the exaltation of the possible." Ironically, to take Jewish ethics more seriously, we need to learn how to play with it more passionately. Lastly, Chapter 11 spells out an optimistic case for the future of Jewish ethics in a post-Madoff world, one rooted in tradition, and at the same time, fully-informed of the facts of our current situation.

THE APATHY IS ONLY A VENEER

In speaking and teaching about ethics to students, business people, and others, I often see a kind of apathy and lack of concern on people's faces. "Yes, this is all very interesting, but what does it have to do with me? Find the bad guys, punish them, and let's get back to real work." I now suspect, though, that this apathy is a thin veneer, masking a deep hunger and a burning desire to help to rebuild a better world, especially among our teenagers and college students. What is missing today is not concern and respect for others, a lack of felt responsibility, or even a passion for making things right. The fiery passion is there, even if it is hidden. I believe what is missing today are the basic abilities, skills, and vocabulary to get started and to talk openly and reasonably about ethics and the rampant ethics failures in our society. Fire can be disorderly and destructive, but when harnessed appropriately, it can be tamed to warm our homes, cook our food, and soothe our nerves.

The overarching goal of this book is to provide and model the use of new tools, a broadened vocabulary, and alternative metaphors, in order to begin to engage in meaningful and passionate dialogues about how to behave and act in ways that promote and protect our human dignity and individuality, even as we live together, productively, in community and harmony.

MEDITATING ON MADOFF: JEWISH ETHICS AS A CALL TO PUT THE HUMAN BACK INTO THE EQUATION

There is a video of Bernie Madoff participating in a roundtable discussion on financial markets that took place on October 20, 2007, about a year before Madoff's empty pyramid finally collapsed upon all of us for good. There is a temptation now, of course, to distance ourselves from Madoff and all he stood for. We rationalize to ourselves that he was an anomaly, a community outlier. But viewing this video (easily available at youtube.com/watch?v=auSfaavHDXQ) of the flawlessly groomed Madoff, sitting so comfortably in his chair, perched in the middle of the room with smiling faces everywhere, perfectly mirroring the widening and narrowing of Bernie's own smile, is a reminder of how much we all *wanted* to believe in his brand of capitalism back in October of 2007. In those days, we were dancing with Bernie, whether we were aware of this or not; he was leading and we were following.

Watch Bernie carefully as he is surrounded by fawning industry experts, bedazzled investors, loyal employees, and naïve and believing academics. He pontificates, slowly, methodically, and so quietly on his philosophy of business (you have to turn your ear to hear him), exploiting his easy, casual, and perfectly-timed, self-deprecating humor. Note to yourself that you are watching a true genius, like the power-hitting Babe Ruth, still in his prime, wowing the crowd with homerun after homerun, in the old Yankee Stadium.

To the delight and excitement of the audience, Bernie notes casually, as an aside, business is "one big turf war." But, not to worry, he assures us more boldly, "In today's regulatory environment it is virtually impossible to violate rules..." Coyly, he adds, almost as an afterthought, "this is something the public doesn't really understand." He continues, perhaps trying to convince himself as much as us, that "when you look at the scope of the trading that goes on today on Wall Street, and when you look at the infractions, they are relatively small primarily because of all of the regulations... It is impossible... for a violation to go undetected... certainly not for a considerable period of time." Although Alan Dershowitz is usually associated most strongly with the term chutzpah, perhaps viewing this roundtable discussion on Youtube will convince you that Bernie Madoff is now the reigning world champion.

At one point in the conversation, Bernie jokes about his mistake in hiring math experts from MIT to work for him as traders, following advice from his wife (who knew how involved in the business his wife was?). Bernie notes that the problem with the academics from MIT was that "They spent too much time thinking..." And, right on cue, the audience knowingly laughs along with Bernie about how impractical it is to think and do business at the same time! As we imagine ourselves transported back to 2007, as we watch this video, we should ask ourselves, would *we* have challenged such blatant anti-intellectualism? Might we have caught an insincere and telling twitch of his eyes as he regaled us with his war stories?

Having worked with him in his capacity as chairman of the Sy Syms School of Business, where I have taught for more than 20 years, and having personally heard him make similar assertions in different contexts, unfortunately I know that *I* would have missed the microscopic facial tics (recognizable to me now only if I watch the video in slow motion) and would have remained silent and intimidated in his presence.

At the time, Madoff's rhetoric and theatrical delivery were a soothing comfort. We might have been anxious, but uncle Bernie surely must have known what he was talking about. Looking back with the aid of 20–20 hindsight, though, his was a chilling message to all of us. In his exact words worth meditating upon:

"Let's take the human factor out of the equation."

"The best thing for us to do was basically to take the human being out of the equation."

"When you take the human being out of the equation you solve your regulation problems because the nature of any human being is the better deal you give the customer the worse deal it is for you."

"As honest as you try to get people to be there's this normal pull, you know, that you have to deal with. So by taking the human being out of the equation to a great extent and turning it over to a computer to make your decisions...by doing that you're able to automate the process."

"I guess you could also program the computer to violate regulations (big laughs from the audience) but we haven't gotten there yet, you know, by taking the human being out of the function..."

At one point in his conversation, Madoff asks rhetorically "What do human beings contribute to the market place?" He offers no attempt at an answer.

In recent years, philosophers have begun to point out how our thinking is constrained by the "metaphors we live by." Madoff was obsessed by a zero-sum mentality ("the nature of any human being is the better deal you give the customer the worse deal it is for you"). This most social of men, who could close a million dollar deal with a wink of an eye, was haunted by a pervasive misanthropy and lack of trust. Over and over again, he openly advised "to take the human being out of the equation." We heard the words, but to our collective shame, we failed to discern the melody beneath the words.

For Madoff, business was like a war. We know he thought this way because he stated this openly and explicitly. Listening to Bernie Madoff, given everything we now know about him, can we agree to jettison the business as war metaphor, once and for all? Can we further agree that his favorite phrase, his mantra, "taking the human being out of the equation" is literally a form of madness? The very purpose of business is to serve and promote human needs. If so, why would anyone ever want to take the human being out of this equation? Business ethics, and Jewish business ethics, in particular, must turn Madoff's philosophy on its head. The question is surely not how to take the human out of business, but how to put the human being back into business, the rest is commentary.

Jewish ethics is both a contemporary and an ancient project. As the Jewish sage Hillel famously asked, "If I am not for myself, who will be for me? And, being only for myself, what am I? And, if not now when?" These are still the questions, in whatever key they are formulated, which continue to both haunt and motivate us as both Jews and as citizens of the world.

CHAPTER 1

JEWISH ETHICS IN A NEW KEY

> Had your Torah not been my plaything, then I would have perished for my affliction.
>
> Psalms 119:92

> Oh, how I love Your Torah! All day long it is my conversation.
>
> Psalms 119:97

The purpose of this chapter, and the chapters that follow, is not to describe Jewish ethics as it existed in some imagined past or as it is now, nor is it to prescribe lists of ethical rules, principles, or rubrics. Rather this chapter is an invitation to the reader to participate in an ongoing, living, and open-ended process. The attempt here is to introduce new ways of thinking about old problems and old ways of thinking about new problems.

The goal is, to borrow a phrase from the psychoanalyst Adam Phillips, to "elicit" new metaphors and alternative images to help us think and feel our way through today's ethical dilemmas, moral conundrums, social crises, and lack of authentic faith and personal meaning (1994, p. 160). This is not a search for single solutions, permanent answers, universal truths, or knockdown arguments. It is a passionate quest for provocative questions, playful answers, new vantage points, continuous dialogues, multiple stories, and usable (and useful) models.

Perhaps the first step in ethical thinking today is to hold ourselves in check; not to quickly and cleverly resolve ethical questions, but to tolerate their complexity, to appreciate and suffer them, to explore them, and to learn how to speak about them with one another in nonreductive, interesting, and productive ways. As a general rule of thumb, the more we feel a sense of urgency to do something (anything), the more hesitant we should be to act.

We almost always prefer to deal with one ethical crisis at a time. So we focus on political, legal, business, or personal ethics, child abuse, cheating in the classroom, Ponzi schemes, whistle-blowing, and so on, searching, most of the time, for top-down solutions. This chapter is a call for an alternative approach, one that looks for conscious and unconscious connections and underlying causes. It is not that we are searching for single solutions and grand schemes (just the opposite), but that we should become more aware of the fact that every proposed solution has unforeseen side effects. As often as not, today's proposed solutions become tomorrow's intractable problems.

There is an almost overwhelming temptation today to look for mechanical solutions—clean, clever, linear, and simple—to help us solve the ethical crises we face. In fact, in many circles, the search for the optimum contract in light of conflicts between principals and agents is the *only* important *ethical* question to ask (see, for example, Jensen and Meckling, 1976 and 1994). There is a place for these kinds of mechanical solutions (often quite brilliant) based on individual utility maximization and the rational models of decision-making, but if this is all we are doing when we are doing Jewish ethics, we are squandering some significant opportunities presented by today's crises.

It is my hope to seduce the reader into imagining and seeking alternative relationships with his or her tradition or traditions. Today it is time to take ethics, Jewish or otherwise, more seriously than ever. The paradox, however, is that to do so requires us to hold onto to our ethical traditions more lightly than ever.

PLAYING WITH ETHICS

A playful attitude, when it comes to ethics, asks us to tolerate ambiguity, contingency, hypocrisy, and plain old stupidity (both our own and that of others). It asks us to become less judgmental, less knowing, less critical, and more improvisational and open to new ideas. It views ethics as imaginative, emergent, experimental, and provisional. Ethics is both a cognitive and bodily function, from this point of view.

Avivah Zornberg, in her new book, *The Murmuring Deep: Reflections on the Biblical Unconscious*, believes that the kabbalistic idea of *tzimtzum* is appropriate here:

> God withdraws from the presumption of total power and knowledge to leave *a play area in which human worlds can be created*. Gaps open up, absences, where God, apparently is not…Within that potential space, however, as worlds crystallize, they harden, become occluded, self-possessed. *Klipot* form, crusty accretions, husks, lifeless surface phenomena, dense and empty at

once. If one's world becomes constricted in this way, a kind of sorcery blocks access to other selves, within and without. Having a defined self is sanity; too densely packed, it becomes madness—without self-division, or motive for change. (2009, p. 71, emphasis added)

"Crusty accretions, husks, lifeless surface phenomena, dense and empty at once..."—are these not apt yet sad descriptions of our own ethical lives in a post-Madoff world? To recover the wellsprings of Jewish ethics, we need to rediscover Zornberg's gaps, tolerate the absences, and celebrate the potential space. If we are to revive Jewish ethics in a serious, real, and substantial way, it will require us to move into "a play area in which human worlds can be created."

To be able to play together, to possess the freedom to imagine a better world, to be able to talk openly to one another about things that really matter to us, to pursue meaning in ways that make sense to us, to include everyone inside the loving circle of ethics, means to make and accept mistakes and errors. The rabbis of the Talmud captured this when they stated, "One never gets the true sense of the words of Torah except after mistakes." As Zornberg explains this, "Stumbling, slipping becomes the condition for stability. It is by way of errors, misconceptions, inadequacies that one moves beyond the banality of first assumptions" (2009, p. 75).

To think about ethics in a more playful way is a tall order. It is counterintuitive in today's world. Is it possible, for example, to teach high school students to make more and better mistakes rather than fewer? Is there time enough, in competitive global markets, to allow college students to explore many different disciplines and areas of potential interest before locking in on a single chosen profession? Is it conceivable to hire employees and then let them play? Principals, teachers, deans, and managers will necessarily respond to these seemingly odd requests: "Yes... but how does one measure the effectiveness of play?"

We live in a culture that worships outsize heroes, and that compensates doers and schemers rather than thinkers and dreamers. Playfulness calls for a strange kind of courage—not the kind of one-dimensional courage one relies on in war and battle—but the kind of complex courage displayed by comics, artists, musicians, and cultural critics. It is the courage to chance appearing weird, slow, odd, and different in front of those who speak so knowingly and with such certainty exclusively in support of the status quo. Playfulness includes a tolerance for ambiguity, complexity, contradictions, and uncertainty. It is built upon "the turbulence of, at best, a partially known self" (Zornberg, 2009, p. 19). It calls for curiosity, forgiveness, humor, and wonder, even while others around us are eager to decide and to move on with business as usual. It is through play that we find the space to grow and to evolve over time.

I believe that the call of the hour is for a Jewish ethics in a new key. This is a call not only for a change in behavior, but a change in consciousness. It asks for a reevaluation of values, and a playful opening up of our beliefs, our ways of relating to self and to others, and to set habits. As Zornberg put it in the above quote, "Having a defined self is sanity; too densely packed, it becomes madness..."

Further, Jewish ethics in a new key is not just a call for a change in consciousness, but it is a call for a change in cultural expectations, as well. We need new kinds of heroes, the plain and everyday ones who show up to work on time, "people who choose responsible, behind-the-scenes action over public heroism to resolve tough leadership challenges" and who, in Joseph Badaracco's sensible phrase, "lead quietly" (Badaracco, 2002). We need heroes who engage in open and frank dialogue with one another and who recognize that it is through such dialogues, in a democracy, that ethics is explored, identified, interpreted, and ultimately, legitimated (Pava, 2009). If we begin to believe with Zornberg and her kabbalistic teachers that it is possible for God to withdraw "from the presumption of total power and knowledge," can we not also start to imagine that it is possible for ourselves to withdraw from these same presumptions?

Woody Allen, playing Alvy Singer in *Annie Hall*, tells the following joke:

> This guy goes to a psychiatrist and says, "Doc, uh, my brother's crazy, he thinks he's a chicken," and uh, the doctor says, "well why don't you turn him in?" And the guy says, "I would, but I need the eggs." Well, I guess that's pretty much now how I feel about relationships. You know, they're totally irrational and crazy and absurd and, but uh, I guess we keep going through it...because...most of us need the eggs. (As quoted at http://www.whysanity.net/monos/annie.html)

Well, I guess that's pretty much how I sometimes feel about the possibility of a playful Jewish ethics, too. At the end of the day, will we ever really grow into a new consciousness? Can we really alter cultural expectations? And, will we obtain the almost magical "access to other selves, within and without..." implicitly promised by Zornberg? Why not just abandon the paradoxes and seemingly impossible promises of Jewish ethics in favor of more mature, mundane, realistic, and reachable goals? Perhaps, like Alvy Singer, though, we need the eggs.

Some critics might suggest that it is inappropriate to combine ethics and play (eggs or no eggs). To these critics, it is a kind of contemporary *shatnaz*, an inappropriate and combustible mixture. I suggest however, that an ethical philosophy that is certain in its beliefs, completely realistic in its aspirations, total in its coverage, absolute in its faith, and purposely devoid of humor is a far darker and scarier scenario to contemplate.

Asking Provocative Questions

Jewish ethics in a new key is playful, but it also must be provocative. Its intention is to push the envelope. We need to figure out how to ask better and more critical questions of ourselves and others. Even as we faithfully teach the tradition to a new generation of students, we must alert them that "the very possibility of interpretation arises when language holds more than one possible meaning" (Zornberg, 2009, p. 19). We must learn how to encourage students not only to rehearse the familiar and comfortable questions that we already have the answers to, but we must support them in formulating their own questions, those unofficial, strange, and unscripted questions that push all of us forward.

I believe that there is an ancient art to asking provocative questions in a constructive way, from inside the tradition. How do we proceed, for example, when we intuit a clash between the minutiae of the law and its larger purposes? How does one raise questions when one senses deep contradictions between the spirit of the law and the practical consequences of its everyday applications? How does one critique a culture that one loves when one comes to believe that some of its laws, rituals, and morals are now serving the interests of the powerful and entrenched, and has become blind and deaf to the needs of the less powerful and the less well-placed?

Consider the biblical case of Korah's rebellion. On the surface, this narrative reads like a straightforward conflict between right and wrong. Moses's first cousin and second fiddle is painted as a disgruntled opportunist who uses the unfortunate circumstances of the aftermath of the sin of the spies to foment a rebellion against Moses and Aaron for his own personal gain and glory.

Korah and his followers "stood before Moses with two hundred and fifty men from the children of Israel, leaders of the assembly... men of renown. They gathered together against Moses and against Aaron and said to them, 'It is too much for you! For the entire assembly—all of them— are holy and God is among them; why do you exalt yourselves over the congregation of God?'" (Numbers 16: 2–3).

Korah's attempted rebellion, according to the text of the Torah, is put down quickly, publicly, and decisively. We read:

> The ground that was under them split open. The earth opened its mouth and swallowed them and their household, and all the people who were with Korah, and the entire wealth. They and all that was theirs descended alive to the pit; the earth covered them over and they were lost from among the congregation. All Israel that was around them fled at their sound, for they said, "Lest the earth swallow us!" (Numbers 16: 31–34)

At first glance, the book on Korah is (quite literally) open and shut.

The rabbis of the Talmud, however, read more into this story than meets the eye. There are several creative embellishments that imagine Korah asking Moses rabbinic-style questions and trying to get the better of Moses and Aaron. One such midrash has Korah telling the following challenging story to the entire congregation of Israel:

> In my [Korah's] neighborhood there was a widow, and with her were her two fatherless daughters. The widow had only one field, and when she was about to plow, Moses said to her, "Thou shalt not plow with an ox and an ass together" [Deut. 22:10]. When she was about to sow, Moses said to her, "thou shalt not sow thy field with two kinds of seed" [Lev. 19:19]. When she was to reap the harvest and stack the sheaves, Moses said to her, "Thou shalt not harvest the gleanings, the overlooked sheaves, and the corners of the field" [cf. Lev. 19:9; Deut. 24:19]. When she was about to bring the harvest into the granary, Moses said to her, "Give heave offering, first tithe, and second tithe." She submitted to the law and gave them to him. What did the poor woman do then? She sold the field and bought two sheep, so that she might clothe herself in the wool shorn from them and profit by the production of lambs. As soon as the sheep brought forth their young, Aaron came and said to the widow, "Give me the firstling males, for this is what the Holy One said to me, 'All the firstling males that are born of thy herd and of thy flock thou shalt sanctify unto the Lord thy God'" [Deut. 15:19].

Korah's imagined story does not end here. Aaron comes back again and again, asking for the first portion of the shearing, and finally carrying the sheep away leaving the widow "weeping—her and her two daughters" (as quoted in Bialik and Ravnitzky, 1992, p. 92).

According to the rabbis, "Korah was a scorner and spoke in scorn against Moses and Aaron." But, wait a moment. To whom does this story really belong? It is true that the rabbis are putting this story into Korah's mouth, but are not the rabbis the true authors of this story and the originators and protectors of these "scornful" thoughts? Are not the rabbis just using Korah as a ventriloquist might use a dummy? To the extent that we read this story as raising real and provocative questions about the justice and fairness of God's law (and, how else can we read this story?), it is not Korah who asks these questions at all, but we ourselves imagining that it is Korah.

Can we allow ourselves to become a tiny bit more self-conscious about our own doubts and questions, especially when we don't have all the answers? Can we use the example and precedent of this rabbinic midrash, a midrash that perhaps picks up on the partial truth of Korah's legitimate democratic instincts ("—all of them—are holy and God is among them") to express our own uncertainties and ambivalences? Is Rabbi Nilton Bonder correct when he writes in his illuminating book *Our Immoral Soul,* that "it is necessary to err, transgress, and violate the status quo in order to achieve a transcendence that is secretly desired by the very tradition that has been betrayed"? (2001, p. 10) It is well to remind ourselves that Korah's own sons survive Korah's rebellion and go down in Jewish history as heroes and psalmists, while no one ever hears again about Moses's sons and descendants. In fact, the prophet Samuel, one of the great leaders of the Jewish people, is described in the Book of Chronicles, as a direct descendant of Korah.

Sometimes we would like it if our traditions were monolithic and spoke with a single, self-interpreting, and simple voice. But, traditions are more complex than this. As Avivah Zornberg would have it, we need to learn how to listen not only to the conscious mind of the Torah, but to the unconscious mind, as well. In perhaps her boldest formulation to date, Zornberg suggests that if God "is to be intimately connected to human beings, His messages cannot be transparent to Himself, even as their meanings transcend the comprehension of those for whom they are intended" (2009, p. 32).

The kind of Jewish ethics that we need for today's world requires us to listen more deeply to widows, single mothers, orphans, foreign workers, and all of those victims whose voices have been silenced, and forgotten. It calls upon us to view ourselves simultaneously as both consummate insiders and masters of the law, on the one hand, and as ignored outsiders and powerless strangers, on the other hand. "The self, is at the very least, double: one self to think with and one to think about" (Zornberg, 2009, p. 16). As Moses himself cries out in a poignant and powerful moment of self-revelation, "I have been a stranger in a strange land" (Exodus 2:22).

ROMANCING THE TEXT

> In play we manifest fresh, interactive ways of relating with people, animals, things, ideas, images, ourselves. It flies in the face of social hierarchies. We toss together elements that were formerly separate. Our actions take on novel consequences. To play is to free ourselves from arbitrary restrictions and expand our field of action. Our play fosters richness of response and adaptive flexibility... By reinterpreting reality and begetting novelty, we keep from becoming rigid. Play enables us to rearrange our capacities and our very identity so that they can be used in unforeseen ways.
> Nachmanovitch, 1990, p. 43.

Sometimes, when I am studying by myself, speaking about Jewish ethics with others, or teaching undergraduate students, I wonder if we, as a community, have lost a kind of special zeal, a unique relationship to ethics that in other historical periods seemed to be our natural inheritance. For sure, there always remains a deep familiarity, a respect, and even a comfort in what we are reading or saying. But there is also a repetitiveness, a knowingness, the same old questions and answers over and over, and, I wonder to myself, what happened to the passion? Is the desire still real, or are we merely going through the mechanical motions of study and speech?

Each day we recite the words of the *Shema* prayer, "You shall love the Lord your God, with all your heart, with all your soul, and with all your might" (Deuteronomy). Jewish ethics in a new key is nothing if it is not passionate, and even romantic."The more zeroing of self, the more 'room' for light and fire" as Michael Eigen has put it in his book, *Ecstasy* (2001, p. 97) .

To regain our ethical footing, we need to learn new ways of relating to our inherited tradition and texts. For some of us, some of the time, this means moving closer to traditional sources and ancient texts and seeing them for the first time. For others, this means moving away, extricating ourselves from our own education and upbringing, looking elsewhere for a time, and coming back to tradition with fresh eyes, a second naiveté (Kula, 2006)." There can be no tradition without betrayal, nor betrayal without a tradition (Bonder, 2001, p. 11).

Here is how the ancient rabbis conceived of the power and energy of Torah study at its most profound:

> Ben Azzai was sitting and expounding and fire was burning around him. They went and said to Rabbi Akiva: Our master, Ben Azzai is sitting and expounding and fire is burning around him! He went to him and said to him: I have heard that you were sitting and expounding and fire was burning around you. He said to him: Yes. He said to him: Perhaps you were engaged in "esoteric ideas of Torah?" He said to him: No, rather, I was sitting and stringing words of Torah together, and from Torah to Prophets, and from Prophets to Writings, and the words were as joyous as when they were given on Sinai, and were as sweet as the root of their being given. And wasn't the root of their being given with fire?

Can we recapture Ben Azzai's fire today by "stringing words of Torah together"?

Stephen A. Mitchell is one of the founders of the relational school of psychoanalysis.[1] He asks an analogous question in his brilliant book *Can Love Last? The Fate of Romance Over Time*. Mitchell's focus, as a practicing psychoanalyst, is on interpersonal relationships, but his insights spill beyond these boundaries. According to Mitchell, each of us possesses an almost wired-in sense of home." It is difficult for me to imagine a person—or a human culture, for that matter—who doesn't orient himself around some sense of home: my place, where I am from, where I belong, where I long to return" (Mitchell, 2002, p. 36). At the same time, however, Mitchell notes that there is also a kind of push away from home."Homes turn into prisons; enclosures become confinements..." (p. 38). Mitchell elaborates:

> There seems to be a fundamental contrast between the ordinary and the transcendent, safety and adventure, the familiar and the novel that runs throughout human experience. Scholars of comparative religion, such as Mircea Eliade, have written of the distinction between the profane and the sacred; theories of cognitive development, such as those of Jean Piaget, stress the dialectic between *assimilation* of new stimuli to established schemata and *accommodation* of those schemata to new stimuli… Each of these dichotomies points to fundamental, conflictual, human needs: on the one hand, a need for a grounding that feels completely known and predictable, a reliable anchoring, a framework, as Erich Fromm put it, for "orientation and devotion"; on the other hand, a longing to break out of established and familiar patterns, to step over boundaries, to encounter something unpredictable, awe-inspiring, or uncanny (pp. 38–39, emphasis in original).

It is the energy created through the rubbing together of these two contradictory impulses that sparks and fuels romantic love in interpersonal relationships. When it comes to love, we want to eat our cake and have it, too.

Over time, however, for many (if not most) couples, romantic passion dissipates. Familiarity swallows novelty, orientation and devotion kill the unpredictable and the awe-inspiring. The usual explanation for this is that over the course of a long relationship partners learn everything there is to know about each other. After just a few short years, there are no more strange surprises." The obvious solution in this traditional account is renunciation: the rationality of adult maturity must triumph over the illusions of infantile fantasy. The ill-fated lover is enjoined to grow up and rededicate himself to the drab, predictable familiarity of his ordinary life!" (Mitchell, p. 43).

Mitchell, however, points out that while this prevailing story contains a kernel of truth, it is not the only plausible description of events nor does it provide the best prescription for how to proceed. According to Mitchell's unorthodox view, the sense of safety and security that one feels with one's partner is not a natural outgrowth of years of living together, but is itself a kind of fantasy. Mitchell would surely agree with Cristina Nehring that "to love is to risk. We do not always know how much… we are launching into a free fall; it can be ecstatic or deadly, depending on factors only partly under our control. We are the more vulnerable for being more feelingful; the more vulnerable for being more courageous; the more vulnerable for having a fine temperament" (2009, p. 144).

We tell ourselves and we reassure ourselves that we know everything there is to know about each other, but to what extent is that really the case? Mitchell writes, "I have invariably discovered that the sense of safety is not a given but a construction, the familiarity not based on deep mutual knowledge but on collusive contrivance, the predictability not an actuality but an elaborate fantasy" (p. 43). It is not that there are no more surprises; it is that together we *pretend* there are no more surprises.

How well do we know *each other*? Or, for that matter, how well do we know *ourselves*? From Mitchell's point of view, the interesting question to ask about long-term couples is not what happened to adventure, risk, and passion, over time, but rather how do we "deceive" ourselves into thinking we know so much more than we really do about one another? And, is there anything that we can do about this?

There are certain kinds of knowing that are coercive and detrimental, according to Mitchell. They "strive to fix the fluidity and multiplicity of the other into a predictable pattern. This form of knowing kills romantic passion, and this is a kind of knowing that is very prevalent in long-term relationships. It has strong appeal. It seems to be security-enhancing. But it is coercive and illusory" (p. 45). I suggest that similar dynamics are at work in all kinds of relationships.

To the extent that we strive to fix religious traditions as our points of "orientation and devotion," it is conceivable that we begin to collude with one another into thinking we know and understand inherited traditions and traditional texts better than we really do. We possess a strong psychological need to feel safe and secure, to extinguish Ben Azzai's fire as fast as possible, and thus to tame tradition by declawing it.

In many ways, many of us obtain this highly sought-after feeling of at-homeness living within a religious tradition, familiar since birth. We do so, however, by agreeing (consciously or unconsciously) to ignore the strange and by bracketing off the unfamiliar and challenging in our own traditions and texts. The problem with this approach (if there is a problem at all) is that when we fix the meaning and multiplicity of the text, we sacrifice the passion and excitement that comes from real learning and accommodating ourselves to that which is foreign. Motivation and desire are diminished. The heady and transcendent feeling of "surrender" in the presence of the text is forfeited (Ghent, 1990). Study becomes a dull and dreaded routine, when it might have been a highly desirable and novel adventure. Teaching and learning can easily (and often do) slip into a coercive relationship, when teachers begin to force students to "accept" the official and politically preferred meanings. In seeking the safety of the same, we celebrate the status quo, while the paths to transformation and to new identities are boarded-up and locked closed.

To counter this tendency is first to recognize that our knowingness, seemingly so real, is often an illusory construction. As Emerson wrote, "No truth so sublime but it may be trivial tomorrow in light of new thoughts." We can, if we so choose, begin to *romance the text*. This means:

- Search not only for what is familiar and soothing in our tradition, but actively seek what is strange and different.

- Recognize that even the borders, separating what is inside the tradition and from what is outside the tradition, are often vague, ambiguous, and contested.
- Remind ourselves that traditions contain many, and often conflicting, voices, and at the very same time, they are fragmentary rather than complete, like a book with missing pages. Traditionally, women's voices (among others) have generally been silenced and/or edited out.
- Listen better and playfully reconstruct these seemingly lost voices in constructive and provocative ways as many feminist scholars have been doing for several decades (see, for example, Adler, 1998; Bal, 1987, 2008; Boyarin, 1993; Greenberg, 1981; Plaskow, 1990, and Ross, 2004, among many others).
- Emphasize that all attempts at closure are always a kind of fiction, trying to wrap things up prematurely. "There is always another story, one we haven't necessarily bargained for" (Phillips, 1994, p. xxv). In romancing the text, all endings are temporary endings, good enough for the time being.
- Make your own novel contributions. Traditions are works-in-process, partially built monuments, awaiting our own active voices.
- Participate in ethical dialogues, remembering that it is only through open communication that ethics is interpreted and legitimated.

The goal in romancing the text is to find just enough security and safety in order to grow and to develop. "It asks us to take a giant leap precisely at the times when we find ourselves most immobilized by fear" (Starr, 2008, p. 65). Its point is to take Jewish ethics more seriously precisely by holding on to it more lightly. This approach strives to *idealize* the tradition without *idolizing* it. It seeks to broaden the boundaries and possibilities of tradition by making the familiar strange and the strange more familiar. Romancing the text is not without its self-constructed fantasies and risks. But it seeks to willingly and self-consciously exploit our imaginative capacities in order to ignite passion, desire, and a motivation for the excitement and pleasures of living an ethical life in the community.

LOVING THE STRANGER

"The stranger that sojourns with you shall be unto you as the homeborn among you, and you shall love him as yourself; for you were strangers in the land of Egypt" (Leviticus 19:34). This mitzvah, although traditionally interpreted in a relatively narrow and specific way, can be reimagined as a dynamic and generative principle, seeking to challenge the status quo and to provoke growth and change.

Consider the biblical story of Ruth as a powerful example of how this mitzvah, at its best, might work. Philip Birnbaum describes the Book of Ruth as follows:

> The narrative is one of idyllic beauty. It is the most charming short story in the Bible. It presents a pleasing picture of life in Eretz Yisrel during the period of the Judges, about two generations before King David. Approximately two-thirds of the narrative is in dialogue. The principal characters of the story are amiable, courteous, unassuming. They all show how a religious spirit may pervade the conduct of daily life. (Birnbaum, 1973, p. vii)

In this brief description, however, Birnbaum merely skims the surface of this text.

Bubbling up beneath the idyllic beauty and charm of this all-too familiar, Hebrew-school version of the story, is a much more complex narrative. It includes famine, exile, and the sudden and unexplained deaths of Elimelech, Machlon, and Chilion. It describes the deep depression of Naomi—"Call me Mara for the Lord has made it very bitter for me." There is Ruth's willingness to surrender her existing relationships to her parents and to her native land and come to a people that she "did not know before." There is the pure contingency of Ruth who "happened to come upon that part of the field which belonged to Boaz, of the family of Elimelech."

Further, there is the mysterious and overwhelming kindness and desire on Ruth's part to cling to her mother-in-law. In the most famous and unforgettable lines of the book, we read some of the most passionate words of the Bible:

> Wherever you go, I will go: wherever you stay, I will stay; your people shall be my people, and your God shall be my God; wherever you die, I will die, and there I will be buried.

In Avivah Zornberg's words, it is here that Ruth "commits herself to the unmitigated rigors of her desire" (2009, p. 358).

Finally, and most importantly for present purposes, there is the unasked question of the text, driving the entire narrative, of how it is even possible for Ruth to enter into the covenantal community and for Boaz to marry "Ruth the Moabitess," a marriage seemingly prohibited explicitly by Mosaic law. Ruth herself is baffled by this thought and she asks Boaz directly, "Why have I found favor in your eyes to recognize me, though I am a stranger?"

Avivah Zornberg elaborates on the complexities of this text:

> In her *stickiness*—her passionate desire, her bold modesty—Ruth poses a disconcerting challenge to the world of Bethlehem. On the one hand, she is

obedient, malleable: according to the midrash, she is submissive to all the legal stringencies with which Naomi tries to deter her... On the other hand, her very existence challenges the imaginative boundaries that have defined the world she desires to penetrate... we can say that it is precisely this complexity that arouses hostility and suspicion in a solidly demarcated world. As one who *clings*—serially, to Naomi, to the servants in the field, to Boaz during the night on the granary floor—Ruth is perceived as disturbingly anomalous. (2009, pp. 365–366)

While the text of Ruth ignores the normative question, the rabbis of the midrash seize upon it. This should not be surprising at all as King David's legitimacy and, in turn, the future Messiah's legitimacy, hinge upon the legality of Boaz and Ruth's marriage.

> And Doeg the Edomite was present at that time, and he said, "Even if he [David] is a descendant of Perez, is he not of impure descent? Is he not a descendant of Ruth the Moabitess?" Avner said to him, "But has the law not been revised: Ammonite but not Ammonitess, Moabite but not Moabitess?" He answered to him: "But if so, we could also say Edomite but not Edomitess, Egyptian men but not Egyptian women? Why were the men repudiated? Was it not 'because they did not meet you with bread and water'? (Deut. 23:5) The women ought to have met the women!" And for the moment, Avner forgot the law.

> Saul said to him, "Go and inquire about that law which you have forgotten from Samuel and his court." When he came to Samuel and his court, he said, "Where did this come from? Not from Doeg? Doeg is a heretic and will not leave this world in peace! And yet I cannot let you go without an answer: 'All glorious is the king's daughter within the palace' (Ps. 45:14)—It is not for a woman to go out and bring food, but only for a man. 'And because they hired Balaam against you' (Deut. 17:5)—a man hires, but not a woman."

It is the disturbing anomaly of Ruth's "stickiness," her *chesed* [kindness], and modesty, which finally force the tradition to take note of the claims of this stranger. "This interpretation was never made until Ruth came on the scene; she is the first Moabite woman to benefit from this change in the law" (Zornberg, 2009, p. 361).

Is she *in* or is she *out*? And, why bother to "revise" the law for Ruth the Moabitess? Ruth, as an individual, bears almost no resemblance to her biblical progenitors who in their stinginess refused to meet the Israelites with bread and water, and in their immodesty tried to ensnare them. Her singular piety and devotion coupled with her openness and courage are unnerving and challenging to the original biblical stereotypes and to the status quo categories. Her kindness, as defined by Phillips and Taylor (2009) as "the ability to bear the vulnerability of others, and therefore of oneself..." (p. 8), might have been wrongly interpreted as a weakness. Boaz and Ruth, however, eventually understand this as her great strength. But, even so, how does an ethical tradition expand? I believe, first, that it is by the "bold modesty" of self-reflexively recognizing its own limitations. Second, it is by recognizing each person as an entire world, and tolerating their fantasies, but more than tolerating, from time to time, playfully entering into their fantasies and elaborating upon them together. Finally, the tradition endures and expands by taking risks in the face of uncertainty—"Wherever you go, I will go..."

Taking the tradition more seriously, as we must begin to do today, if we are to do Jewish ethics in a new key, requires us to hold on to it more lightly. In the case of Ruth, this meant creatively reinterpreting the inherited text to fit the contingencies of the real world, despite the social resistance that was still felt, even generations later in the time of David. In the end, Ruth is read into the tradition because the tradition itself, from time to time, is able to expand and live up to its very highest aspirations. "The stranger that sojourns with you shall be unto you as the homeborn among you, and you shall love him as yourself; for you were strangers in the land of Egypt" (Leviticus 19:34). It is through Ruth's desire, the dangerous act of Boaz choosing to love the stranger, and the tradition's ultimate endorsement of his choice that Judaism revitalizes and regenerates itself. In loving the stranger, the seeds for the Messiah are planted. Ruth's story is not a quaint and nostalgic story, but it is a cutting edge, paradigmatic narrative pregnant still with untapped meaning for our own purposes.

Phillip Birnbaum oversimplifies when he describes the story as charming and the principal characters as amiable, courteous, and unassuming. He is correct, however, perhaps for reasons he himself did not quite consciously comprehend, when he states that "They all show how a religious spirit may pervade the conduct of daily life."

TOLERATING THE COMPLEXITY

Adam Phillips asks, "What would it be like to live in a world in which people welcomed their own, and therefore other people's complication; in which people did not allow their children to be simplified by conventional education, or coercive belief systems? Traditionally the numinous thing has been to simplify the moral life" (1994, p. 160).

We read about the Boeskys, Abramoffs, Spitzers, Madoffs, and so many others with an almost perverse and smug satisfaction. We think to ourselves how different we are from these people. But, don't we really know that Bernie Madoff, for example, was not acting alone? He, as we all do, had his many enablers. There are those who invested with Madoff almost certainly knowing that all was not kosher, but assumed that they were earning real profits with inside information or by front-running. There are others who invested other people's money with him and did not engage in the due diligence their position of responsibility required (Pava, 2008). While I am not suggesting that we let criminals off the hook, I am suggesting that we need to realize that there is often more that connects us to these people than separates us. We are all complex beings with multiple and contradictory motivations, both conscious and unconscious. Who knows how any one of us would act, if given the right (or wrong) set of circumstances?

If, in the past, Phillips is correct and there has been a tendency "to simplify the moral life," Jewish ethics in a new key questions the effectiveness of this strategy. Traditionally, we take so much pride, particularly those among us calling for "moral clarity," in the fact that our forefather Jacob is described in Genesis "as a simple man [*eesh tam*] dwelling in tents," especially when we compare this to how the Bible describes his twin brother Esau's character, "one who knows trapping, a man of the field" (Genesis 25: 27).

Jacob is the truthful son, the opposite of his older brother Esau. "However," Avivah Zornberg notes, "to be a *tam*—whole, simple innocent, sincere—may eventually be felt to restrict a richer consciousness of self" (2009, p. 287). And, in fact, we see that within a few short verses, Jacob is already banging up against the preset boundaries of his own youthful identity. Jacob, responding to his father's question about who he is, answers flatly "I am Esau your firstborn." When Esau, expecting to receive Isaac's blessing, returns from his successful hunt just a few moments later, Isaac explains to him that "Your brother came in guile [*mirmah*] and took your blessing." Rashi, the preeminent Jewish biblical commentator, however, rejects the literal interpretation of *mirmah* [guile] and explains that Isaac is telling Esau (and the reader) that Jacob came in "wisdom and cleverness." Zornberg, provides an insightful and thought-provoking extension:

> Jacob has adopted the improvisational mode of language in order to elaborate his own repertoire of identity; "I am Esau your firstborn" is spoken with a new and perilous ambition of self-creation. The unequivocal innocence and sincerity of an earlier stage yields to a more complex struggle for authenticity. The Sages strikingly express the moral and developmental issue: "When *chochmah* [wisdom] enters a person, cunning enters with it." If Jacob is to move from simplicity to wisdom, his identity, his *anokhi* [his I], will have to be exposed to the duplicities, the improvisations of consciousness. No longer all of a piece, he will bring imagination and desire to bear on shaping a self that may often seem incoherent, troubling, enigmatic... the dynamic sense of *anokhi*, the instinct to elaborate himself, can no longer be denied. (2009, pp. 287–288)

Can we not assume that we, too, "are no longer all of a piece?" Can we not generalize from this that if *we* are to move from simplicity to wisdom, our identities will have to be exposed to duplicities, *we* will need to bring imagination and desire to bear on shaping a new self, and *we* too can no longer deny the instinct to elaborate ourselves. In short, we will need to accept much more complex versions of ourselves than we are perhaps used to.

Rabbi Irwin Kula describes all of this with the striking phrase "sacred messiness." He elaborates, using ancient biblical imagery, on the complexities of living an ethical life in our postmodern world and what this entails:

> In Hebrew the opposite of holy is *chol*, which is translated not as "profane" but as "empty"; in other words, "not yet filled." The word for holy in Hebrew is *kedusha*. A more accurate translation of *kedusha* is "life intensity." To be holy is to be intensely dynamic, ever-changing, and ever-realizing. The Biblical command "You shall Be Holy" is an invitation to celebrate what philosopher Mark Taylor calls "a maze of grace that is the world." Live as richly and passionately as possible; that's as close to meaning as you will get. And the *messes* are the point. (2006, p. 45, emphasis added)

One of the lessons, from both Zornberg's and Kula's imaginative reading of tradition, I suggest, is that Jewish ethics, both its processes and its contents, needs to be at least as complex and as messy as the world in which we operate.

Not everyone agrees with this emerging viewpoint. Natan Sharansky, in his book, *Defending Identity*, for example, celebrates the fixed and concrete nature of identity, rather than its more fluid aspects. In his view, identity is not about self-creation, but is a sincere discovery of what is already there. He writes, "I discovered that only by embracing who I am—by going back to the *shtetl*, by connecting to my own people...could I stand with others (Sharansky and Wolosky, 2008, p. 15) The goal, in his view, is not to cultivate complex identities, nor to hold onto ourselves more lightly, but to possess "strong identities." Such identities provide us with the necessary "barriers" separating individuals and ethnic groups from one another.

One of Sharansky's favorite and often repeated metaphors throughout the book is to view identity as the "armor" that protects us from "our" enemies. He warns, for example, "A society that abandons identity sheds its protective armor..." (2008, p. 205). Not surprisingly, Sharansky views international hostilities as grounded in fixed and unchanging ideologies rooted deeply in the mists of history. In his view, it is useless or worse to try to understand "the underlying reasons for the hostility" or to address stated "grievances" (p. 94). "Focusing on grievances rather than ideology creates a basis for cooperation between two forces *that should be inherently inimical to each other*" (2008, p. 94, emphasis added). Dialogues and conflict-resolution groups, according to Sharansky's view, are the naïve and dangerous fantasies of those "useful idiots" (p. 62) advocating "a post-identity" position (p. 67).

I did not choose Sharansky here as a straw man to easily defeat. In fact, in other writings, I have described him as a contemporary Jewish hero (Pava, 2006). There is much to agree with in Sharansky's book. First, and most importantly, I wholeheartedly endorse his attempt to find a strong and authentic voice for religion in the public sphere. I, too, believe with him that such a voice can potentially be a positive source to support and to undergird democratic institutions. Second, his seemingly full endorsement of pluralism is a view I share. In addition, Sharansky is clear that "where democratic norms and identity have clashed, *identity must give way* (2008, p. 133, emphasis added).

In the end, I do not think that Sharansky's view is completely wrong. In fact, he paints a plausible view of ethics, appropriate for survival in the Soviet Gulag, and in other extreme situations. Sharansky's mistake is to insist that his view of ethics is the only appropriate one.

Sharansky, himself, once wrote in his brilliant memoir, *Fear No Evil*, how difficult the transition from life in the Soviet Union to life in Israel was for him. In words worth meditating upon, Sharansky said that he "soon learned that defending one's freedom in the ocean of love can be no less challenging than defending it in the sea of hatred" (1988, p. 419). No less demanding, but I imagine it calls for a much more complex approach. In the sea of love, to conceive of one's identity as protective armor, is a sure recipe for failure. Stephen Mitchell has written that "each of has become a kind of variegated psychic community. Being a person seems now to be much more complicated and involving than ever before; it requires discovering ourselves as well as shaping ourselves, exploring ourselves as well as controlling ourselves" (2002, p. 24). From this point of view, we are "multiplicitous" (2002, p. 24). It is worth contemplating, at least, whether or not identities might not only be usefully compared to armor but usefully compared to connecting-bridges, as well.

Sharansky oversimplifies by choosing to compare his own views only with the most extreme views of those who disagree with him. In a complex world such as ours, we must recognize that there exists a menu of options that we must choose from. This is why we cannot give up on dialogue and conflict-resolution groups, as quickly as Sharansky would have us do. I side with the contemporary Israeli novelist David Grossman when he notes, "But even if we are doomed to years of violence and animosity, to fragile peace agreements that will be violated over and over again, we must keep creating an alternative. We must reiterate the possibility, denied and repudiated today, of peaceful coexistence" (2003, p. x).

We can no longer afford the luxury of assuming that there are ideologies that "should be inherently inimical to each other." *Should be?* From whose point of view? Even if today we cannot find a way to love the stranger yet, we must, from a Jewish ethics point of view, continue searching. Identities can be too strong. When we start acting on the belief that there is "meaning beyond life itself" (Sharansky, 2008, p. 5), we have transgressed one of Judaism's most sacrosanct ethical principles—"Now choose life so you and your children may live" (Deuteronomy 30:19). To violate this principle even unconsciously, when we already know better, is unconscionable.

"What would it be like to live in a world in which people welcomed their own, and therefore other people's complication?" Adam Phillips asks. To be honest, we don't know the answer to this question yet. Perhaps, though, to promote the quest to locate an authenticity beyond mere sincerity, it might be worth our time to find out.

Living in the Moment

> Habit devours everything, objects, clothes, furniture, your wife and the fear of war...That which we call "art" exists in order to remedy our perception of life, to make things felt, to make the stone stony. The purpose of art is to evoke in man a sensation of things, to make him perceive things rather than merely recognize them.
> Victor Shklovsky as quoted by Zornberg, p. 257.

So, too, one of the purposes of Jewish ethics is to make us "perceive things rather than merely recognize them." To do so, we use both the ancient and modern traditions and texts of Judaism to live more fully in the moment, to recognize the rights of the least powerful members of society, and to be able to step outside of our own culture in order to both appreciate it and critique it. Jewish ethics is as much art as it is science; it is a source of overflowing meaning, joy, and beauty. Its purpose is not to have us live our lives looking back nostalgically, but to help us journey onward, to live in the moment.

The children of Israel were thrown out of Egypt, almost against their will. But, as the Torah tells us, Pharaoh changed his mind one last time."What is it we have done that we sent Israel away?" (Exodus 14:5), Pharaoh rhetorically asked, as he ordered the final attack on his former slaves. The children of Israel are pinned against the sea. The strong scent of rebellion was in the air. "Moses, let us alone so that we may serve Egypt?" (Exodus 14:12).

Every man said to the other, "I will not go down into the deep waters." Nachshon ben Amminadab, alone, stood up and silently plunged into the raging sea. The entire tribe of Judah followed his courageous example. The Talmud, at Sotah 36b, in the name of Rabbi Yehuda, fills in the details and teaches us that it is because the tribe of Judah "sanctified God's name" at the sea that Judah was granted dominion in Israel. Nachshon, until now, a relative unknown, demonstrated his unswerving faith. His *emunah* was a spark for others so much so that the chapter concludes by stating that the entire people of Israel "believed in God" (Exodus 14:31).

Nachshon overcame any doubts he may have had. He alone obeyed Moses's command to "journey onwards" (Exodus 14:15). Nachshon certainly must have feared for his own life, but in overcoming this fear, Nachshon demonstrated his worthiness. Leaving it here, however, misses the real point of this famous *midrash*. Nachshon and all of the children of Israel faced an even greater fear than that of drowning in the sea. An interpretation closer to the spirit of this text and the surrounding verses suggests that every man said to the other "I will not go down into the deep waters" not because of a fear that the waters would *not* split, but just the opposite. The real fear was that it just might be the case that the waters *would* split. Let me explain.

The children of Israel correctly sensed that this was not just any old moment in time, but this was *the point of no return*. If the waters split and they passed through to the other side of the sea, they would never be able to go back to Egypt. In the future, they may dream of returning, but the way back to where they have lived their entire lives has been forever closed. This is scary!

The splitting waters are a path to freedom, but they also represent a permanent barrier to returning to Egypt. The Torah is explicit on this point. That is why God took them on a long-cut. "God guided them not through the land of the Philistines, although that was near, for God said, perhaps the people will repent when they see war, and they will return to Egypt" (Exodus 13:17). Choosing the path of no return is no easy task.

The "sanctification of God's name" does not reside in the fact that Nachshon believed in and relied on miracle. That cannot be it. This story follows the dramatic ten plagues. Who other than a Pharaoh, whose heart has been hardened by God, might still doubt God's ability to perform miracles? Miracles, it turns out, are the easy part. Mindfully choosing a life of freedom over slavery, today over yesterday, is the real test here. Rabbi Nilton Bonder describes this process beautifully:

> When the body finds itself in a narrow spot, and when it is aware that discomfort is caused by this narrowness, it becomes possible to make camp in front of the sea. From this unsuitable, anxiety-provoking place, we look toward the horizon. Reaching it will be no longer a process of the body but one of the soul. It is here on this bank that you "give in" and divest yourself of everything, revealing not only the body but changing it as well. This metamorphosis frightens us, we may be relinquishing our integrity and our very identity. (2002, p. 43)

In plunging into the sea and journeying onward, Nachshon overcame his fear—not that the waters would *not* split—but the greater fear that the waters *would* split. Nachshon's soulful action is a direct response to the explicit suggestion that the children of Israel return to Egypt. In jumping into the sea, the option of returning to Egypt is removed as a real option, once and for all. Nachshon and everyone else know that the sea will part once, but never again (Pava, 2006).

Even today it is difficult to give up on the attractive fantasy of returning to a lost but glorious past. Consider the example of the Temple Institute, founded in 1987, and located in the heart of Jerusalem's old city. Under the leadership of its founder, Rabbi Yisrael Ariel, the Temple Institute's museum has grown into a well- known and fascinating tourist stop for visitors from all over the world. But the Temple Institute is much more than a typical museum. Here is how the Institute describes its goals and principles:

> Our short-term goal is to rekindle the flame of the Holy Temple in the hearts of mankind through education. Our long-term goal is to do all in our limited power to bring about the building of the Holy Temple in our time... The major focus of the Institute is its efforts towards the beginning of the actual rebuilding of the Holy Temple. Towards this end, the Institute has begun to restore and construct the sacred vessels for the service of the Holy Temple. These vessels, which G-d commanded Israel to create, can be seen today at our headquarters in Jerusalem. They are made according to the exact specifications of the Bible, and have been constructed from the original source materials, such as gold, copper, silver and wood. *These are authentic, accurate vessels, not merely replicas or models. All of these items are fit and ready for use in the service of the Holy Temple.* Among the many items featured in the exhibition are musical instruments played by the Levitical choir, the golden crown of the High Priest, and gold and silver vessels used in the incense and sacrificial services. After many years of effort and toil, the Institute has completed the three most important and central vessels of the Divine service: the seven-branched candelabra, or Menorah, made of pure gold; the golden Incense Altar, and the golden Table of the Showbread. (http://www.templeinstitute.org/about.htm; emphasis added)

Although Rabbi Ariel recognizes certain *halachick* [legal] questions surrounding his project, he is confident that these issues can be resolved. For example, in the absence of a ritually acceptable red heifer, he admits his institute's artifacts are "made in impurity." But, he quickly adds, "If no red heifer is available, then the High Priest must even serve in the Holy of Holies on Yom Kippur in a state of impurity." The ultimate purpose of fashioning these items is not educational at all. It is "for the fulfillment of Torah commandments in the Holy Temple" (www.israelnationalnews.com/News/News.aspx/12443). The possibility that a new Temple might not be identical, in every way to the old one, is presumably a thought not worth considering from Rabbi Ariel's point of view.

I am truly fascinated by this project. If this phenomenon was simply the work of a few fanatics, it would not require much comment. However, I believe that relatively large segments of traditional Jews today, even if they do not fully accept the goals of the Temple Institute outright, are certainly more than willing to openly flirt with them. As evidence for my view, I suggest that the institute's golden menorah "suitable for use in the Holy Temple" was moved in 2007—without great controversy—from the Cardo section of the Old City to the much more public landing of the staircase that leads from the Jewish Quarter to the Western Wall. As Arutz Sheva (www.israelnationalnews.com) described this, "The Menorah moves closer to the Temple Mount."

All of this is fascinating, but it is deeply troubling, as well. It is simply disingenuous to claim that the Temple Institute has no "political" agenda as some of its defenders claim.

Several years ago, Michael Walzer raised similar concerns:

> There is a price to be paid for what I can only call this dishonesty. Thus, the tiny sect of Israeli Jews (Americans too?) who are preparing for the resumption of the sacrifices, designing the priestly robes and writing a code for the rituals: I am sure that they claim to be acting in the name of Jews generally. What if, one day, some other fanatics try to blow up the mosques, so as to clear the way for the immediate rebuilding of the Temple? The rest of us will insist rightly that nothing would be further from our minds. We only hoped that God would come... and do what? (2000).

Defenders and admirers of the Temple Institute have a moral responsibility to both the Jewish people and to the world at large to explain fully the practical steps they intend on taking (and those steps that they will not take) to further their agenda to "bring about the building of the Holy Temple in our time." In addition, they must explain—in real terms—what kinds of reactions (from both friends and foes) they anticipate in response to their actions. There is no room to be coy here, as there is so little room for error in today's overheated political environment. Critics and bystanders have a moral responsibility to demand such accountability now.

There is reason to tolerate and encourage more fantasy in Jewish life today. But as these fantasies begin to impinge on our communal existence in dangerous ways, putting our lives in peril, there is a need to translate these fantasies into language that is understandable to all. Our fantasies, once they are no longer private, must be subject to the scrutiny and criticism of open and free dialogue. Even at our most playful, we must try our best not to confuse the symbol for the symbolized, as perhaps the Temple Institute and its supporters are now doing. Judaism's ethical call to live in the moment reminds us that history is a one-way street. Its categorical imperative is not to return to Egypt, because that is impossible, once the sea is no longer split, but it is to always "journey onwards."

SUSTAINING THE DIALOGUES

> So instead of getting to heaven at last, I'm going all along!
> Emily Dickinson.

Imagining Jewish ethics as a kind of dialogue is an authentic, useful, and fertile way of conceiving of what it is we're doing when we're doing Jewish ethics. This dialogue can be thought of as an internal conversation that one has with oneself, but more importantly it is through the give and take with others, the back and forth *flow of meaning*, that the content and authority of ethics is established. It is by remaining in the space of dialogue that we learn about ourselves and others and *together* craft a workable and practical vision of the ethical life and the responsibilities such a life entails (Pava, 2009).

Jewish ethics as dialogue is complex and multidimensional. It is a give and take with history and tradition. Although history cannot speak for itself, we ourselves imaginatively give it a voice. It is a local conversation among those we love most, while it is simultaneously a global discussion among both neighbors and strangers. Jewish ethics as dialogue is also an exchange with our children and grandchildren. It must constantly ask, "What are our responsibilities to future generations? Are we leaving this planet to the future in better condition, or at least no worse condition, that we received it?"

Natan Sharansky correctly reminds us that it is impossible to "engage the world as a lone individual." He elaborates:

> What you do contributes to a larger picture: linking your life to the lives of contemporaries who are part of the same community or to past and future generations of that community. History becomes as Burke described it: a pact between the dead, the living, and the yet unborn. Being part of such a community gives you great strength to defend your values and vision: a strength that comes not only from inside yourself but also in your ties to others who share with you these ideals and who are working to advance them. What you gain is solidarity—the sense of what is common among the members of this mutually committed community, from which each person draws support and strength. (2008, p. 7)

If this vision of solidarity, however, is closed, static, parochial, lacking in humor, single-minded, intolerant of differences, and inhospitable to strangers, it quickly transforms itself into a wicked and idolatrous orgy of self-satisfaction. As Richard Titmuss reminds us, "to love oneself, one must love strangers" (as quoted in Phillips and Taylor, 2009, p. 100).

Ethics is not a game which we either win or lose, rather it is a game where the only rule is that we keep on playing. An overarching goal of ethics then is to sustain the many and varied ethical dialogues. In fact, our very resistance to these dialogues may be a sure sign that we want them and need them now more than ever (Phillips and Taylor, 2009). We must be ever vigilant in keeping them open, dynamic, hospitable, and self-reflexive. To do so, it is helpful for each of us to imagine ourselves as "strangers and settlers" as the Torah describes the human predicament (Leviticus 25:23). Each one of us has earned the right to speak simply by virtue of being part of the human family. Ultimately, not one of us has the final say, regardless of credentials, because there is no final say, only temporary and good-enough agreements.

Conclusion

"We have just enough religion to make us hate, but not enough to make us love one another." So wrote the satirist Jonathan Swift in the eigthteenth century. Is there a kernel of truth to this observation, even in the twenty-first century? If so, the call of the hour is to become more religious and not less so. But we must tread carefully here. Perhaps the issue of religiosity is not a question of more or less at all, but a question of quality. How does one relate to ones religion? Do we hold onto it like one desperately holds on to an anchor in a rough sea? Or, do we hold on to it more like an experienced sailor who knows that in holding the sail too tightly she will stall the sail power and in holding it too loosely she will lose the wind altogether?

In Genesis, God introduces himself to Abraham with the simple command *lekh lekha* [go forth]. To reenergize Jewish ethics, we too, must hear the echo of this call. Avivah Zornberg asks a critical and most relevant set of questions here."When God calls Abraham—*Lekh lekha*—is this Abraham's own thought? Why then does God speak it to him? Or is it not his own thought? How then can it benefit him?" Zornberg immediately answers her own query:

> It is neither exactly his nor not his. It represents his "further, next, unattained but attainable self." God speaks, Abraham listens; he rejects the rejecting mechanism so well developed in others—perhaps in himself till now. *Lekh lekha* evokes his difference from himself. A new majesty is born, a citadel rises into the air... (2009, p. 168)

Zornberg's vision is an optimistic one, "a citadel rises into the air..." Zornberg herself resides, however, not in any citadel, but she is situated in the gap between today's status quo and the "unattained but attainable." It is precisely to this gap that Jewish ethics in a new key is playfully, but passionately aiming and striving.

NOTE

1. This perspective emphasizes that "Human relations...constitute the basic stuff of experience, and the pursuit and maintenance of relatedness is seen as the essential motivational thrust both in normality and in psychopathology" (Mitchell, 1988, p. 169). See also Aron, 2001.

REFERENCES

Adler, Rachel, *Engendering Judaism: An Inclusive Theology and Ethics* (Boston: Beacon Press, 1998).
Aron, Lewis, *Meeting of the Minds: Mutuality in Psychoanalysis* (Hillsdale, NJ: The Analytic Press, 2001).
Badaracco, Joseph, *Leading Quietly: An Unorthodox Guide to Doing the Right Thing* (Boston: Harvard Business School Press, 2002).
Bal, Mieke, *Lethal Love: Feminist Literary Readings of Biblical Love Stories* (Bloomington: Indiana University Press, 1987).
Bal, Mieke, *Loving Yusuf: Conceptual Travels From Present to Past* (Chicago: Chicago University Press, 2008).
Bialik, Hayim Nahman and Ravnitzky, Yehoshua Hana, *The Book of Legends: Sefer Ha-Aggada: Legends from the Talmud and Midrash* (New York: Schocken Books, 1992).
Birnbaum, Philip, *Five Megilloth* (New York: Hebrew Publishing Company, 1973).
Bonder, Nilton, *Our Immoral Soul: A Manifesto of Spiritual Disobedience* (Boston and London: Shambhala, 2001).
Boyarin, Daniel, *Carnal Israel: Reading Sex in Talmudic Culture* (Berkeley: University of California Press, 1993).
Eigen, Michael, *Ecstasy* (Middletown, CT: Wesleyan University Press, 2001).
Ghent, Emmanuel, "Masochism, Submission, Surrender: Masochism as a Perversion of Surrender," *Contemporary Psychoanalysis,* 1990, Vol. 6, Number 1, pp. 108–136.
Greenberg, Blu, *On Women and Judaism: A View From Tradition* (Jewish Publication Society, 1981).
Grossman, David, *Death as a Way of Life: Israel Ten Years After Oslo* (New York: Farrar, Straus and Giroux, 2003).
Jensen, Michael C., and William H. Meckling, "The Theory of the Firm: Managerial Behavior, Agency Costs, and Ownership Structure," *Journal of Financial Economics,* 1976, Vol. 3, pp. 305–360.
Jensen, Michael C., and William H. Meckling, "The Nature of Man," *Journal of Applied Corporate Finance* 1994, Vol. 7, No. 2, pp. 4–19.
Kula, Irwin, *Yearnings: Embracing the Sacred Messiness of Life* (New York: Hyperion, 2006).

Mitchell, Stephen A. *Relational Concepts in Psychoanalysis* (Cambridge: Harvard University Press, 1988).

Mitchell, Stephen A. *Can Love Last? The Fate of Romance Over Time* (New York: W.W. Norton and Company, 2002).

Nachmanovich, Stephen, *Free Play: The Power of Improvisation in Life and the Arts* (New York: The Putnam Publish Group, 1990).

Nehring, Cristina, *A Vindication of Love: Reclaiming Romance for the Twenty-First Century* (New York: Harper, 2009).

Pava, Moses L., *The Jewish Ethics Workbook* (Published online at the Edah.org, 2006).

Pava, Moses L., "We are all Madoff Enablers," *The Jewish Forward* (December 24, 2008).

Pava, Moses L., *Jewish Ethics as Dialogue: Using Spiritual Language to Reimagine a Better World* (New York: Palgrave, 2009).

Phillips, Adam, *On Flirtation: Psychoanalytic Essays on the Uncommitted Life* (Cambridge: Harvard University Press, 1994).

Phillips, Adam, and Taylor, Barbara, *On Kindness* (New York: Farrar, Straus and Giroux, 2009).

Plaskow, Judith, *Standing Again at Sinai: Judaism From a Feminist Perspective* (New York: Harper Collins, 1990).

Ross, Tamar, *Expanding the Palace of Torah: Orthodoxy and Feminism* (Waltham MA: Brandeis University Press, 2004).

Sharansky, Natan, *Fear No Evil* (New York: Random House, 1988).

Sharansky, Natan, with Weiss, Shira Wolosky, *Defending Identity: Its Indispensable Role in Protecting Democracy* (New York: Public Affairs, 2008).

Starr, Karen E., *Repair of the Soul: Metaphors of Transformation in Jewish Mysticism and Psychoanalysis* (New York: Routledge, 2008).

Walzer, Michael, "Learning to Sacrifice the Temple Mount," *The Jewish Forward* (September 29, 2000).

Zornberg, Avivah Gottlieb, *The Murmuring Deep: Reflections on the Biblical Unconscious* (New York: Schocken Books, 2009).

CHAPTER 2

TEMPTATIONS OF TRADITION

> Temptation: The act of influencing by exciting hope or desire; "his enticements were shameless"
>
> www.wordreference.com
>
> Most dangerous is that temptation that doth goad us on to sin in loving virtue.
>
> William Shakespeare

Jewish ethics in a new key is self-consciously tentative, reflective, critical, and selective in its use of tradition to help resolve ethical problems. We survey, recover, and interpret tradition for the many lost but usable treasures it contains, but we must also be wary of its perennial temptations, risks, and dangers. Religious traditions are full of dire warnings about the many temptations "out there." "But you must not eat from the tree of the knowledge of good and evil, for when you eat of it you will surely die" (Genesis 2:17), the Torah commands Adam and Eve in Eden. But, what about tradition's own built-in temptations, and the negative effects these can have on our desire to live an ethical life?

"TERRIBLE IS THE TEMPTATION TO BE GOOD"

These internal temptations are just as real and dangerous as the more familiar external ones. Tradition's temptations, however, are often more subtle and beguiling. Appearing with no obvious labels, almost invisible, these temptations masquerade not as lewd, talking snakes, but as angels, kings, prophets, rabbis, and priests. Crowned with esoteric learning, rich and luxurious garments, long-familiar customs, and unquestioned powers, these temptations usually do not even look like temptations, at all. There is certainly a profound truth to Nahmanides' observation that it is possible to "be a scoundrel with the full permission of the Torah" just as there is much wisdom to Bertolt Brecht's even more radical observation, "terrible is the temptation to be good."

Jewish ethics in a new key is neither a turning away from tradition nor a complete embrace of the status quo. It is first and foremost a call for a new way of relating to tradition. We approach tradition today, not as those who are submitting to a powerful invading army, but as equal, responsible citizens—accountable, covenantal partners—in an ongoing and open-ended dialogue. History's hard won lessons have a vote in this process, but not a veto. According to Rabbi Irving Greenberg, the contemporary Jewish theologian, "Setting limits on truth claims and ethical norms reduces the chances that good values will 'run away' for the sake of good and lead to evil" (2006, p. 220). Our own life experiences, contemporary scientific knowledge, intelligent processes, our particular histories, gifts, insights, desires, and aspirations for the future are not bracketed off in this process (or, at least, they should not be), but are most central to its functioning properly. "Since the Torah was not given to angels but to human beings, and since it depends on interpretation and understanding by human beings, whatever is discovered in it by human beings who accept the Torah as God's revelation to the Jewish people at Sinai and study it is indeed the truth of the Torah," wrote the late Rabbi Eliezer Berkowitz more than 25 years ago (1983, p. 51).

For those of us who speak in favor of tradition because we continue to view it as a positive source for goodness and growth (with no equivalent substitute), but are shocked by the frequency and magnitude of today's ethical crises and social breakdowns both inside and outside our own communities, it is not sufficient to always look elsewhere to place the blame. Tradition itself contains weeds that if ignored, left unattended, and unmanaged, can ultimately destroy the garden upon which all of us depend.

Irving Greenberg employs the metaphor of brokenness to understand the inherent limitations of tradition. In his words:

> The broken system recognizes that it is partial: perhaps it sees itself as a diminished fragment from a larger whole and, for that reason, necessarily incomplete. The brokenness may stem from flaws in the system/truth/paradigm; recognition of failings is an important source of modesty and openness to others. The brokenness may also reflect a whole that has been wounded or damaged by reality. In such a case, the break/wound is a tribute to the high standards or the deep commitment to human reality of the wounded one. Thus, the wound is a mark of nobility, even though it may reflect a weakness and vulnerability to a hard blow from refractory reality. (2006, p. 220)

Whichever metaphor one chooses to describe the limits and dangers of tradition, it is important to specify and describe carefully these stumbling blocks inherent to tradition. The unbound love of our own history and an uncritical embrace of tradition often transform themselves into the *temptation of nostalgia* and an unthinking evasion of today's problems. The legitimate desire for safety and security morphs into the *temptation of certainty* and the arrogance that always accompanies this. The opposite side of the coin of choseness is the *temptation of exclusivity* and worse. The overwhelming desire to live a life in accord with God's commandments, left unchecked, evolves into the *temptation of total submission* and the ultimately impossible lure of self-abnegation. A rich and meaningful ritual life is wrongly translated into the *temptation of uprooting desire* completely and the perverse ideal of living a life untouched by secular contaminations. Finally, the practical, tested, and this-worldly idealism of tradition often is converted into the dangerous *temptation of messianism,* forcing out the possibility of reasonable discussions, practical decision making, and hope of achieving an ethical and workable equilibrium among opposing parties.

Like all temptations, there is an excitement in the promises of nostalgia, certainty, exclusivity, submission, uprooting desire, and messianism. These temptations speak to deep human needs, legitimate hopes, and thrilling desires. What is more exciting, in the moment, than the complete sacrifice of one's autonomy and freedom to a higher power? How alluring is the thought of membership in a completely exclusive club? What could be more attractive than living in utopia? No doubt, there are payoffs in succumbing to these temptations, but these are always short-run rewards that come with long-run costs. Each of these temptations upset the possibility for long-term growth and transcendence. They pull us in, juvenilize us, ensnare us in a status quo from which it is difficult, if not impossible, to escape. In the end, the promises of these temptations are mirages. These temptations—sacrificing one's autonomy, belonging to exclusive clubs, and living in utopia—rather than liberating us, imprison us in impossible paradoxes and lock us into self-defeating behaviors.

TEMPTATION'S TRADITIONAL GARB

There is a difficult to understand verse in Genesis often interpreted as describing a strange kind of powerful and mysterious temptation. "And the sons of God [also translated as the sons of the mighty] saw the daughters of men that they were fair; and they took them wives, whomsoever they chose" (Genesis 6:2). The *midrash* interprets the phrase "daughters of men" as, among others, Naamah, "the fairest of all women who seduced the sons of the mighty" (Soloveitchik, 1964). Rabbi Joseph Soloveitchik elaborates in detail:

> Her seductive charms captivated the sons of the mighty and led to their appalling disregard for the central divine norm enjoining man from reaching out for the fascinating and beautiful that does not belong to him. The sons of the mighty yielded to the hedonic urge and were unable to discipline their actions. They were a nonconfronted, non-normative group. They worshipped beauty and succumbed to its overwhelming impact. Naamah, the incarnation of unhallowed and unsublimated beauty, is, for the Midrash, not so much an individual as an idea, not only a real person but a symbol of unredeemed beauty. As such, she appears in the Biblical drama in many disguises. At times her name is Delilah, seducing Samson; at other times she is called Tamar, corrupting a prince. She is cast in the role of a princess or queen, inflicting untold harm upon a holy nation and kingdom of priests whose king, the wisest of all men, abandoned his wisdom when he encountered overpowering beauty. The Book of Wisdom (Proverbs) portrays her as the anonymous woman with an "impudent face" who "lieth in wait at every corner" and the Aggadah—also cited here by Nachmanides—as the beautiful queen of the demons tempting man and making him restless.

Rabbi Soloveitchik reads Genesis 6:2, following the ancient midrashic tradition, as a warning against the temptation of hedonic pleasure. "Her seductive charms captivated the sons of the mighty..." I suggest that we proceed cautiously here.

Just as Naamah, the fairest of all women, is charmingly captivating so too is Rabbi Soloveitchik's traditional but single-minded interpretation of Genesis 6:2. In the paragraph cited above, there is almost an obsessive and misogynistic focus on a single form of sexual temptation. I suggest such obsessive attention and the overt fear of the feminine Other it demonstrates obscure other forms of temptation. In addition to these hedonic urges of the individual triggered by external stimuli, there are tradition's own seemingly hardwired, internal urges to worship the past as a kind of lost paradise, to see certainty even in the face of uncertainty, to submit to authority when we certainly know better, to view our own community as superior to others, to strive for complete purity and perfection even when we know we live in an imperfect world, and, perhaps worst of all, to rely upon messiahs of our own inventions to save us from ourselves.

I fully believe that a reengagement with tradition is a necessary step in improving the quality of ethical dialogue and behavior in today's world. Tradition must seize its legitimate place in contemporary conversations and debates. Nevertheless, such a reengagement with tradition comes with its own costs. This chapter examines tradition's own temptations and limitations. Temptation is not always an external threat. It does not only reside outside of the "holy nation and a kingdom of priests" in the guise of alluring, overpowering, foreign princesses and exotic queens, as implied by Rabbi Soloveitchik above, but the desire for holiness and perfect purity can themselves become dangerously tempting diversions leading us away from goal of leading an ethical, balanced, and meaningful life as individuals and as a community. When Rabbi Soloveitchik writes "*She is cast* in the role of a princess or queen, inflicting untold harm upon a holy nation..." (emphasis added), we must pause and ask, who is doing this *casting*? Is it some external power that is testing us? Or, is it, perhaps, we ourselves, hallucinating that it is we who are the "mighty sons of God," consciously or unconsciously, doing the casting here?

THE TEMPTATION OF NOSTALGIA

> Humpty Dumpty sat on a wall,
> Humpty Dumpty had a great fall.
> All the King's horses, And all the King's men
> Couldn't put Humpty together again!

Nostalgia, the love of a time and place that never was, is a common human pathos. For those of us who embrace tradition, nostalgia possesses a particularly strong pull. The exodus from Egypt, the forming event of the Jewish experience, almost compels one, against one's conscious will, to fantasize about returning there. "We remember the fish which we ate in Egypt freely; the cucumbers, and the melons, and the leeks, and the onions, and the garlic: But now our soul is dried away: and there is nothing at all, besides this manna, before our eyes" (Numbers 11:5–6), cry the Israelites still in the dessert on the way to the Promised Land.

I remember, as a 15-year-old, visiting Israel for the first time. I was sitting with my friends at the summit of a Jerusalem hill with a beautiful view of the old city, listening to familiar stories I had heard many times before, and singing sad songs accompanied by a lone acoustic guitar. The night was clear and cool after an unusually hot summer day. More than anything, I remember the unique smell of Jerusalem's trees and summer flowers. It was the Ninth of Av, the saddest day of the year in the Jewish calendar. One of our tour guides, a young and charismatic rabbi, was teaching us a lesson about the destruction of Judaism's holy Temples. Both destructions had occurred on this date we were told, and today, all of us were fasting and mourning, neither eating nor drinking for 25 hours, to commemorate the tragic events. Our tour leader was crying as he reached the climax of his story about the ancient catastrophes, and he invited us to join with him.

But it was more than an invitation. It was a kind of challenge. "How deeply do we feel the loss of the Temple?" he asked us teenagers, pointing out that we can no longer offer animal sacrifices on the Temple Mount and celebrate Jewish holidays in the precise way the Torah originally prescribed. "Are we truly connected to our ancestors?" he wondered aloud, "or, are we simply going through the motions?" Some of my friends began to cry, tears rolling down their cheeks. I, too, *tried* to cry. But, I couldn't. "Is there something wrong with me?" I worried. I *wanted* to weep. I *wanted* to belong to the Jewish people and to demonstrate my membership tangibly, proof for everyone else to see, with real tears. But, I couldn't. The only emotion I truly felt at the time, and even afterward, was a kind of gnawing guilt. "Don't I care about my ancestors and their overwhelming tragedies? How can we get closer to God if we can't offer the appropriate sacrifices?"

With 20–20 hindsight, I now believe that there was an unreal theatricality to this rabbi's performance that night. He was selling us a tempting and captivating emotion. It was a con game, and we were the intended dupes. He was exploiting the Ninth of Av as a tool to imprint upon us an identity that rightly should have been ours to choose freely or not through discussion, thought, and critical analysis. As our cognitive skills were developing, this was a carefully orchestrated attempt to bypass them in favor of more primitive emotions and tribal longings. He was painting a picture of an idyllic time, destroyed by our enemies, which had never really existed in the first place. In a word, he was selling the pleasures of nostalgia.

The problem with nostalgia, from an ethical point of view, is that it removes us from the here and now and fantastically places us in an imaginary past. As Bruce Springstein sings, "Glory days well they'll pass you by…Glory days in the wink of a young girl's eye Glory days…" Even at 15, I knew that I really did not want a return to animal sacrifices. And, although, I had not yet read Maimonides nor had I been taught about the corrupt priests of the Temple period, I sensed that other forms of worship such as prayer and meditation were far more appropriate to my own situation as a contemporary Jew. There is no arguing, though, with nostalgia.

I do care about my ancestors and their overwhelming tragedies, but we do them no favor by whitewashing history and neglecting our own responsibilities to ourselves and to future generations. In fact, the only way to truly honor our past, is to study it truthfully, to cherish the present, and to plan together reasonably for the future. William James, the American philosopher, once said that "looking forward instead of backward, looking to what the world and life might become instead of what they have been, is an alternation in the 'seat of authority'" (as paraphrased by Dewey, 1929, p. 285). This change in perspective is precisely the kind of change that Jewish ethics in a new key is calling for, and, unfortunately, it is exactly the kind of change that spinners of nostalgia such as the Ninth of Av rabbi are so afraid of. There are plenty of good reasons to mourn with the Jewish people on the Ninth of Av. It has been a tragic day in our history filled with untold misery. Nevertheless, we should not indoctrinate our students and children with false memories and fake emotions in the service of rebuilding a past that never was to the neglect a future that still might be.

THE TEMPTATION OF CERTAINTY

"Doubt is not a pleasant condition, but certainty is absurd." Voltaire, the French enlightenment philosopher who first penned these words, may very well have been correct in his assertion that certainty is absurd, but it is, no doubt, a very attractive absurdity. Certainty promises stability, security, and confidence in the face of instability and danger. It promises a stable foundation upon which to build a worldview. Certainty cuts through complexity and yields the gift of utter simplicity. It stops critical thinking and dialogue and views these actions as time-wasters or worse. Those who possess certainty have a huge advantage over the rest of us who live in and must contend with an inherently risky and unpredictable world (or, so it may seem).

Historically, religious traditions, including Judaism, have provided a fertile environment for the unchecked growth of certainty in one's beliefs and actions. It is not obvious why tradition should provide such a hospitable environment to an idea so at odds with our real world experiences. I suggest a couple of possibilities. First, at the heart of tradition is the process of education. Tradition, by definition, must be passed down from one generation to the next in an efficient manner. Complex and nuanced ideas, tentatively held, however, are extremely difficult to pass on. There is a temptation then for teachers and parents to simplify core ideas and streamline one's beliefs in such a way as to make them easier to learn through rote repetition. By transforming the probable into the definite and presenting the likely as certain, the educational process is dramatically altered and eased. Further, religious traditions demand huge investments in time and energy from their adherents. Tradition is a high cost proposition especially in an era in which there are seemingly viable substitutes and alternatives. By promising certainty to the next generation, traditional leaders make their product much more appealing than they otherwise would be. In a turbulent and dangerous world, tradition's stability and seemingly perfect confidence are an incredibly attractive option for young people fearful of an unknown future.

Whatever the real reasons are for tradition's embrace of certainty even in the face of obvious risk and unpredictability, there can be no denying the tight and familiar link between tradition and certainty. The problem with holding one's beliefs with certainty is the extremism in behavior that follows. For those of us who cave into the temptation of certainty, it always necessarily follows that "I am right and you are wrong" and there are literally no reasons to discuss this further. To the extent that Jewish ethics demands confrontation, discussion, and back and forth dialogue among those who disagree with one another in the first place, holding onto one's beliefs with certainty is an insurmountable barrier to improving ethical behavior over time.

For advocates of Jewish ethics in a new key, we must learn how to hold onto our beliefs more lightly. We must continue to have our beliefs, but our beliefs must not have us. We must learn how to educate our children not only to accept authority, but students must learn to question authority when appropriate as part of the pedagogical process. Classrooms must model the kinds of real dialogue that we hope constitute the essence of democratic decision making. Further, a call of the hour is to find a way to make tradition, even in the absence of the promise of certainty, an attractive choice in a world of so many other options. As the psychoanalyst Michael Eigen correctly notes, "We should take the rise of emotional certainty as a signal for humility" (2006, p. 58).

The good news is that the Jewish tradition grounds us in a heritage of great accomplishments. The tradition contains noble and time-tested values including modesty, a deep respect for learning, and a full acceptance of our creatureliness and our ultimate mortality. The dominant strand of Judaism reflects a realism earned over millennia. These are tools internal to tradition that we can use to overcome the temptation of certainty. Rabbi Emanuel Rackman, a former president of Bar Illan University in Israel and one of the great Jewish leaders of the last century, expressed the best in the Jewish ethical tradition when he warned:

> A Jew dare not live with absolute certainty, not only because certainty is the hallmark of the fanatic and Judaism abhors fanaticism, but also because doubt is good for the human soul, its humility, and consequently its greater potential ultimately to discover its Creator. (p. 17)

Thinking in probabilistic terms is a modern invention. Traditionalists, when they are not being traditionalists, have no difficulty using the science of probability and statistics to make decisions both at work and at home. The problem is that when we begin to speak from inside the tradition, we often revert to a more familiar black and white style of thinking and speaking. Everything is yes and no instead of more or less likely. A renaissance in Jewish ethics demands that we learn how to integrate old and new styles of thinking. "Our tradition makes room for the honest doubter, for without such doubt questions would never be asked, prejudices never challenged, and science would come to a halt" (1998, p. 17), Rabbi Norman Lamm, another great leader of the last century and former president of Yeshiva University, wrote several years ago in words that are even more relevant today.

The Temptation of Exclusivity

> The Israelites, upon whom the Holy One, blessed be He, bestowed the favor of the Law and laid upon them statutes and judgments, are a merciful people who have mercy upon all.
>
> Maimonides, Law of Slaves 9:8

"Understand, then, that it is not because of your righteousness that the Lord your God is giving you this good land to possess, for you are a stiff-necked people. Remember this and never forget how you provoked the Lord your God to anger in the desert. From the day you left Egypt until you arrived here, you have been rebellious against the Lord" (Deuteronomy 9:6–7). The tradition itself, from its very inception, is self-conscious and explicit about the dangers inherent in the concept of choseness. Moses, in one of his farewell speeches to the Israelites, before they enter the land, directly states that it is not because of righteousness that God has chosen them. And, yet, even with this explicit and clear warning the sense of specialness, uniqueness, distinctiveness, and exclusivity are seemingly built-in hazards of the tradition.

Today, the temptation of exclusivity is arguably more overwhelming than ever. Consider the following items taken from recent newspaper reports:

Item 1
"At least 100 students of Ethiopian origin in Petah Tikva do not know what school they will be attending in the fall, with the opening of the school year just two and a half weeks away. The uncertainty stems from the fact that the city's private schools with an ultra-Orthodox or national Orthodox bent have refused to accept children of Ethiopian origin" (www.Haaretz.com, August 26, 2009).

Item 2
"A gunman shot dead two people and wounded at least 15 others in an attack at a central Tel Aviv gay and lesbian center Saturday night before fleeing the scene. Israel Police said that the incident at the club on Nahmani Street did not have a terror motive. The two victims were initially identified as a 24-year-old man and a 17-year-old woman" (www.Haaretz.com, August 1, 2009).

Item 3
The Syrian Jewish community in the United States issued an edict in 1935 prohibiting its members to marry converts to Judaism. No conversion, according to this edict, is acceptable according to Jewish law. According to the New York Times, "They wanted to build an iron wall of self-separation around the community. They couldn't do this the Hassidic way, dressing the men in costumes of ancient design, physically segregating women and making sure that children received nothing in the way of useful secular education. After all, the Syrian men couldn't be expected to make money if they looked like figures from 18th-century Poland" (*New York Times,* October 14, 2007).

Item 4
"Thirteen Austrian bishops were barred from praying at Jerusalem's Western Wall last week by Jewish religious authorities when they refused to take off their crosses, according to Austrian officials. On a planned visit on Thursday to the wall—the holiest place where Jews can pray—the bishops were given an ultimatum by the rabbi of the site: Either remove the crosses or stand behind a fence several meters (yards) from the site. The bishops refused the request and watched people praying from behind the fence, according to an Austrian official" (http://catholicforum.fisheaters.com/index.php?topic=2292248.0,
November 13, 2007).

Item 5
"Earlier this month, the Israeli Supreme Court, in a 5–4 decision, refused to permit women to pray out loud at the Western Wall ("the Wall") in Jerusalem." Known in Hebrew as the "Kotel Ha'Maaravi," the Wall is all that remains of the second Jewish Temple destroyed by the Romans almost 2000 years ago. It is one of the holiest sites in existence for Jews around the world. The plaintiffs in the case called themselves the "Women of the Wall." They asked the Israeli Court to recognize their right to pray out loud at the Kotel, after they had repeatedly encountered physical and verbal abuse from the Ultra-Orthodox each time they tried to do so on their own" (www.Findlaw.com, April 23, 2003).

Exclusivity is a pernicious meme that has attached itself to tradition. It is a value easily passed down from one generation to the next. There are, of course, the undeniably sweet pleasures of exclusivity. Who doesn't want to belong to a private club with special rights and prerogatives? But exclusivity too easily slips into racism, sexism, xenophobia, and fear of the Other as the five cases identified above illustrate.

"There is always a danger that the language of intimacy that conveys the experience of God's passionate love for Israel can create a narcissistic frame of mind in which the reality of God revolves exclusively around *my* people's history, *my* rituals and *my* traditions," writes Rabbi David Hartman. He continues, "The passionate attitude that characterizes covenantal communal religious intimacy can overshadow the religious importance of the universal spirit of creation" (2000, p. 131, emphasis in original).

In Hartman's view, Maimonides recognized the problem of exclusivity and offered a viable solution. By emphasizing the universal story of creation, tradition's tendency toward exclusivity can be managed. Torah obligations and ethical responsibilities, seemingly directed only toward Jews, are expanded through creative interpretation to include non-Jews, too.

> Maimonides reveals how the theme of Creation affects the application of the Sinaitic revelation. If we understood and applied the mitzvoth in keeping with

the universalistic spirit of Creation, we would realize that the true intent of God's revelation is to create a people who would embrace and feel responsible for and compassionate toward all human beings.(Hartman, 2000, p. 135)

Contemporary problems demand a broadening of the ethical circle. Hartman's project of *returning to tradition to critique and enlarge tradition* is a model to be emulated. To the extent that we have finally had enough of business as usual in the realm of ethical behavior at the individual, organizational, and national levels, Hartman's reading of Maimonides is a useful launching off point.

The case for Maimonides's position here should not be overstated. It has historically been a minority and elitist one at tradition's periphery. It is not, nor has it ever been, the only view held by traditionalists. Yehuda Halevi and his contemporary followers reject, or at best, downplay the "universalistic spirit of creation." They prefer particularistic interpretations emphasizing the unique experiences of the Jewish people in history and focus on more parochial issues concerning group solidarity, ritual purity, and the singularity of the Jewish people. The problem with Yehuda Halevi's position, today, however is the very real danger of succumbing almost completely to the temptation of exclusivity. In a period of ethical crisis, a position that celebrates the specialness of the Jewish tradition but does not simultaneously provide a time and a place, a vocabulary, and a grammar to critique and improve it, must remain passive and mute. Such deafening silence, however, is a big part of the contemporary ethical meltdown in the first place.

THE TEMPTATION OF TOTAL SUBMISSION

A person should never give all his property to the sanctuary. He who engages in this practice transgresses the intent of Scripture... This is not piety but folly because he loses all property and will have to depend upon others... It is with regard to him and similar other cases that the Rabbis stated that pious fools destroy the world.
Maimonides as quoted by Wurzburger, 1994, p. 56

Surrender is a legitimate and central experience and goal of a religious life grounded in tradition. In Emmanuel Ghent's description, surrender is not a giving up but "a *longing* for the birth, or perhaps re-birth of true self" (1990, p. 110, emphasis in original). It is an experience of being in the moment. It is characterized by an absence of domination and control, and while one may surrender in the "presence of another," one never surrenders "to another." Surrender is a form of active acceptance of all that is, but not resignation. It is felt as joyful and life-affirming. According to Ghent, surrender may even be a universal human need. It promotes fundamental change, positive transformation, and real growth. "Its ultimate direction is the discovery of one's identity, one's sense of wholeness, even one's sense of unity with other living beings" (p. 111). Although Ghent did not use the term spirituality in his original formulation of this concept (he did use the term faith), his descriptions of the process of surrendering are consistent with many contemporary descriptions of the spiritual process (Pava, 2007 and Starr, 2008).

The purpose of Ghent's original paper, however, goes beyond a mere description of surrender. His thesis is that there is a counterfeit version of surrender. He labels this alternative as submission, or as masochism. In his words:

> Submission, losing oneself in the power of the other, becoming enslaved in one or other way to the master, is the ever available lookalike to surrender. It holds out the promise, seduces, excites, enslaves, and in the end, cheats the seeker-turned victim out of his cherished goal, offering in its place only the security of bondage and an ever amplified sense of futility. By substituting the appearance and trappings of surrender for the authentic experience, an agonizing, though at times temporarily exciting, masquerade of surrender occurs; a self-negating submissive experience in which the person is enthralled by the other. (pp. 115–116).

As Ghent notes, submission, the giving up of one's freedom, control, and power to an overwhelming other, in the moment, is exciting and deeply compelling. In the end, though, it is always a distortion or a perversion of the life-affirming desire to surrender.

I suggest, here, that religious traditions may contribute to this mixing-up of surrender and submission. From a religious perspective, I believe, there often exist confusions between the quest for legitimate spirituality, on the one hand, and an attraction for an unhealthy masochism (broadly conceived), on the other hand. From inside a tradition, there are damaging temptations to move beyond the search for a sense of wholeness and a sense of unity with other living beings, desires often painted as too temperate, mundane, and this-worldly. Religious seekers are tempted not to just "knock on heaven's door," but to barge right in.

The point emphasized here is that from an ethical perspective, submission—as opposed to surrender—represents an abdication of our own individual responsibility and an attempt to sidestep moral accountability. The temptation for total submission leads to extremism in ideologies and in behaviors. It justifies and strengthens authoritarian leadership and mocks democratic initiatives. When submission is wrongly substituted for surrender, individual freedom and autonomy are seen as dispensable values. Rabbi Soloveitchik writes, for example, that God "wills man to be free in order that he may commit himself unreservedly and forfeit his freedom." This call for man to "forfeit his freedom" to God, from traditional perspectives, is gripping and often extremely persuasive. It is a tantalizing and exciting offer. To forfeit one's freedom even to God, however, is too high of a price for anyone to pay. In choosing to forfeit one's freedom, humanity is not enlarged but sadly diminished and regressed. Without the constant aspiration for freedom, ethical growth is permanently halted. Can this really be God's wish for us?

Deeply buried in tradition is an almost unspeakable desire for human sacrifice and death. Nadab and Abihu, two of Aaron's sons, succumbed to the temptation of total submission in an eerie narrative included in the book of Leviticus. The Israelites had just completed the construction of the Tabernacle in the desert. On the eight day, they began to offer sacrifices to God. It was a day of great celebration, a culmination of the people's joint efforts to build the Tabernacle together. "Moses and Aaron came to the Tent of Meeting, and they went out and they blessed the people—and the glory of God appeared to the entire people" (Leviticus 9:23). The text continues, "and the people saw and sang glad songs and fell upon their faces" (Leviticus 9:24). This text describes one of the great high points in Jewish history. It is precisely at this awesome moment that Aaron's sons step forward onto the stage of history:

> The sons of Aaron, Nadab and Abihu, each took his fire pan, they put fire in them and placed incense upon it; and they brought before God a *strange fire* that God had not commanded them. A fire came forth from before God and consumed them, and they died before God. Moses said to Aaron: Of this did God speak saying: "I will be sanctified through those who are nearest me, thus I will be honored before the entire people" and Aaron was silent. (Leviticus 10:1–3, emphasis added).

For Nadab and Abihu, the sacrificial service, as prescribed by God here in Leviticus, was an intoxicating inducement for an even greater offering. The majesty of the moment was misinterpreted. For them, it was not enough to catch a glimpse of God's glory like everyone else had. The strange fire of Nadab and Abihu symbolizes the misplaced passion for total submission. It represents a masochistic desire for complete self-abnegation. Above all, theirs was the urge to erase themselves completely through their service to God.

There is still an open question, even today, about how to best understand these mysterious verses. On the one hand, traditional interpretations are clear that Nadab and Abihu sinned in their zealous behavior that "God had not commanded." On the other hand, there are the seemingly plain words of Moses to Aaron that somehow God has been "sanctified" and "honored before the entire people" as a result of Nadab's and Abihu's actions.

How one answers this question is not merely a theoretical or academic debate. For those of us who are traditionalists, how we choose to read Scripture affects how we see the world around us and how we perceive our own responsibilities and ethical aspirations in today's world. In turn, it affects our ultimate decisions and actions. Interpretation is not only about history, but it helps to create our future both for ourselves and descendants. Does God really ask us to erase ourselves? And, in doing so, do we bring honor to God? This story suggests that indeed there is a great temptation, among the best and the brightest, to answer these questions affirmatively. I believe, though, that ultimately the only reasonable response is to resist such temptation, "choose life," and get on with the messiness of our everyday lives. "Pious fools destroy the world," as Maimonides describes those who wish to give away their entire wealth to God. How much more so, when one wishes to give away even more?

THE TEMPTATION OF DESTROYING DESIRE

> Nahman in the name of Shmuel [said]: Behold it was good [Gen. 1:31]. This is the Good Desire. Behold it was very good [ibid.]. This is the Evil Desire! Is the Evil Desire indeed good? Incredible! Rather, without the Evil Desire a man would not build a house or marry a woman or beget children.
>
> As quoted in Boyarin, 1993, p. 63

Religious rituals, performed precisely, serve as a counterweight against the temptation of total submission discussed above. Immediately following the narrative of Nadab and Abihu, the Torah warns against drinking strong wine when you come to the Tent of Meeting to perform the sacrificial rites. "... This is an eternal decree for your generations. In order to distinguish between the sacred and the profane, and *between the contaminated and the pure*, and to teach the Children of Israel all the decrees that God had spoken to them through Moses" (Leviticus 10: 9–11, emphasis added).

The goal of purity, such as the pursuit of surrender, is an essential aspect of religious experience. But just as surrender is often wrongly replaced with submission, so too purity has its counterfeit in the powerful desire to uproot desire. This temptation lures one to deny our essential creatureliness and mortality. It proposes and then accepts the idea that there exists a complete break between physical and spiritual realms. According to this approach, "spiritual development is contingent upon *detachment* from materialism and corporeality" (Rothenberg, 2009, p. 2, emphasis added). It is a view that exaggerates the legitimate and ethically sound proposition that it is possible to channel one's energy and passion toward appropriate ends. It falsely teaches that if it is good to *control* desire, it is even better to *destroy* it.

This has been an extremely tempting idea for both religious and philosophical traditions. It is also a very dangerous proposition from an ethical standpoint for the simple reason that it represents a basic denial and a refusal to accept human limitations.

As with all of the temptations enumerated here, its embrace makes ethical dialogue unreal and impossible. Its acceptance as an ideal to be vigorously pursued leads to a dangerous extremism in behavior and an unrealistic overreaching in aspirations. The temptation to uproot or destroy desire fuels the contemporary orthodox world to embrace ever more stringent ritual rules even to the neglect of ethical concerns. From this point of view, more ritual is *always* better than *less*. In addition, like nostalgia, the attempt to detach oneself from materialism and corporeality always changes the subject from the here and now to the there and never. To quote Philip Roth's fictional character Nathan Zuckerman in *Exit Ghost* we cease "to inhabit not just the great world but the present moment. The impulse to be in it and of it I had long since killed" (2007, p. 1)

The Talmud, at Yoma 69b, gives classic expression to both the temptation to destroy desire and the dire consequences of actually doing so:

> They said, "Since this is a time of [God's] favor, let us pray regarding Desire for sexual sin." They prayed and he was committed into their hands. He said to them, "Be careful, for if you kill that one, the world will end." They imprisoned him for three days, and they looked for a fresh egg in all of the Land of Israel, and they did not find one. They said, "What shall we do? If we kill him, the world will end. If we pray for half [i.e. that people will only desire licit sex; Rashi] in heaven they do not answer halfway prayers. Blind him and let him go." At least a man does not become aroused by his female relatives. (As quoted in Boyarin, 1993, p. 61)

It is desire then, according to the rabbis, which keeps the world going. In this story personified Desire is captured in order to destroy him. Fortunately, instead of killing Desire immediately, his captors imprisoned him for three days. After the three days passed, there are no eggs to be found in all of Israel. Eggs, of course, symbolize reproduction and generativity. Halfway prayers are not answered, so the best that can be done is to blind Desire in order to reduce incest with one's closest relatives. The crucial point of this story is that "in order for there to be desire and thus sexuality at all, there must also be the possibility of illicit desire. *Desire is one*, and killing off desire for illicit sex will also kill off the desire for licit sex, which is necessary for the continuation of life" (Boyarin, p. 62, emphasis added).

The Talmudic material quoted above represents a particular view within tradition. The point here is not that this is the only view expressed there. In fact, the point is just the opposite. There are indeed other views where the temptation to destroy desire completely overwhelms the more sober aspiration of channeling desire. This temptation is not something external to tradition and foreign to our own cultural inheritance. "The lust for purity" (Eigen, 2006, p. 15) is an attractive temptation built right into tradition and one that we must begin to talk about more openly and honestly. We today must make *our* choices. In a tradition such as Judaism with many voices, there is no getting around this hard fact of life. We must be both perfectly honest about tradition and, at the same time, as clear as we can be about what we can take from it and what we can not.

THE TEMPTATION OF MESSIANISM

A sprout will come forth from the trunk of Jesse
King David's father

> ... The spirit of God will fill him,
> A spirit of wisdom and understanding...
> With righteousness he will judge the poor
> And bring justice to the lowly of the land
> ... The wolf shall dwell with the lamb,
> The leopard lie down with the kid...
> No one shall hurt or destroy
> In all My holy mountain... (Is.11:1–9)

Consider the following chilling words of Rabbi Moshe Manis Friedman of Chabad Lubavitch, published in response to a question about how the Israeli Defense Forces should approach a war in which enemy combatants attack from among civilian populations. Speaking in the name of tradition, Friedman wrote:

> I don't believe in western morality, i.e. don't kill civilians or children, don't destroy holy sites, don't fight during holiday seasons, don't bomb cemeteries, don't shoot until they shoot first because it is immoral. The only way to fight a moral war is the Jewish way: Destroy their holy sites. Kill men, women and children (and cattle). The first Israeli prime minister who declares that he will follow the Old Testament will finally bring peace to the Middle East... Living by Torah values will make us a light unto the nations who suffer defeat because of disastrous morality of human invention. (As quoted in Moment Magazine, May/June 2009)

This quote is not from a fringe member of the Lubavitch movement. In fact, Rabbi Friedman served as a translator for the Lubavitcher Rebbe until 1990, and he has about 200 articles and videos posted at chabad.org. His Women's

Yeshiva in Minnesota is listed in the official online directory of Chabad outposts (www.FailedMessiah.com).

These words, I believe, reflect what can go wrong when one succumbs fully to the temptation of messianism, the certain belief that the promised messianic period is here or has already begun. This last temptation is often accompanied with the symptoms of exclusivity, certainty, submission, and exaggerated purity discussed above, and almost all of which are illustrated in Rabbi Friedman's brief quote above. This kind of extreme thinking not only makes it difficult to engage in ethical dialogue, these views come perilously close to an outright rejection of ethics!

The temptation of messianism is the flip side of the temptation of nostalgia, discussed above. Where nostalgia looks back, messianism looks forward, and like nostalgia, succumbing to the temptation of messianism removes us from the complexities of the here and now. Real world politics, strategy, and reasonable decision making become irrelevant. Fantasy takes hold, and, at the very extreme, death is both celebrated and denied.

In the first century, Rabbi Akiva, arguably the greatest sage of his time, succumbed to this temptation by embracing the military leader Bar Kochba as the messianic redeemer. History proved Rabbi Akiva wrong, and one of his colleagues correctly censured him when he memorably stated, "Akiba, grass will grow from your cheeks— you'll be long in your grave—and the Messiah will still not be here" (T.J. Ta'anit IV).

From my point of view, the definitive statement in Judaism on the appropriate attitude toward messianism is the view of the great Rabbi Yochanan ben Zakkai, who combined his unswerving belief in tradition with a pragmatic and real world vision and strategy for its future. He is most famously remembered for clashing with the Jewish zealots of his own time during the siege of Jerusalem by the Romans. Arguing in favor of peace, he snuck out of Jerusalem inside of a coffin and arranged for a meeting with the Roman General Vespasian. At this meeting, Yochanan Ben Zakkai negotiated for the establishment of a permanent, safe haven in Yavneh so that rabbinic Judaism could continue to develop there even after the predicted fall of the Temple. He stated: "If there be a sapling in your hand when they say to you: 'Behold the Messiah!—First, go and plant the tree, and afterward go out to greet him.'" Yochanan ben Zakkai does not deny the possibility of Messiah, to the contrary, he is a firm believer. Nevertheless, there is a patient and realistic attitude on his part grounded in the natural world. His principle focus is not on the next world, but this one. "First, go and plant the tree..."

Perhaps the best way to think about messianism is similar to how we view capital punishment in Judaism today. It is something we necessarily keep on the books for good reasons, but it is not something that we act upon. We must learn to disentangle our messianic hopes and desires so beautifully captured in the Prophetic writings from our ethical responsibilities in the here and now. Messianism leads to disastrous ethical decision making. In some historical periods, the temptation of messianism becomes almost overwhelming. The infamous episode of the false Messiah Shabbatai Zevi in the seventeenth century is perhaps the best known and most notorious example of how bad things can get. We fool ourselves, however, when we start thinking that we are immune to such thinking.

Today, we need, more than ever, to somehow find a way to continue believing that justice will be brought to the lowly, as Isaiah promises. Maintaining this belief is not an easy task to accomplish as we read newspapers and follow the blogs. We must continue to be inspired by the idealistic writings of Isaiah, Micah, Amos, and others, but at the same time we cannot afford to lose sight of the real world for even a brief moment. Explicit calls to abandon "western morality" are a sick and suicidal symptom of indulging in a temptation we can ill afford at this historical moment. There is an attraction to the idea that history, as we know it, has ceased. Such thinking allows us to indulge in fantasies about pure free market capitalism, or, alternatively, a full embrace of socialism, or even an outright rejection of all political solutions in favor of miracles. This is a temptation that is not external to tradition and brought on by others, but it is one that is part and parcel of our traditional inheritance.

CONCLUSION

> We try to localize weapons of mass destruction and destructive thoughts exterior to ourselves as if they are not somehow central to our beings.
> Eigen, 2006, p. 91

Tradition's temptations are not like the more familiar external ones like cheating on your taxes or your wife. While there are often ingenious attempts to rationalize these more familiar temptations, there is also a tacit knowledge that these actions are wrong and need rationalizing to justify them, in the first place. It is relatively easy for adults to see how cheating on your taxes or your wife eats away at the shared moral capital and makes living together in society more difficult. Tradition's temptations, however, are more subtle. In thrall to nostalgia, exclusivity, and certainty, and mesmerized by the excitement of submission, the fantasy of destroying our own desires, and the intoxication of messianism, there is no need to rationalize anything. From inside tradition, these temptations are often coded as positive values. These temptations are shared among many in the community, and one does not have to hide one's aspirations. These are values that are often encouraged by authoritarian leaders who have much to gain from their acceptance. So unlike cheating on your taxes or your wife, there is no need to bury these indulgences.

Followers who submit completely to leaders don't feel guilt, but pride. Traditionalists who refuse to admit the existence of legitimate doubts are not blamed but praised. Those who celebrate exclusivity are themselves celebrated by their co-religionists. For those overcome by the temptations of tradition, it is almost impossible to see why one would ever want to extricate him or herself. There is always a verse, a story, a law (interpreted appropriately), and a good "friend" who will justify nostalgia or messianism. Besides, indulging in these temptations feels so good in the moment.

This is not to say that there are no antidotes. Tradition itself has many voices and recognizing this obvious and simple truth is a first step out of the labyrinth. For every source that seemingly encourages exclusivity, certainty, and submission there are counter-sources that question these values. The tradition teaches us to love the stranger, to choose life, and to walk humbly before God. We are warned that if we hear rumors about the Messiah, plant the tree in your hand first and then go out to greet the Messiah. We have been taught that you will be long in your grave and the Messiah will not be here. There is Nahmanides who warned about the possibility of being a scoundrel with the Torah's approval. There is Maimonides whose universal focus tempers many of the internal desires outlined here. There are contemporary voices such as Hartman, Greenberg, and Lamm.

Even the antidotes, however, can be co-opted by the power of tradition's temptations. The mitzvah of loving the stranger is read as narrowly as possible. Maimonides's universalism is painted by internal critics as external to tradition. Critical contemporary thinkers are labeled as enemies rather than as teachers.

There are no permanent, pre-packaged solutions to temptation. Each generation, and each person in that generation searching for an ethical and meaningful life, must find his or her own balance between fitting in and being true to oneself. Each of us must discover our way of muddling through the maze. If we are not just true to tradition, but if we are to allow tradition to grow and mature to meet the needs of today's ethical crises, tradition's temptations must be named, faced, and overcome (at least, from time to time). The temptations outlined above, harm our humanity, belittle our intelligence, and denigrate our creatureliness and mortality. It is important to keep in mind with Michael Eigen that "more important than imaginary purity is the concrete reality of every human being" (2006, p. 17). Jewish ethics in a new key must learn to be vigilant and as sensitive to internal threats as we have always been to external ones. In the attempt to protect ourselves at all costs from, Naamah, "the fairest of all women who seduced the sons of the mighty," we begin to alter ourselves beyond recognition. My deepest fear is that in trying to keep ourselves whole, we begin to slowly destroy ourselves.

REFERENCES

Berkowitz, Eliezer, *Not in Heaven: The Nature and Function of Halakha* (New York: Ktav Publishing House, 1983).

Boyarin, Daniel, *Carnal Israel: Reading Sex in Talmudic Culture* (Berkeley: University of California Press, 1993).

Dewey, John, *The Quest for Certainty: A Study of the Relation of Knowledge and Action* (New York: Capricorn Books, GP Putnam and Sons, 1929).

Eigen, Michael, *Lust* (Middletown, CT: Wesleyan University Press, 2006).

Ghent, Emmanuel, "Masochism, Submission, and Surrender: Masochism as a Perversion of Surrender," *Contemporary Psychoanalysis*, Vol. 26, 1990, pp. 108–136.

Greenberg, Irving, "Theology After the Shoah: The Transformation of the Core Paradigm," *Modern Judaism* (2006).

Hartman, David, *Israelis and the Jewish Tradition: An Ancient People Debating its Future* (New Haven: Yale University Press, 2000).

Lamm, Norman, *The Shema: Spirituality and Law in Judaism* (Philadelphia: Jewish Publication Society, 1998).

Pava, Moses L. "Spirituality In (and Out) of the Classroom: A Pragmatic Approach," *Journal of Business Ethics,* 2007, Vol. 73, No. 3, pp. 287–299.

Rackman, Emanuel, *One Man's Judaism* (Tel Aviv: Greenfield Publishers, no date).

Roth, Phillip, *Exit Ghost* (New York: Vintage, 2007).

Rothenberg, Naftali, *The Wisdom of Love: Man Woman & God in Jewish Canonical Literature* (Boston: Academic Studies Press, 2009).

Soloveitchik, Joseph B, 1964, "Confrontation," *Tradition*, Vol. 5, No. 2.

Starr, Karen E., *Repair of the Soul: Metaphors of Transformation in Jewish Mysticism and Psychoanalysis* (New York: Routledge, 2008).

Wurzburger, Walter S., *Ethics of Responsibility: Pluralistic Approaches to Covenantal Ethics* (Philadelphia and Jerusalem: The Jewish Publication Society, 1994).

CHAPTER 3

SACRED COMPROMISE

Be holy for I am holy.

Leviticus 11:44

Then God said, "Let us make man in our likeness, and let there be a creature not only the product of earth, but also gifted with heavenly, spiritual elements." Truth then appeared, falling before God's throne, and in all humility exclaimed: "Deign, O God, to refrain from calling into being a creature who is beset with the vice of lying." Peace came forth to support this petition. "Wherefore, O lord, shall this creature appear on earth; he will bring about war and destruction in his eagerness for gain and conquest."

Whilst they were pleading against the creation of man, there was heard, arising from another part of the heavens, the soft voice of Charity: "Sovereign of the universe." The voice exclaimed, in all its mildness, "vouchsafe thou to create a being in thy, likeness, for it will be a noble creature striving to imitate thy attributes by its actions." The Creator approved of the pleadings of Charity, called man into being, and cast Truth down to the earth to flourish there; and he dignified Truth by making her his own seal.

Midrash Rabba

From the perspective of an outsider looking in, the belief that religious individuals and communities should *not* compromise on matters sacred or holy is seemingly obvious and self-evident. The well-known Israeli philosopher Avishai Margalit, in his recent book, *On Compromise and Rotten Compromises* (2010), describes this belief clearly and unequivocally. He writes, "The religious picture is in the grip of the idea of the holy. The holy is not negotiable, let alone subject to compromise. Crudely put, *one cannot compromise over the holy without compromising the holy*" (p. 24, emphasis added). Or, just one page later, he writes, "The logic of the holy as an ideal type is the negation of the idea of compromise." The purpose of this chapter is to challenge Margalit, and both those outsiders and religious insiders, who share this belief. In my view, from a Jewish perspective, the assertion that the holy is unalterably opposed to the idea of compromise is both false and dangerous.

Compromise, or as its etymology suggests—to promise together—is one of the necessary building blocks of a Jewish ethics in a new key. Removing the possibility of compromise from large chunks of our lives, or even believing that others have done so, significantly diminishes our ability to work together to build and to sustain an ethical world. I suggest that religious individuals and communities can and must be open at all times to the possibility of profound and radical compromise. Further, it is important that secularists recognize this possibility for growth, even for believers, who explicitly claim to reject any compromise on holy matters.

Contrary to Margalit, sacred compromise is a key ingredient of holiness and not an anathema. Further, sacred compromise, while never commonplace and certainly never entered into casually, is a Jewish concept with roots deeply buried in our ancient traditions. To aspire to authentic holiness is not to be walled-in and fully-protected or fixed once and for all, rather it is to be open and ready for life's great mysteries and unfoldings. Religious sacrifice, properly understood, *always* entails a sacred compromise. So too, forgiveness and repentance are *wholly dependent* upon the possibility of sacred compromise.

No-Compromise: The Holy is Not Negotiable

While I believe that Avishai Margalit's assertion that the holy is not negotiable is a false and ethically dangerous conception to hold (for both religious outsiders and insiders), it is also an understandable and quite plausible view. As the Bible plainly teaches, "You shall make no covenant with the inhabitants of this land [Canaan], but you shall break down their altars" (Joshua 2:2). Or as the Talmud states, "let the law bore through the mountain, as it is said, 'judgment belongs to God'" (Sanhedrin 6b). Indeed, there is ample evidence to document and support the no-compromise stance in both biblical and rabbinic sources. Further, even a cursory glimpse at today's Jewish newspapers undeniably suggests that a large number of contemporary rabbis proudly cling to this position.

In the Bible, two narratives stand out as particularly strong evidence against the possibility of religious compromise. Pinchas, the grandson of Aaron the high priest, is remembered in Jewish history as an especially vivid symbol of strength and inviolability in the face of loosening moral standards and religious corruption. According to the Book of Numbers, it happened once that an Israelite man brought a Midianite woman "near to his brothers in the sight of Moses and in the sight of the entire assembly of the children of Israel..." (25:6) Pinchas, a bystander to this highly provocative event, reacted with immediacy and a zealous vengeance. Taking his spear in hand, he followed the couple into the tent and "pierced them both, the Israelite man and the woman into her stomach..." (25:7) With a single thrust of his spear, he killed them both. His outsized and bloody deed halted a deadly plague in which 24,000 people had already died.

The rabbis of the Talmud noted the unusual events recounted in this story. There was no warning (as is required in all capital cases), no formal court case to determine guilt or innocence here, and strangely Pinchas completely ignored his "teacher" Moses, even though, as the text goes out of its way to mention, the brazen act took place "in the sight of Moses." This was vigilante justice at its most extreme. And, if there is any lingering doubt on the reader's part concerning the correctness of Pinchas's no-compromise stance, the text of Torah clarifies by noting that Pinchas and his descendants are rewarded with the "covenant of eternal priesthood, *because* he took vengeance for his God" (25:13, emphasis added).

"On all counts of the holy, the domain of the holy should be free from human manipulation and human interests. It is the domain of God, his sanctuary. Violating God's honor by compromising what is due to God alone is anathema, an act of worshipping evil" (Margalit, p. 72). Margalit's words here provide an apt explanation to help understand and explain the motivation of Pinchas in this story. In publicly dishonoring God, it was as if this couple was worshipping evil, and such an act must be stopped, *come what may.*

An even more famous and extreme narrative is recounted in I Samuel. Saul, the king of Israel, is commanded to utterly destroy the people and wealth of Amalek because of the particularly heinous way this nation attacked the Israelites after the exodus from Egypt. "Now go, attack the Amalekites and totally destroy everything that belongs to them. Do not spare them; put to death men and women, children and infants, cattle and sheep, camels and donkeys" (15:3).

Saul carried out these instructions quickly and efficiently. He and his army attacked Amalek and unflinchingly destroyed the men, women, children, and cattle, and so on. "But Saul and the army spared Agag [the king of the Amalekites] and the best of the sheep and cattle, the fat calves and lambs—everything that was good. These, they were unwilling to destroy completely, but everything that was despised and weak they totally destroyed" (15:9).

"What then is the bleating of sheep in my ears?" (15:14) Samuel bluntly asked Saul, after Saul claimed to have carried out all of God's instructions. Although Saul stated that the reason he saved the best of the animals was precisely so he could sacrifice them to God, God is grieved with Saul's decision, unmoved by his rationale, and sorry that he anointed him as king of Israel. This is a seemingly small difference of opinion and an excusable improvisation, *from Saul's perspective. From God's point of view,* however, it is a grave act of disobedience that will necessarily alter Jewish history forever. Because he and his men were "unwilling to destroy completely" when commanded to do so by God, Saul is to be replaced as king of Israel by David.

The prophet Samuel explained the grave nature of this blasphemous affront as follows: "For rebellion is like the sin of divination, and arrogance like the evil of idolatry. Because you have rejected the word of the Lord, he has rejected you as king."

It is not possible to argue that either of these two narratives is peripheral or tangential to Judaism. These are core stories, essential to a full and complete understanding of Jewish history. How is it that Pinchas and his family became the high priests in Israel? How is it that David and his descendants became the kings of Israel? The answers are recorded for posterity in these much studied stories, passed on from one generation to the next.

Extremism in the name of the holy and sacred represents a strong and unbroken strand in Judaism. In these two texts, and many others, the domain of the holy is understood as something set above and separate from the routine and normal. The holy commands special attention and complete and total devotion. The holy stands apart from the normal give and take of the secular world.

Echoes of Pinchas and Samuel can be heard in intense debates in Israel to this day about giving up sacred land in exchange for peace with its Arab neighbors. Extremists claim that it is absolutely impossible, from a religious perspective, to justify handing over sacred land to non-Jews, and it is prohibited to obey army orders to evacuate Jewish citizens from Israeli settlements. Consider the words of the twentieth century Rabbi Yaacov Moshe Harlop, former head of the Mercaz HaRav Yeshiva in Jerusalem, written in 1936 before the establishment of the state of Israel, in response to Britain's proposed Partition Plan:

> Behold, the matter is simple and clear—Heaven forbid that the Jewish People relinquish any tiny concession of any iota of land that is sanctified with the holiness of Eretz Yisrael [land of Israel]... There is no doubt that if the matter reaches the point where we will need sign an international agreement that includes any form of surrender of our rights to Eretz Yisrael, it is preferable for those signing to chop off their thumbs, rather than to chop up the garden of Zion. Just like a person who states that the entire Torah is from Heaven, except for one letter, he is considered a heretic, so too one who states that all of Israel belongs to the Jewish People except for one footstep, behold he is totally cut off from the holiness of the Land and he violates the soul of Israel... for Israel is undividable. (Published in Techumin, Vol. 9, p. 272)

Rabbi Harlop's position is all-or-nothing. This kind of highly-charged and controversial rhetoric should be taken with the utmost seriousness as it entails dire political effects. This is not to say, though, that one must agree with these statements, nor must one always accept and interpret these dramatic statements at face value.

The harsh and uncompromising tone of this proclamation—"Heaven forbid...any tiny concession of any iota of land that is sanctified"—and many others is an attempt by contemporary rabbis to conjure up the memory and to invoke the authority of biblical and rabbinic predecessors. The 1936 directive to "chop off their thumbs" is reminiscent of Pinchas's own fury and uncompromising actions to destroy sinners. Rabbi Harlop's passion mimics the style of Samuel castigating King Saul, no holds barred. But was Rabbi Harlop's expression meant to be taken literally? And, even if he did intend all of this in a literal sense, must we necessarily read and understand it in this same way?

HOLINESS AS AN EXTERNAL FORCE

Rabbi Harlop's loud and shrill voice does communicate a deeply felt *emotional* truth. It expresses a combustible mixture of love of one's people and homeland, hate for one's enemies, a sense of historical entitlement, fear, shame, and an intense desire and commitment to continue fighting for what one believes is right. It conveys the belief that what is at stake in this struggle between Israelis and Palestinians is not just about who gets what, but what is in play here is the very *identity* of the Jewish people. What the voice tries to obscure, however, consciously or unconsciously, is the unalterable fact that, regardless of how loud it is, this remains Rabbi Harlop's *own* voice. Like all human utterances, it is a specific interpretation of events, authored at a particular historical moment, and subject to the potential for change and alteration over time.

The philosophy of no-compromise, come what may, is attached to a unique and partial vision of the holy. It is a vision of holiness, like all visions, grounded in metaphor. When we say holiness is x (whatever x is), it is always to be understood that what we are really saying is that holiness is *like* x. This is why the prophet Ezekiel, for example, when he reports his ecstatic vision of the chariot, is always cautious and repeatedly states "it had the appearance of" or the "the likeness of" and never attempts to directly describe holiness in itself (see especially Ezekiel Chapter 1).

Those who insist on no-compromise experience the holy *as if* it is an external force imposing itself upon them. Holiness is *like* a mysterious, incomprehensible, transcendent, wholly other power. There is almost a magical quality to holiness experienced through the lens of this metaphor. It represents a commanding power. It presents a *vertical* vision of holiness.

Holiness is dangerous and one can choose to submit to it or to defy it, but if one chooses defiance, calamitous consequences will necessarily follow. This is Job's experience of the holy, poignantly described in his description of God speaking to him through the whirlwind. "Who is this that makes the purpose of God dark by words without knowledge?" (38:2) This type of experience of holiness is reminiscent of a child in the presence of a strict and stern father. This is the dominant metaphor through which Pinchas, Samuel, and Rabbi Harlop interpret their life's events and circumstances.

When Avishai Margalit writes that "the religious picture is in the grip of the idea of the holy," it is more precise to qualify this statement as follows: *for some people, at some points in time*, the religious picture is in the grip of *a particular metaphor* of the holy. This metaphor is a powerful human tool. It is an attractive and extremely sticky meme. It dovetails with some of our most intimate and profound experiences. It can be an enriching metaphor that lends meaning and purpose to life's most intimate activities. At its best, it provides a way of navigating our way through the world that enlivens everyday occurrences, sharpens our sensibilities, deepens our attachment to others, and provides a framework for decision making. It is a safety net, an insurance policy, and a protective shield. It provides a sense of continuity, security, and certainty in a discontinuous, insecure, and uncertain world. It is not an invention of any single individual or even any single religion. It is a vast multicultural accomplishment, thousands of years in the making. But, it is not the only metaphor, nor is it costless.

Experiencing the holy as a vertical presence, as if one is in the presence of a strict father, is both enriching and constricting. Ultimately, though, it locks out more of life, than it opens up. From the perspective of this metaphor, we hear God punishing us for "refusing to destroy completely" and somehow this makes perfect sense to us! From the perspective of this metaphor, we hear our own voice speaking, but refuse to take authorship or responsibility for our own words and their effects. But, this is only part of a bigger story about holiness.

Holiness in Time

> Let him kiss me with the kisses of his mouth for your love is better than wine.
>
> Shir Ha-Shirim 1:2

An alternative metaphor imagines holiness in more naturalistic and human terms. It is horizontal and not vertical. To experience holiness, from this point of view, is to resonate with the deep and primal rhythms of life; it is to be in sync with the very blood pumping through our veins. To be holy is to be mindful and appreciative of each and every breath of air we inhale and exhale. It is to experience the mysteries of life and to flow with them. To experience holiness requires both wisdom and practice that feel like gifts from God.

There is a way of experiencing holiness, not from a God's eye perspective, but from a wholly human one. Holiness is like dancing, making music, or making love. As the twelfth century Jewish philosopher Maimonides wrote, "What is the proper form of the love (of God)? It is that he should love the Lord with great, overpowering, fierce love to the extent that his soul is bound to the love of God and he dwells on it constantly, *as if he were love-sick for a woman and dwells on this constantly*, whether he is sitting or standing, eating or drinking" (Teshuva 10:3, emphasis added).

This is not holiness as experienced through the metaphoric whirlwind of Job, the rage of Pinchas, or the incomprehensible judgment of Samuel, but this is holiness as imagined by Rabbi Akiva in his description of *Shir Ha-Shirim* [the Song of Songs], a collection of ancient love poems, as the holy of holies:

> For all the ages are not worth the day on which the Song of Songs was given to Israel; for the *Ketuvim* (Writings) are holy but the Song of Songs is the holy of holies. (*Yedaim* 3:5)

It is certainly true as Rabbi Louis Jacobs has noted, that "the standard Rabbinic view, and the reason why Rabbi Akiba declared the book to be 'the Holy of Holies,' is that the Rabbis saw the 'lover' as God and the 'beloved' as the community of Israel" (1995, p. 475). But what is important to emphasize for the present purposes is that in order to symbolize and better understand the relationship between God and Israel, the rabbis, in this instance, boldly applied *metaphoric language* in which "sexual desire is expressed exquisitely but with the utmost frankness" (Jacobs, 1996, p. 475). According to the Song of Songs, the experience of holiness *is like* sexual desire. Or, loosely restated, spirituality *is like* sensuality.

Holiness is not always experienced as an external force imposed upon us as described above, but it can be experienced as a unique and special quality of time. No one has written about this with more elegance, authority, and poetry than the great twentieth century theologian Rabbi Abraham Joshua Heschel:

> One of the most distinguished words in the Bible is the word *kadosh*, holy; a word which more than any other is representative of the mystery and majesty of the divine. Now what was the first holy object in the history of the world? Was it a mountain? Was it an altar?

> It is, indeed, a unique occasion at which the distinguished word *kadosh* is used for the first time: in the book of Genesis at the end of the story of creation. How extremely significant is the fact that it is applied to time: "And God blessed the seventh day and made it holy." There is no reference in the record of creation to any object in space that would be endowed with the quality of holiness.
>
> This is a radical departure from accustomed religious thinking. The mythical mind would expect that, after heaven and earth have been established, God would create a holy place—a holy mountain or a holy spring—whereupon a sanctuary is to be established. Yet it seems as if to the Bible it is *holiness in time*, the Sabbath, which comes first. (1959, p. 272, emphasis in original)

From a traditional Jewish perspective, experiencing the Sabbath fully is to be in tune with the most profound rhythms of creation. Experiencing the Jewish holidays is to be in sync with the changes of the seasons. In fact, nearly every activity is Jewish life, including all significant life-events, can be heightened and elevated through practice, religious ritual, and mindfulness.

The contemporary Rabbi Irwin Kula defines holiness as follows:

> In Hebrew the opposite of holy is *chol*, which is translated not as "profane" but as "empty"; in other words, "not yet filled." The word for holy in Hebrew is *kedusha*. A more accurate translation is "life intensity." To be holy is to be intensely dynamic, ever-changing, and ever realizing. The Biblical command "You Shall Be Holy" is an invitation to celebrate what philosopher Mark Taylor calls "a maze of grace that is the world." Live as richly and passionately as possible; that's as close to meaning as you will get. (2006, pp. 44–45)

Eating, drinking, making love, and even eliminating can be accomplished in consonance with the natural cycles of life and not in opposition to them. There is even a prayer to be recited after elimination that expresses our appreciation and thankfulness for the body's rhythmic and continuous openings and closings:

> Blessed art thou, Lord our God, King of the universe, who hast formed man in wisdom, and created in him a system of ducts and tubes. It is well known before thy glorious throne that if but one of these be opened, or if one of those be closed, it would be impossible to exist in thy presence. (Birnbaum, 1977, p. 14)

There is a real paradox here, what Douglas Hofstadter called a *strange loop*. "Whenever, by moving upwards (or downwards) through the levels of some hierarchical system, we unexpectedly find ourselves right back where we started" (1979), the strange loop phenomenon is present. In the case at hand, to experience heightened levels of holiness requires us to deepen our engagement with the everyday and mundane activities of life. But, in deepening our engagement with everyday life, we gain access to a broadened dimension of holiness. The holy and the secular may be opposites, but they are opposites that are completely dependent upon one another for their meaning, like down is to up and empty is to full.

Sacred Compromise

In Judaism (as I assume in most world religions), holiness is a complex and ambiguous phenomenon. It is not like any one thing or any one experience, but it is multifaceted. Alternative values are identified with alternative metaphors. For those who experience holiness as a kind of resonance with the rhythms of life, horizontal holiness, the notion of compromise is not equated with disobedience to God's word, but it is *reimagined* as a necessary, albeit difficult, accommodation to life's realities. The experience of holiness is constituted, in part, by the experience of compromise, "intensely dynamic, ever changing and ever realizing."

A sacred compromise can be defined formally as breaking a seemingly inviolable and deeply-held principle for the sake of a previously unimagined and unimaginable principle, a more encompassing vision, a higher-order principle, perhaps even a principle not yet fully comprehended or understood. Arthur Green does not use the phrase sacred compromise, but he does describe a nearly identical process as both necessary and inevitable aspects of the religious journey:

> At any given point where the seeker stands in his religious life, his mind is filled with some particular content of understanding: he conceives of God in some specific way. This conception is the *penimi,* that which is "within" the mind at that moment. This *penimi,* however, is inevitably attached to a *maqqif,* a conception beyond the mind's present grasp, one which at the same time both challenges the *penimi* and offers a conception on a higher level. Man's task is to seek out this *maqqif,* to bring into his mind as a new *penimi,* and thus to seek a still-higher challenge and resolution.

Sacred compromise sometimes feels, from the inside, like a giving up, such as Moses smashing the stones upon which were written the Ten Commandments, but it is better envisioned as *a moving on.* It is always a real and extremely excruciating psychological and (sometimes even) social sacrifice, but a sacrifice always offered in the name of a more complex, "still-higher challenge and resolution," just out of our present reach.

BIBLICAL MODELS OF SACRED COMPROMISE

> Is it not true that wherever there is truth and justice there is no peace, and wherever there is peace, there is no truth and justice? But what is justice that also contains peace? That is compromise.
>
> R. Yehoshua ben Korcha

It is relatively easy to find both ancient and contemporary examples of the no-compromise position. Pinchas, Samuel, and Rabbi Harlop are cited above as illustrative examples and not with the intention of providing a comprehensive list of every example. What, perhaps, is less well-known is the ease in identifying examples of sacred compromise, both in the Bible and in rabbinic sources. In the Jewish tradition, it is Aaron, Moses's older brother, who is identified most closely with compromise. Aaron's motto was "love peace and pursue peace and make peace between man and man, as it is written: 'The law of truth was in his mouth, unrighteousness was not found in his lips, he walked with Me in peace and uprightness and did turn away many from iniquity'" (Sanhedrin 6b).

In turning to the Bible, first, let us consider the case of the daughters of *Zelophehad*. Just before the people were about to enter the Promised Land, these five women, now orphaned, approached Moses in front of the entire congregation, with a complaint. Since their father had no sons and only daughters, the law, as it was understood at that moment, stated that his inheritance would be lost from the family forever, and the name of *Zelophehad* would be forgotten among his family. This, in the daughters' view, was simply not fair, especially since *Zelophehad* had not taken part in the sin of *Korach* and his congregation.

Moses was uncertain as to how to answer them and he turned to God. God replied:

> The daughters of Zelophehad speak right: thou shalt surely give them a possession of an inheritance among their father's brethren; and thou shalt cause the inheritance of their father to pass unto them. And thou shalt speak unto the children of Israel, saying: If a man die, and have no son, then ye shall cause his inheritance to pass unto his daughter. (Numbers 27:7–8)

Later on, the leaders of the tribe of *Menasseh*, *Zelophehad's* tribe, brought a new complaint to Moses. They pointed out that if the daughters of *Zelophehad* were to marry men from a different tribe, the land would be lost to the tribe of *Menasseh*, and this, in *their* view, was not fair. They argued to Moses as follows: the land "will be added to the inheritance of the tribe whereunto they shall belong; so will it be taken away from the lot of our inheritance" (Numbers 36:3).

Ultimately, a final compromise was reached and implemented. The daughters were to inherit their father's land but only on the condition that they marry within the tribe. "So shall no inheritance of the children of Israel remove from tribe to tribe; for the children of Israel shall cleave every one to the inheritance of the tribe of his fathers" (Numbers 36:7).

It is the holiness of the land of Israel that is in play in this story, and we have moved some distance from the no-compromise position. In this case, the appropriate understandings of the laws of inheritance are adjusted back and forth until an equilibrium is reached, and everyone's legitimate concerns are met. The principle of letting the "law bore through the mountain" is sacrificed in favor of social cohesion and perceived equity. As Rabbi Shlomo Riskin has recently written, this is a case where the "strict letter of the law must be *further interpreted*. Law speaks eternally only when justice takes into account the interest of peace" (2008, emphasis added). There is certainly still an element of the holiness as a top-down phenomenon here, but authentic holiness now must conform to a broader and more complex conception, one that includes dialogue and a human perspective, as well. Presumably, had everyone remained silent, the law, as originally understood, would never have been altered, and (even from a God's-eye perspective) we would have gotten this "wrong."

A second biblical example also deals with the holiness of the land of Israel. This is the case of Reuben and Gad. This case, too, is understood best, as an example of holiness being experienced as an unfolding process and thus subject to change (albeit difficult) and compromise over time. After 40 years of circling in the wilderness, the children of Israel were finally ready to enter the Promised Land. Two of the 12 tribes, however, had other ideas. The tribes of Reuben and Gad expressed a desire to remain on the eastern side of the Jordan River; "the place was a place for cattle," and these tribes had "a great multitude of cattle" (Numbers 32). Moses, upon hearing this request was angry with them. It undercut the "bottom line" purpose of the entire narrative, as Moses understood it until that time. The very purpose of the Exodus of Egypt and the revelation at Sinai, it was understood and taken as self-evident, could be realized only on the western bank of the river, that is, in Canaan proper. In response to their request, Moses's initial reaction was to call the leaders of Reuben and Gad a "brood of sinful men." These words, spoken in haste, derive from the no-compromise perspective.

Despite this initial reaction, Moses had second thoughts and invoked a solution consistent with an alternative conception of holiness, one that explicitly recognizes the human element. At this point in his career, he demonstrated the best of what covenantal leadership entails (for more about the unique characteristics of covenantal leadership see Pava, 2003). In order to maintain social organization and to promote moral growth, Moses accepted an imaginative compromise. The tribes were permitted to "build sheepfolds for the cattle and cities for their little ones" on the eastern bank, but only if they promised that they would not return to inhabit these cities "until all the children of Israel have received their inheritance." The special needs of these two tribes were balanced against the needs of the entire people. The original plan was altered in real time, and it is holiness, the sanctity of the land of Israel, that is in play once again.

In this narrative, Moses suddenly discovered himself out of sync with the conditions on the ground. In his ability to improvise in the moment, Moses reconnected with the changing rhythms of his people, *and* without surrendering his own integrity. Compromising on what is considered in and what is considered out is not something apart from holiness, but compromise—to promise one another—contrary to Avishai Margalit's assumption, on this model is constitutive of holiness.

RABBINICAL MODEL OF SACRED COMPROMISE

> Doing righteous deeds of charity is greater than offering all of the sacrifices, as it is written: "Doing charity and justice is more desirable to the Lord than sacrifice."
>
> Sukkah 49

A final example taken from the rabbinic literature concerns Yochanan ben Zakkai, a student of Hillel and considered his most promising rabbinic protégé. Until the year 68 CE, two years before the eventual destruction of the Temple in Jerusalem, Yochanan ben Zakkai, was known as a dedicated scholar, founder of an academy known as the "great house," and a stern and strict interpreter of Jewish law. One tradition has is that he sat in the shadows of the Temple and lectured to his students all day. Another tradition quotes him as castigating the residence of Galilee for their lax religious observance. "O Galilee, Galilee, thou hatest the Torah; hence wilt thou fall into the hands of robbers!"

In 68 CE, the Roman army, the most powerful in the world at the time, held Jerusalem in its death-grip. The Romans had surrounded the city and rather than attack the well-fortified target, they chose to patiently wait out Jerusalem's inhabitants. The situation inside the besieged city became increasingly desperate. Food was in short supply and hope was scarce. The zealots, a group of extremists, literally called the bandits by the Talmud, staged a military coup and took political control of the city. Believing that God would miraculously save them, the zealots destroyed much of the food supply and blockaded the gates of Jerusalem from the inside, preventing anyone from escaping the city. The zealots believed, as a matter of faith, that it was better to die a martyr's death, or even to commit suicide, than to surrender to the vastly superior Roman Army and to give up Jerusalem and the holy Temple.

Yochanan ben Zakkai, universally respected as a teacher of Torah, counseled peace, but realized that this was an impossible dream under the current political circumstances. "How long will you carry on like this, and starve everyone to death?" he asked his own nephew, Abba Sikrah, the titular leader of the zealots. But, by now, even Abba Sikrah had lost control of his followers. "What can I do?" He rhetorically responded, "if I tell them anything they will kill me." Realizing that this was his defining moment, Yochanan ben Zakkai, with his nephew's help, devised a plan to escape the city, leaving his coreligionists behind.

He feigned his own death and was carried out in a coffin through the gates of Jerusalem to be buried by his students outside the city limits, as prescribed by Jewish law. Once outside the walls of Jerusalem and the irrational control and blind zeal of his coreligionists, he arranged a meeting with Vespasian, the Roman general in charge of the army. During the meeting, Yochanan ben Zakkai predicted Vespasian's imminent rise to Emperor of Rome. Later, upon receiving news of his elevation, Vespasian granted Yochanan ben Zakkai his modest request to build a Torah Academy in Yavneh, on the Mediterranean coast. In his understated and memorable words, "Give me Yavneh and her sages."

Although Yochanan ben Zakkai *pretended* that he had died in order to escape the Roman siege and the Jewish zealots, his old world would, *in actuality*, be destroyed in just two short years. The Romans finally breached the walls of Jerusalem in 70 CE. Ultimately, they destroyed the Temple completely, brutally killed thousands, took others as slaves, and triumphantly marched home to Rome with the holy vessels, including the *menorah*, proudly displayed and memorialized to this day on the Arch of Titus. But like Yochanan, the rumors of Judaism's death were premature.

Yochanan ben Zakkai's bold innovations at Yavneh would prove to be the seeds for Judaism's renewal, even in the face of seemingly utter destruction. Yochanan ben Zakkai does nothing short of re-envisioning God's relationship to his people. With the Temple in ruins, the sacrificial rites, the centerpiece of religious practice as it was known among the Jewish people until then, were no longer possible. It would seem then the connection between God and Israel had been severed. Grounding his new interpretation in the Prophets, Yochanan ben Zakkai expansively reread the Hosea's statement, "I desired deeds of lovingkindness and not sacrifice," to mean "deeds of lovingkindness on the part of a nation have the atoning power of a sin-offering."

Further, Yochanan ben Zakkai made several specific enactments at Yavneh to promote his new vision. He ruled, for example, that the shofar should now be blown in Yavneh on the Sabbath, a practice that had been restricted before the destruction to Jerusalem only. Similarly, he ruled that the four species should now be taken on all seven days of the holiday of Sukkot, another practice that had been, until then, restricted to Jerusalem. He determined that Jews should continue to eat the bitter herbs on the Passover holiday "to remember the Temple Service," even though the biblical requirement to do so was abrogated with the Temple's destruction. Further, Ben Zakkai established the practices of washing one's hands before eating bread, eating bread with salt, and lighting the Sabbath candles. These practices were designed to emphasize that the table at which one eats his or her meals is like the altar upon which the priests of the past offered sacrifices.

It is hard to fathom, from today's vantage, the revolutionary nature of Yochanan ben Zakkai's, new philosophy. Literally, within months of the destruction of the Temple, he was able to stem the tide of depression among his people, and convincingly offer them an altogether new paradigm. Commenting upon his belief that deeds of lovingkindness can have the same atoning power of sacrifice, Jacob Neusner wrote:

> What Yohanan demanded was that Israel now see, in its humble day-to-day practice, deeds of so grand a dimension as to rival the sacred actions, rites, and gestures of the Temple. If we appreciate the force of powerful emotions aroused by the Temple cult, we may understand how grand a revolution was effected in the simple declaration, so long in coming, that with the destruction of the Temple the realm of the sacred had finally overspread the world. Man must now see in himself, in his selfish motives to be immolated, the noblest sacrifice of all...If one wants to do something for God, in a time when the Temple is no more, the offering must be the gift of selfless compassion. The holy altar must be the streets and marketplaces of the world...In the end he accomplished a revolution of the spirit, which has not yet run its course. Yohanan recovered the whole of what was best in ancient teachings and reshaped it for the future (1975, p. 173).

"How grand a revolution" was effected by Yochanan ben Zakkai's decision to compromise and request Yavneh instead of Jerusalem (a compromise diametrically opposed by his contemporaries). "How grand of a revolution" was his statement proclaiming that deeds of lovingkindness can themselves atone. And, "how grand a revolution" were his many innovative enactments, imagining each Jew as a "Priest" in his own home.

Underlying this revolution, was a new experience of holiness. Here was an alternative perspective, a perspective with antecedents in biblical and rabbinic thinking, but never before so explicitly articulated. Rather than imagining holiness as an external force imposing itself upon the Jewish people, such as a father demanding gifts from his children, holiness resides in the ability to find meaning in everyday actions and rituals such as washing one's hands before a meal, study of Torah, daily prayers instead of animal sacrifices, eating one's bread at one's own table with family and friends emulating the priests of old, and through deeds of lovingkindness. In short, Yochanan ben Zakkai rediscovered holiness through living in harmony with the daily, monthly, and annual rhythms of life.

"Woe to the children who have been exiled from their father's table" (Berachot 3a) the Talmud states, mourning the destruction of the Temple and its sacrificial rites. This is how the loss was described in the calamitous aftermath of Rome's victory. A way of being in the world, a way of experiencing the holy—it had been like children in the presence of their father—had been stolen away from the Jewish people. But with the destruction, also came opportunity, growth, and renewal. With the calamity, a new articulation of holiness was explicitly put forward and took hold of the Jewish people," a revolution of the spirit which has not yet run its course."

THE NO-COMPROMISE RESPONSE

How might Avishai Margalit and religious insiders like today's followers of Rabbi Yaacov Moshe Harlop (of whom there are many) respond to the suggestion that rabbinic Judaism, from its inception, has not only tolerated compromise on matters holy, but is founded upon compromise?

Margalit suggests that while one can never compromise on the holy, it is possible to temporarily rezone the holy. "The claim about the uncompromising nature of the holy may be *hedged significantly*, especially with respect to holy sites," writes Margalit. "One hedge, typical of religions that have lost political and military power is to spiritualize the holy—to remove the holy from the physical space... Retreat to the spiritual is one way in which the holy is negotiated" (2010, p. 74, emphasis added).

From this point of view, Yochanan ben Zakkai did not embrace an alternative understanding of holiness, but he discovered a temporary location in which to retreat (this does, of course, stretch the meaning of temporary well-beyond normal usage). Yochanan ben Zakkai did not mean to revolutionize anything. He was no more willing to compromise than his fellow zealots were. His difference with the zealots was that he was willing to significantly "hedge" (*The New Oxford American Dictionary* writes that to hedge is to "avoid making a definite decision, statement, or commitment") his claims about the uncompromising nature of the holy and patiently wait for another day.

"Retreat to the spiritual is one way in which the holy is negotiated," but all such negotiations are *temporary* in duration, and therefore can never constitute real compromise. When Yochanan ben Zakkai says, "Give me Yavneh and her sages," this is a strategy, conceived under duress and against

Ben Zakkai's will, in order to buy more time. Margalit makes this point, in general terms, in the most clear and emphatic language:

> When forced to make concessions, the believers view their concessions as a temporary setback. In their weakness, they may opt for truce but only for the sake of regaining strength, not for the sake of peace. The politics of the holy may include cessation of violence, but never cessation of the expectation of violence. *Thus the politics of the holy, I maintain, is inherently irredentist* [an irredentist is a person or group who support the return to their country of territories that used to belong to it but are no longer]. Religious irredentism can be dormant and can erupt violently, but it cannot be discounted, even when dormant. (2010, p. 73, emphasis added)

Margalit is making an extremely strong claim here, and it is not without its supporting evidence, even in the case of Yochanan ben Zakkai. Ben Zakkai's last words, for example, "Prepare a throne for Hezekiah, the King of Judah, who is coming," can be interpreted as a declaration of his belief that the Messiah's coming was imminent, and soon everything would be back to normal.

Judah Goldin, a twentieth century Judaic scholar, described Yochanan ben Zakkai's project as "revolutionary" in scope. He stated that Ben Zakkai showed that "it *is* possible to worship God and to show one's love for and to Him, without giving him a material gift... We can win [God's good opinion] by acts of lovingkindness to our fellow man." This idea, however, "takes a long time to sink in..." Goldin continued, however, *providing direct support for Margalit*, by noting that this idea "never entirely displaces the primary impulse. If only there were the Temple: what a busyness would go on, what a tangible reassurance it would be to see the High Priest change from one set of garments to another" (as quoted in Neusner, 1975, p. 172).

The most impressive evidence for Margalit's position, however, is not from the pen of an academic pining for "tangible reassurance," but it is the current rhetoric of many of today's rabbis and Jewish leaders, the spiritual and religious followers of Rabbi Harlop and his school of thought.

WHY SHOULD WE ALLOW THE FUNDAMENTALISTS TO DEFINE OUR TERMS?

The politics of the holy is inherently irredentist, claims Margalit. This means that despite political agreements, it is *impossible* for believers to give up their claims to the sacred. Any political agreement believers might sign onto that involve sacred compromise are, at best, the result of a calculated political strategy intended as temporary in nature. I believe that this *is* a true statement, but only from a singular point of view that not only continues to view holiness as an external force and foreign imposition, but also insists that this perspective *is* God's perspective. In other words, holiness is inherently irredentist, but only for fundamentalists who refuse to recognize the metaphoric underpinnings of their experience of holiness. There is nothing to prevent Margalit, or anyone else for that matter, to pick out from tradition itself a broader, multiplicitous, and more complex definition of holiness. In fact, as heirs to a multivocal tradition, traditionalists *must choose* how best to understand the experience of holiness.

To deny choice here is to deny both our humanity and the humanity of the other. It is also to severely limit our ability to negotiate with one another in order to reach workable and good enough compromises. If we believe with Margalit that it is impossible for religious believers to negotiate and compromise on things holy, strangely, we, too, adopt a position close to fundamentalism. It is not only impossible for believers to compromise with nonbelievers in a substantial and significant sense from Margalit's perspective, but, perhaps even more troubling, it is also impossible for nonbelievers to compromise with believers. How can a nonbeliever trust a believer, if one is certain that the believer will always renege on his or her agreements, when it is in his or her interest to do so? There is a negative vicious cycle at work here that is seemingly impossible to break. If believers can never really be trusted, neither can nonbelievers, and if nonbelievers can never really be trusted, neither can believers.

For those who believe in the possibility of ethics, including the possibility of compromise among enemies, we must accept the possibility of both our own growth and development and the growth and development of others, even those with whom we have strong disagreements. We must believe that fundamentalism is not a permanent status, but a temporary stage in development. To think that it is impossible to compromise on the holy is a radically pessimistic philosophy. It is no wonder then that in describing the Israeli-Palestinian conflict that Margalit concludes, "To believe that, in this situation, compromise is within reach requires a great leap of faith" (2010, p. 167). From Margalit's perspective, the *only* hope for peace is that everyone gives up on the notion of holy all together. Short of this, we can never really trust one another.

I suppose, my own vision, is also pessimistic, but less radically so than Margalit's. My hope resides not in the possibility of everyone denouncing holiness, but my hope is for a broadened and deepened view of holiness, a view that might be shared across religious worldviews, grounded in tradition, but tailored to the needs of the contemporary world. This is a view of holiness, that recognizes both its vertical and horizontal dimensions, but one held more lightly, and with less certainty. It is a view fully aware of its own metaphoric underpinnings. It is the subject of constant dialogue and always recognizes the possibility for sacred compromise. It is a view where you allow me to grow and evolve, just as I allow you to do the same. Both repentance and forgiveness *are* possible and necessary. It is hard to be overly optimistic about this, when it seems, at least on the surface, as if we are now moving in the *wrong* direction. Perhaps, in periods of perceived dangers and increased risks, all of us have a tendency to regress to older and more familiar conceptions. If so, this too, must become the subject of dialogue and discussion. There are historical precedents for sacred compromise. The example of Yochanan ben Zakkai is one of these, and it is worthy of study and further contemplation. In the end, though, we study this and similar stories, not to relive the lives of our heroes, but to rekindle a confidence in our own, as yet unwritten futures.

CONCLUSION

> The halakhah...believes that absolute right and wrong can be realized only in heaven. In dealing with imperfect man, we posit that no man is totally wrong or right...both are partially right and wrong.
> Rabbi Joseph Soloveitchik

There is a deep irony in the contemporary no-compromise position, especially if one adopts Maimonides's understanding of the ancient sacrificial ceremonies and rites. According to Maimonides, the reason God commanded the elaborate sacrificial services, in the first place, was as a *concession* to the needs of people who had grown accustomed to these kinds of pagan rituals. Sacrifice, from God's point of view, was never a first best solution, but was a kind of *compromise* on God's part. In his words:

> But the custom which was in those days general among men, and the general mode of worship in which the Israelites were brought up consisted in sacrificing animals... It was in accordance with the wisdom and plan of God... that God did not command us to give up and to discontinue all these manners of service. For to obey such a commandment would have been contrary to the nature of man, who generally cleaves to that to which he is used; it would in those days have made the same impression as a prophet would make at present if he called us to the service of God and told us in His name, that we should not pray to God nor fast, nor seek His help in time of trouble; that we should serve Him in thought, and not by any action. (1956, Book III, Chapter. 32)

The irony in the no-compromise position is that those who hold it are *stricter* than God Himself. The very commandments calling for sacrifice are grounded in God's own compromising nature, as it were.

"We should, I believe, be judged by our compromises more than by our ideals and norms. Ideals may tell us something important about what we would like to be. But compromises tell us who we are" (Margalit, 2010, p. 5). This is a statement that I agree with wholeheartedly. I would only add that the ability to compromise is a skill we should not claim only for ourselves, but it is one that is universally available.

REFERENCES

Birnbaum, Philip, *Daily Prayer Book: Ha-Siddur Ha-Shalem* (New York: Hebrew Publishing Company, 1977).

Heschel, Abraham Joshua, *Between God and Man: An Interpretation of Judaism From the Writings of Abraham J. Heschel* (New York: The Free Press, 1959).

Hofstadter, Douglas R., *Godel, Escher, Bach: An Eternal Golden Braid* (New York: Basic Books, 1979).

Jacobs, Louis, *The Jewish Religion: A Companion* (New York: Oxford University Press, 1996).

Kula, Irwin, *Yearnings: Embracing the Sacred Messiness of Life* (New York: Hyperion, 2006).

Maimonides, Moses, *The Guide for the Perplexed* (Dover Publications, 1956 edition, translated by Friedlander, M.).

Margalit, Avishai, *On Compromise and Rotten Compromises* (Princeton and Oxford: Princeton University Press, 2010).

Neusner, Jacob, *First Century Judaism in Crisis* (Abingdon Press, 1975).

Pava, Moses L., *Leading with Meaning: Using Covenantal Leadership to Build a Better Organization* (New York: Palgrave, 2003).

Riskin, Shlomo, *Parhat Pinchus* (http://www.ots.org.il/parsha/5768/pinhas68.htm, 2008, downloaded on December 27, 2009).

CHAPTER 4

RENEWING JEWISH ETHICS

> They impose the Word meant for yesterday and thus miss hearing the Word that the eternal validity of the Torah was planning for today, for this generation, for this new hour in the history of the Jewish people.
> Rabbi Eliezer Berkovitz, 1983, p.118

Rabbi Aharon Lichtenstein, in his seminal paper, "Does Judaism Recognize an Ethic Independent of *Halakhah?*"[1] identifies two domains of decision-making in Judaism. On the one hand, there is *din*, the sphere of strict law, and on the other hand, there is *lifnim mishurat hadin* (usually translated as beyond the letter of the law), the sphere of Jewish ethics. From Lichtenstein's point of view, Jewish ethics plays a relatively minor role in Jewish life. This is because Judaism is *essentially* a religion of law. This view is expressed most clearly in a statement by Maimonides in his Commentary on the Mishnah: "What you must know is that [as regards] anything from which we abstain or which we do today, we do it *solely* because of God's commandment conveyed through Moses..." (2004, p. 36, emphasis added), This means, according to Lichtenstein, that while a kind of natural morality predates Sinai, as a sanction in Judaism, natural morality has been effectively superseded by the *Halakhah* (Jewish law).

According to Lichtenstein, the need for a Jewish ethics (or, a *halakhic* morality, as he puts it) arises *only* in those situations where the law is silent. Jewish ethics *supplements* Jewish law and serves as a *complement* to it. Quoting Nachmanides favorably, Lichtenstein writes:

> He [God] had said that you should observe the laws and statutes which He had commanded you. Now He says, with respect to what He has not commanded, you should likewise take heed to do the good and the right in His eyes, for He loves the good and the right. And this is a great matter. For it

is impossible to mention in the Torah all of a person's actions toward his neighbor and acquaintances, all of his commercial activities, and all social and political institutions. So after He had mentioned many of them...He resumes to say generally that one should do the good and the right in all matters...(p. 40)

The single purpose of Jewish ethics, as an aid to Jewish law, is to extend the ethos of law into those areas of life where there is no explicit Torah legislation.

In Judaism, according to Lichtenstein's view, Jewish law, as revealed in the Torah is supreme. It consists of 613 specific *mitzvot* or commandments. Despite the extremely broad scope of this Divine law, there remain situations where the law provides no explicit rules. The law itself recognizes this "limitation" and creates a space for ethics. "The demand or, if you will, the impetus for transcending the din is itself part of the halakhic corpus" (p. 40). Jewish ethics is thus the child of Jewish law and operates completely within its jurisdiction. While it is a debatable point whether or not *lifnim mishurat* hadin is itself a *mitzvah* in the most technical sense (most rabbinic commentators say no), it acquires whatever normative force and authority it may possess only through its origination in Jewish law. The posited relationship between law and ethics in Lichtenstein's view is thus clear, unequivocal, and unilateral. To put it most bluntly, Jewish law *creates* and *authorizes* Jewish ethics.

This conception of a one-way relationship between law and ethics, ethics as a mere construction of the law, is entwined with several other basic axioms. In Jewish law, decisions are rule based. "*Din* consists of a body of statutes...that, at the moment of decision, confront the individual as a set of rules...the basic mode is that of formulating and defining directives to be followed in a class of cases...Judgments are essentially grounded in deductive, primarily syllogistic reasoning" (p. 47). In Jewish ethics, by strong contrast, while a set of guiding principles exists, each decision is dependent upon the specific situation. "He (the contextualist) is directed, in theory, at least, only by the most universal and the most local of factors—by a minimal number, perhaps as few as one or two, of ultimate values on the one hand, and by the unique contours of the situation at hand, on the other" (p. 48). Thus, it follows, that there is a sharp line dividing the modus operandi of Jewish law and Jewish ethics, and there can be little room for confusion between these two separate spheres.

Second, rabbinic authorities, as the legitimate interpreters of Jewish law, are *also* the legitimate and final interpreters of Jewish ethics. "The ethical moment we are seeking is itself an aspect of Halakhah" (p. 40). Further, the boundaries of Jewish ethics—which cases are *in* the domain of ethics and which cases are *out*—are strictly defined and defended by *Halakhah*.

Third, Jewish ethics can never overrule Jewish law. "Any ethic so independent of *Halakhah* as to obviate or override it clearly lies beyond our pale" (p. 38). Finally, there is no formal recognition of the possibility for a distinction between the human interpretation and the real world application of Jewish law in a particular situation or a given case, on the one hand, and Torah ideals, on the other. Lichtenstein writes with no qualification, "*Din*...imposes fixed objective standards" (p. 49). Thus Jewish ethics, in this view, can never adopt an independent and critical stance toward a Jewish legal decision (arrived at through the strict and purely logical mechanisms of the law). In Lichtenstein's understanding, we are left with the radical conclusion that any "ethical" critique of Jewish law is, at best, a meaningless pronouncement and, at worst, antinomian in character. In Jewish life, it would seem, at least according to this view, that the conclusions of Jewish law are untouchable and enjoy a monopoly status in Jewish discourse.

THERE IS NO ETHIC INDEPENDENT *HALAKHAH* (FROM RABBI LICHTENSTEIN'S POINT OF VIEW)

Is there an ethic independent of *Halakhah*? The bottom line from Rabbi Lichtenstein's perspective is no! If we understand *Halakhah* in its broadest terms as encompassing both *din* and *lifnim mishurat hadin*, as Lichtenstein encourages us to do, then Jewish ethics is a relatively minor room within the vast citadel of Jewish law. It is true that at one point in the article Rabbi Lichtenstein compares the relationship between law and ethics to a marriage ("the divorce of Halakhah from morality not only eviscerates but falsifies it" p. 38), but, if so, it is a strange kind of marriage where one partner is permanently designated as master and the other is forever considered his subordinate.

Rabbi Lichtenstein's description of the appropriate relationship between Jewish law and ethics is a formidable and important articulation of "the Jewish view." His view has arguably been the single most important statement on Jewish ethics for Centrist Orthodox Jews in the last 35 years. It is rigorously argued, logically coherent, and rooted deeply in rabbinic sources. It possesses strong appeal for those looking for a legitimate (even if severely limited) role for Jewish ethics to play in contemporary life. It provides a strong anchor for ethics in a world that seems to have lost its direction. And, finally, it provides a degree of certainty in an otherwise uncertain world, and a dose of clarity in an otherwise ambiguous environment.

Rabbi Lichtenstein's is a plausible reading of the tradition, but is it the *only* plausible reading? And, further and most importantly, is it the most appropriate one for the contemporary world? Does his one-dimensional view of Judaism do justice to the rich heritage from which he, like all of us, must necessarily pick and choose? In short does Rabbi Lichtenstein's Centrist Orthodoxy provide us with the necessary tools to meet the many complex challenges of today's world?

To be sure, there is a certain personal dignity and power to Rabbi Lichtenstein's thesis, and his open recognition of an area of supralegal conduct that is both "binding" and real, even from a *pan-halakhic* worldview.

> Halakhic commitment orients a Jew's whole being around his relation to God. It is not content with the realization of a number of specific goals but demands personal dedication—and not only dedication, but consecration. To the achievement of this end, supralegal conduct is indispensable. Integration of the whole self within a halakhic framework becomes substantive rather than semantic insofar as it is reflected in the full range of *personal activity*. Reciprocally, however, that conduct is itself stimulated by fundamental halakhic commitment. (pp. 50–51, emphasis added)

Halakhic man consecrates himself fully to God's commandments. It is not enough for him to fulfill the specific *mitzvot* or to realize "a number of specific goals," but his whole being, "the full range of personal activity," is motivated by and is integrated within the halakhic framework.

There is, at times, a melancholic stoicism to Rabbi Lichtenstein's understanding of Jewish law and its admitted limitations and gaps. He poignantly wonders aloud, for example,

> Who has not found that the fulfillment of explicit halakhic duty could fall well short of exhausting clearly felt moral responsibility? The point to be emphasized, however—although this too, may be obvious—is that the deficiency is not merely the result of silence or ambiguity on the part of the sources... The critical point... is that even the full discharge of one's whole formal duty as defined by the *din* often appears palpably insufficient (p. 39).

This melancholic stoicism, from one point of view, seems like an admirable, wise, and mature posture in the face of the real world and the many constraints and limitations it imposes upon all of us. It *is* appropriate to learn how to better tolerate the deep sadness that is felt when I cannot fully discharge my "felt moral responsibility," but this holds *only* when *I* am the one who must bear the cost of my own failure. Is this a fair attitude to cultivate and celebrate when it is the *least powerful members of society* who must suffer because of my inability to fulfill my "felt moral responsibility?"

If we turn our gaze away from our own personal activity and individual character development—Rabbi Lichtenstein's main concern is the personal and not the social—and focus on broader social issues such as the status of the *agunah* (literally the chained woman), gay rights, unthinkable abuse of power in both the conversion process and the divorce process, the high incidence of fraudulent financial behavior, staggering mismanagement of kashrut industry and the kosher slaughtering process, increasingly unfair allocation of income and wealth, the seemingly high tolerance for child sexual abuse in our society, and the weakening of democratic institutions both in Israel and in the United States, melancholic stoicism seems more like a feeble apology for the status quo, at best, if not brutal sadism, at worst. To argue that one cannot offer an ethical critique of *Halakhah*, in today's climate, should be recognized as a convenient but cold, mechanical, and inhumane approach.

RENEWING JEWISH ETHICS

Rabbi Aharon Lichtenstein's article *is* a foundational text of what today is called Centrist Orthodoxy (and below we will discuss its influence on the Rabbinical Council of America's [RCA's] contemporary policy decisions with regard to Agriprocessors). But, before Centrist Orthodoxy emerged as a dominant view in Jewish Orthodox life, there was Modern Orthodoxy. One of the single most important distinctions between these two related, but competing, ideologies, concerns Rabbi Lichtenstein's view of the unilateral relationship between law and ethics. Modern Orthodox writers, often writing *before* Lichtenstein's article, recognized Jewish ethics, not as the handmaiden of Jewish law, nor as its byproduct, but as a legitimately independent and normative force in Jewish life, with none of Lichtenstein's suffocating qualifications. In the Modern Orthodox perspective, Jewish ethics played as much of a role in *creating* Jewish law as Jewish law did in *creating* Jewish ethics. These rabbis also used the metaphor of marriage, like Lichtenstein, but it was conceived of as a marriage between equal and autonomous partners. Just as Jewish law informs Jewish ethics, so too, Jewish ethics informs Jewish law. Rather than viewing the relationship between law and ethics in unilateral terms, Modern Orthodoxy viewed the relationship as one of real reciprocity and mutual exchange.

Among the many leaders of Modern Orthodoxy, Rabbi Eliezer Berkowitz was one of its most articulate, least apologetic, and forceful spokespersons:

> The Torah is eternal because it has a Word for each generation. Every day the Torah should seem as new to you as if it had been given on that day, says the Midrash. One can find the Word that has been waiting for this hour to be revealed only if one faces the challenge of each new situation in the history of the generations of Israel and attempts to deal with it in intellectual and *ethical* honesty. (1983, p. 118, emphasis added)

In this alternative view, Jewish ethics is a filter through which we read, understand, and apply Jewish law. It is only in facing the challenges of each new situation that Jewish law can function properly.

Similarly, Rabbi Emanuel Rackman wrote, "The only authentic Halachic approach must be that which approximates the philosophy of the teleological jurist. The teleological jurist asks: What are the ends of the law which God or nature ordained and how can we be guided by these ideal ends in developing the Law?" (undated, p. 48). It is precisely these ethical ideals, situated in Torah *or* nature, that Lichtenstein claims should have *no voice* in the wholly mechanical legal process.

Rabbi Walter Wurzburger summarized the Modern Orthodox viewpoint in clear and unequivocal language:

> I look upon *Halakhah* as an indispensable component but *not as coextensive with the full range and scope of the Jewish normative system*... In my view, Jewish ethics encompasses not only outright *halakhic* rules governing the area of morality, but also intuitive moral responses arising from the Covenantal relationship with God, which provides the matrix for forming ethical ideals *not necessarily patterned after legal models*. (1994, p. 15, emphasis added)

Arguably this has always been the dominant practice, or at least, a dominant aspiration, among most rabbis of every persuasion, even if it was not always explicated and articulated in this precise way. As Rabbi Eliezer ben Azzaria taught in the Mishna, "if there is no *Derech Eretz* (ethical behavior) there can be no Torah—and without Torah, there can be no *Derech Eretz*." Or, as Rabbi Abraham Joshua Heschel wrote more recently:

> "An ox who gores a cow," is Jewish theology, for Judaism is law and nothing else. Such pan-halachic "theology" claims that in Judaism religious living consists of complying with a law rather than of striving to attain a goal which is the purpose of the law... It claims that obedience is the substance rather than the form of religious existence; that the law is an end, not a way. (Heschel, 1955, p. 323)

The call of the hour today, I believe, is to begin to be more self-conscious about this. This means we must study Jewish ethics on its own terms, not just as an aid to expanding the domain of Jewish law, but as an *independent field of study*, a powerful source of responsibility and aspiration, and as a the subject of continuous Jewish dialogue.

Let us translate what Wurzburger sensed as "intuitive moral responses arising from the Covenantal relationship with God" into clear and explicit moral guidelines, boldly articulated, and actively incorporated into Jewish education and Jewish life, both private and communal. Let us continue to debate the content of the "ideal ends" to which Judaism is aiming, rather than arguing about whether or not such ideal ends even exist in Judaism. Let us recommit ourselves to the "intellectual and ethical honesty" at the heart of Rabbi Eliezer Berkowitz's passionate writings.

In the end, Jewish ethics cannot stand alone anymore than Jewish law. Jewish ethics is inextricably linked to Jewish law, and it lives or dies with it. But, from a practical perspective, it is time to start seeing the world again not only through the eyes of Jewish law, but also through the eyes of Jewish ethics. These are two related, but distinct perspectives, and only when joined together do they begin to give us a glimpse of our highest aspirations and our deepest responsibilities. If Abraham can ask God, "shall not the judge of all the earth act justly?" (Genesis 18:25), can we not ask of human judges and rabbinic decisors, in our own age, is this verdict fair? Is this interpretation or non-interpretation of *halakhah* just?

JEWISH ETHICS IN A POSTMODERN WORLD

Rabbi Aharon Lichtenstein conceptualizes the domain of Jewish law as a rule-based system where "Judgments are essentially grounded in deductive, primarily syllogistic reasoning." Does not this description, though, grossly exaggerate the mechanical nature of legal reasoning? Compare Lichtenstein's view to Rabbi David Hartman's understanding of Judaism as an interpretive tradition.

> This is the distinctive legacy of the Talmudic interpretative tradition: an understanding of revelation in which God loves you when you discover ambiguity in His word. He loves you for finding forty-nine ways to make this pure and forty-nine ways to make it impure. Revelation is not always "pure and simple" but may be rough and complex. Since you may find yourselves arguing interminably, you may decide the law according to such principles as majority rule. But even if God, the Law Giver, were to intervene in a legal debate among scholars and were to reveal that this interpretation was correct or that legal formulation should become law, the rabbis would object and say: "Sorry, God. You may not interrupt and terminate discussions among students of Torah. If our minds appreciate and conceive of the ambiguity of the human situations in which your word must be implemented, you may not interfere to change our minds. Torah is not in heaven." (1999, p. 22)

In Hartman's view, there is not only a divine and supernatural aspect to Jewish law, there is an undeniable human and natural element, as well. In denying the subjective aspect of pure *din*, it is as if Lichtenstein picks out a single strand of a thick rope and claims that this string alone is sufficient to hold the whole tradition together.

In the same vein, Lichtenstein's equating of Jewish ethics with the Jewish concept of *lifnim mishurat hadin* is inadequate to the great legacy of the

Jewish ethical tradition. "Love your neighbor as yourself" (Leviticus 19:18). "Love him [the stranger] as yourself; for you were strangers in the land of Egypt" (Leviticus 19:34). These commandments (among many others) are not only objective rules with precise and specific requirements, but these are broad and commanding principles, inviting continual interpretation and reinterpretation, which should ideally inform every aspect of our lives. These ethical prescriptions are not "beyond the letter of the law," but form the very foundations of the law. As Abbaye said, "the whole of the Torah is for the purpose of promoting peace." *Lifnim mishurat hadin* is an important concept in *Halakhah*, and Lichtenstein's article is a useful reminder of this. But to equate it with Jewish ethics and then to casually note, in passing, that it is not as "binding as shofar or tefillin" (p. 41) according to Nachmanides (and presumably Lichtenstein himself) is to disempower and denude ethics at a moment in Jewish history when it is arguably needed more than ever before.

In drawing a bright line between *din* and *lifnim mishurat hadin*, Jewish law and Jewish ethics, Rabbi Lichtenstein implies that there are no ambiguous cases. In his view, law demands a rule-based approach while ethics is contextual, each case decided in light of the unique contours of the situation. But the fact is that most, if not all, of the important social questions we face in Jewish life today require a mixed approach, a moving back and forth from legal to ethical language. Rabbis and Jewish ethicists do a disservice to the Jewish community when they try to provide definitive answers to questions about end of life, abortion, gay rights, requirements to obey army officers in a time of war, how best to apportion healthcare in today's society, or the appropriate contours of corporate social responsibility (to name just a sampling of issues), with recourse to exclusively legal language *or* exclusively ethical language. Is it not obvious that these kinds of broad social issues require ongoing dialogues that make use of all of tradition's normative resources, and not just an arbitrary subset? Using only rule-based thinking or only contextual analysis in any important case is like asking a person to solve a highly complex problem with only the left or right half of his or her brain.

Jewish ethics in a postmodern world is not a return to Modern Orthodoxy, although it should strive to incorporate its hard won insights. Today, Jewish ethics operates in a dynamic and open environment, not just where change is ubiquitous, but where the *rate of change* is dramatically increasing. Change includes technological innovations such as genetic engineering, cloning, and digitization. It also includes social changes such as feminism, globalization, expanding minority and gay rights, business and medical ethics, environmentally sustainable practices, virtual communities, and an increasing demand for accountability in organizations and political entities of every sort. A Jewish ethics which ignores change is no ethics at all. To study Jewish ethics today is to get your hands dirty by immersing oneself in these and other issues.

A Jewish ethics appropriate for the postmodern world is a work-in-process, as it must be. It is characterized by a jettisoning of the old certainties and a recognition, if not an embrace, of ambiguity. It recognizes the central role for dialogue. This includes dialogues between experts in Jewish law and experts in Jewish ethics, but it also includes dialogues among professionals (doctors, lawyers, accountants, teachers, etc.), practitioners of all sorts, academics experts, and theoreticians. It includes dialogues among Jewish ethicists (from all of Judaism's various branches), ethicists working out of other religious traditions, and secular ethicists. It is still useful to talk about a unique Jewish ethics for some purposes, but talk about this in isolation from other approaches and opinions is now anachronistic.

Most importantly, I suggest, Jewish ethics must align itself with democracy, not as a second best solution, but democracy *lechatchila* (as a first best solution). What happens when we denigrate democracy or simply remain neutral about it? How bad can things get? I keep a newspaper article from the *Jerusalem Post* on my desk at school so that every student who comes into my office can read it. The article appeared in 1996, about a month before Yigal Amir's murder of Yitzhak Rabin. The title of the article is "They Will Share the Guilt."

The article, written by two Jewish writers associated with the Hartman Institute in Jerusalem, hints darkly about the possibility of a Rabin assassination. In the article, the authors document the harsh and incendiary public statements of a prominent rabbi attacking Rabin's political policies, implying that Rabin, a former military hero of Israel, was now, *according to Jewish law*, a traitor to the state. The authors suggested, with deadly accuracy, that if and when Rabin is assassinated, it is precisely these leaders—who are undercutting the most basic premises of Israeli democracy in the name of Jewish law—who will be to blame.

Rereading this article with the advantage of 20-20 hindsight is uncomfortable and disturbing, but it also provides a powerful argument in favor of recognizing our responsibility to strengthen society's fragile democratic institutions and values. These values include respecting others, noncoercion, transparency, equal rights, freedom of expression, pluralism, compromise, individual and communal responsibility, and many others.

It also should remind us how important purely theoretical statements can be. If one were to have read Rabbi Lichtenstein's article literally, and taken him at face value, when he wrote that ethics cannot override *Halakhah*, one might very well have wrongly concluded that these kinds of purely ethical warnings about the absolute prohibition of killing an elected prime minister of the State of Israel are truly meaningless expressions of mere preference or taste (or, in any event, would have *certainly* concluded that ethical pronouncements are always less binding that *Halakhic* pronouncements). Rabbi Lichtenstein, it should go without saying, never condoned the murder of Rabin from a *Halakhic* perspective. The point here, however, is that his theoretical writings severely limit (or, at least, attempt to limit) the ability of the Jewish community, as a whole, to engage in serious discussion and debate. In removing ethics as an independent source of normative authority within Judaism, we are left with a severely truncated critical vocabulary with which to engage one another.

For those who still insist that Yigal Amir was a crazy young man acting alone, this article provides a powerful wake-up call. Amir did murder Rabin, but he did so in order to realize his teachers' antidemocratic ideals. In thinking back about what happened, one can easily trace the slippery slope from a basic lack of respect for a fellow human being (I disagree with your politics to you're a traitor) to cold-blooded murder in the name of a perverse and upside down reading of Jewish law. If the assassination of Yitzhak Rabin has taught us anything at all, surely it has taught us how fragile democracy really is. It needs all the friends it can get.

Does Our "Theory" of Jewish Ethics Really Matter?

The argument about whether or not there exists an ethic independent of *Halakhah* may still seem to some readers as an arcane and academic point, perhaps, simply a matter of semantics, after all. Consider, however, a contemporary case of significant interest to everyone who observes kashrut in the United States and who endorses ethical business practices.

Agriprocessors, located in Postville, Iowa, was, at one time, the largest producer of kosher beef in the United States. It was founded in 1987 by Aaron Rubashkin, managed by his son Sholom, and run as a highly profitable family business until it declared bankruptcy on November 5, 2008. Serious allegations were lodged against Agriprocessors by several different groups for several years before the bankruptcy. Among the many accusations were claims of inhumane treatment of animals, hiring illegal aliens, unfair treatment of workers, environmental pollution, and unfair marketing practices. On November 12, 2009, Sholom Rubashkin was convicted in federal court on 86 counts of financial fraud, including making false statements to a bank, mail fraud, and money laundering, among others.

In response to Agriprocessors' many alleged ethical (and now legal) lapses, the RCA recently issued a document entitled "Jewish Principles and Ethical Guidelines (JPEG) for the Kosher Food Industry," The RCA is one of the largest organizations of Orthodox Rabbis in the world, and is an affiliate of the Orthodox Union, the kashrut agency that supervised Agriprocessors until its ultimate demise.

A close reading of JPEG (easily accessible at the RCA website) reveals it to be a strange document. It is self-described, in part, as an "ethical" statement for the "kosher food industry." In the introductory paragraphs (Section A) it pledges responsibility to "promote ethical conduct in the workplace." In the concluding paragraphs (Section E), the document cites several specific areas of concern including: integrity toward the consumer, honoring commitments to workers, and concern for public safety and animal welfare. In the penultimate paragraph, the document reminds the reader that "Jewish law and ethics require that all Jews strive to facilitate correct business behavior far beyond the limited realm of kashruth itself." However, the substance of the document, sections B, C, and D, focus exclusively on the kosher food industry's responsibility to follow the strict letter of the law and removes any and all ethical responsibility from the certifying kashrut agency.

In Section B, the document clearly states, "Responsibility for regulating the business practices of the kosher food industry lies...with a variety of specialized government agencies" and not with the kashrut supervising agency. Tellingly, the document does not even stipulate that the company itself has any responsibility for self-regulation. Specific action items for the kashrut agencies include the following:

> An agency should require companies seeking its certification to affirm in advance that they are committed to *law-abiding conduct*, and have implemented procedures to comply with legal norms as they understand them...
>
> In its agreements with companies they supervise, an agency should stipulate that *serious legal violations,* as described in...this document, will constitute grounds for sanctions including termination of kosher certification.
>
> An agency *cannot assume responsibility* for monitoring a company for unethical or illegal behavior...
>
> Once suspicions are raised, an agency is not expected to initiate its own investigation.
>
> In assessing allegations, an agency must maintain an attitude of fairness and a policy of *due process.* It should *not act hastily,* and should give the accused company a fair opportunity to respond to allegations whenever possible...
>
> Once an agency has become convinced that *serious legal violations* are occurring at a company, it should act promptly and not remain, or even appear to remain, indifferent to such misconduct... (quoted from the RCA website, emphasis added).

For some readers, this document is extremely disappointing. In fact, it reads almost more like a justification, after the fact, of the Orthodox Union's (OU's) inaction during Agriprocessor crisis, than a document intended to spell out and expand our understanding of ethics and corporate social responsibility.

Its sole emphasis on kosher producers to abide by the strict requirements of the law (and, if there is any doubt about this claim, the chairman of the JPEG Task Force explicitly stated in an interview "Our guiding principle is law-abiding behavior."), and its complete rejection of ethics as a substantive issue with real force in the kosher food industry, perhaps, should come as no surprise. This document, and the attitude it represents, corresponds and is quite consistent with Rabbi Aharon Lichtenstein's views as summarized above.

According to Lichtenstein, Judaism is essentially a religion of law. "Anything from which we abstain or which we do today, we do it *solely* because of God's commandment conveyed through Moses." Given that according to many (if not most) positions, *Halakhah* does not even recognize the formal existence of corporations (only partnerships), how could one expect the RCA to endorse and encourage a sophisticated definition of corporate social responsibility?

Jewish ethics is defined as "beyond the letter of the law." And, here, in the domain of ethics, each case is distinct and unique. "He (the contextualist) is directed, in theory, at least, only by the most universal and the most local of factors—by a minimal number, perhaps as few as one or two, of ultimate values on the one hand, and by the unique contours of the situation at hand, on the other." This particular and rather unique understanding of Jewish ethics as purely contextual and generally discretionary makes it almost impossible to derive broad ethical prescriptions for the kosher food industry, as the RCA presumably would agree.

Further, Lichtenstein's focus on individual ethics as opposed to social ethics turns organizational ethics into a nonissue from the get go. Finally, in both Lichtenstein's view and the RCA's perspective, Jewish ethics is less "binding" than the specifics of Jewish law such as shofar, tefillin, and now, we should add to this list, kashrut. Indeed, if there is no ethic independent of the law, how could we have ever expected the RCA to take business ethics seriously in the first place?

On the other hand, had the RCA chosen to return to its own Modern Orthodox roots, with its insistence that Jewish law is "not coextensive with the full range and scope of the Jewish normative system" and that there does exist a domain of Jewish ethics independent of the law, how might its JPEG statement have differed? Here are some possibilities and suggestions. First, articulate specific ethical guidelines and behaviors expected from all companies who receive a kashrut certification (adjustments can be made to accommodate the size of the enterprise in question). These guidelines could include, among others, specific rules stipulating minimum levels of compensation and benefits to all full-time workers, minimum requirements for safety instruction, stated policies on conflicts of interests and receipt of gifts, a statement on animal rights, and a requirement to include a so-called triple–bottom line report to stakeholders that includes economic, social, and environmental performance metrics. Guidelines for such reports are easily available at the Global Reporting Initiative Website. Second, require all companies receiving kashrut certification to develop their own code of ethical conduct. Almost, all major US and international corporations now have such statements as a matter of good business practice. Require companies to affirm in advance that they are committed to not only *law-abiding conduct*, but *ethical conduct* as specified by JPEG and the company's own ethics statement. Such affirmation should include detailed explanations on the procedures in place to ensure compliance with ethical norms as stipulated in the company's code of ethical conduct. Such procedures include internal control systems and ethics audits by outside consultants or accounting firms on a periodic basis. In assessing allegations, an agency must maintain an attitude of fairness and a policy of *due process*, but stipulate clearly that an agency may take action before arrest and conviction. *The overriding concern of the guidelines should be corporate accountability to the public as part of an ongoing dialogue.* This means clear articulation of the company's own goals, a description of mechanisms used to measure its own performance, and a commitment to full disclosure and communication to all stakeholders, in a timely manner, concerning its economic, social, and environmental performance. While these institutional changes may be new to the kosher industry, these are already best practices in most major industries.

A important litmus test concerning the success or failure of the RCA's JPEG statement is how one would answer the following simple question: Had these guidelines been in effect before the Agriprocessors case reached its critical climax, would they have made any difference in either Agriprocessors' or the OU's behavior? Rabbi Asher Meir, chair of the taskforce, stated in an interview with the Jewish Week, "What we saw at Agriprocessors was that the producers were not aware of what the demands of the supervisors were regarding compliance with US laws" (January 26, 2010). To the extent that one agrees with this diagnosis, then, perhaps, the answer is yes. To the rest of us, who see the Agriprocessors case as, first and foremost, an ethics failure, the RCA's new guidelines are too little and too late.

While the specifics of this case are extremely important, the point to emphasize in closing here is a deeper problem with the RCA's statement. To the extent that it derives from a philosophic foundation which denies

Jewish ethics the right to challenge Jewish law, as a matter of principle, it implies that the RCA's actions are correct, *by definition,* and do not need to be legitimated through reasonable discussion and public debate. Not only does Jewish ethics make a significant difference to the quality and meaning of our lives, but our *underlying theory* of Jewish ethics, makes a difference, as well. If one believes with Rabbi Lichtenstein that *din* is objective and holds a monopoly position in Jewish life, it is more accurate to describe Jewish ethics as eviscerated and, essentially *beside the point* than it is to describe it as *beyond the letter of the law.*

CONCLUSION

Rabbi Aharon Lichtenstein's reading of Jewish tradition is plausible, but it does require him to resort to some interpretive somersaults. "There are, of course, situations in which ethical factors like the preservation of life, the enhancement of human dignity, the quest for communal or domestic peace, and the mitigation of anxiety or pain, sanction the breaching, by preemptive priority or outright violation, of specific norms. However, these factors themselves are halakhic considerations, in the most technical sense of the term, and their entailment implies no rejection of the system" (Lichtenstein, p. 38). Can it be that the preservation of life, the enhancement of human dignity, the quest for peace, and the mitigation of anxiety are meaningful values *only* if reduced to technical terms within a mechanistic legal system? This is Lichtenstein's position, but it is not the only one. Is it not much simpler, truer to tradition, and wiser to understand human dignity and these other values, contested and subjective as they are, as providing the foundations and purposes of the law? These values, surely as eternal as the law itself, and, at the same time, the subject of continuous dialogue and reinterpretation, are the values that help us to promote just laws and to criticize unjust laws. These, among others, are the very values that constitute the *independent* domain of ethics.

The rabbis of the Talmudic period were among the most trenchant critics of the law-only perspective. The rabbinic imagination, historically, was expansive enough to accommodate both law and ethics. And, when one of their own failed to grasp this, the rabbis themselves were the first to point out his profound error. Consider the midrashic story of Kamtza and Bar Kamtza.

It happened once that a certain man had a friend named Kamtza and an enemy named Bar Kamtza. In anticipation of a banquet he was preparing, the man asked his servant to invite Kamtza to the festivities. By mistake, the servant brought Bar Kamtza. Enraged, the host had him thrown out of the party in front of everyone, including the rabbis in attendance. This happened in spite of the fact that Bar Kamtza, to save face, offered to pay the host for the full cost for the entire banquet.

Bar Kamtza thought to himself that since the sages sitting there did not stop the man from throwing him out, that they must have approved of the man's actions. Bar Kamtza wanted revenge and he went to Caesar and said to him that the Jews were about to revolt. Caesar wanted some proof. So Bar Kamtza suggested that he send an offering to the Temple in Jerusalem and see whether or not the Jews would be willing to offer it as a sacrifice to God. On the way, Bar Kamtza secretly cut the upper lip of the calf that Caesar had sent, rendering it unfit for the Jews to sacrifice (but still fit for heathens).

> The sages were inclined to offer it in order to maintain peace with the government. But R. Zechariah ben Avkulas protested, "People will say that blemished animals may be offered on the altar." Then it was proposed to have Bar Kamtza assassinated, so that he would not continue to inform against them. Again R. Zechariah ben Avkulas demurred: "Is one who makes a blemish on consecrated animals to be put to death?" (as quoted in Bialik and Ravnitzky (1992, p. 189)

In this story, R. Zechariah ben Avkulas twice asserts the theory that the law is supreme and that even the highest of values, if not explicitly articulated in the language of specific rules (like maintaining peace with the government for the sake of one's own survival), carry no weight or authority in decision making.

Years later, in the aftermath of the Temple's destruction by the Romans, Rabbi Yochanan singled out for his strongest possible condemnation, not Bar Kamtza nor the Romans themselves, but R. Zechariah's decision not to sacrifice Ceasar's animal. Rabbi Yochanan believed that he (R. Zechariah) "destroyed our [holy] house, burned our Temple hall, and caused us to be exiled from our Land" (as quoted in Bialik and Ravnitzky (1992, p. 189). Decisions can have profound and lasting consequences, Rabbi Yochanan taught. One of the lessons here is that one should think very carefully about whether or not a society based only on law can even survive. Jewish law independent of Jewish ethics makes no more sense than Jewish ethics without Jewish law.

NOTE

1. This paper was first published in *Modern Jewish Ethics*, edited by Marvin Fox, published by Ohio State University, 1975. It was reprinted in *Leaves of Faith: The World of Jewish Living* (Lichtenstein, 2004) from which all quotes are taken.

REFERENCES

Berkovitz, Eliezer, *Not in Heaven: The Nature and Function of Halacha* (Jersey City: Ktav, 1983).

Bialik, Hayim Nahman and Ravnitzky, Yehoshua Hana, *The Book of Legends: Sefer Ha-Aggada: Legends from the Talmud and Midrash* (New York: Schocken Books, 1992).

Hartman, David, *A Heart of Many Rooms: Celebrating the Many Voices within Judaism* (Woodstock, VT: Jewish Lights Publishing, 1999).

Heschel, Abraham Joshua, *God In Search of Man: A Philosophy of Judaism* (New York: Harper and Row, 1955)

Lichtenstein, Aharon, *Leaves of Faith: The World of Jewish Living* (Jersey City: Ktav, 2004).

Rackman, Emanuel, *One Man's Judaism* (Tel Aviv: Greenfield LTD., undated).

Wurzburger, Walter, *Ethics of Responsibility: Pluralistic Approaches to Covenantal Ethics* (Philadelphia: Jewish Publication Society, 1994).

PART 2

ON THE GROUND

CHAPTER 5

LEARNING TO SPEAK ABOUT THE ELEPHANT IN THE ROOM

Rabbi Israel Meir HaCohen Kagan was born in Poland in 1838. Although his name is not well-known, his book, the *Chofetz Chayim*, a compendium of Jewish laws aimed against *lashon hara* (literally evil tongue), has had a huge and lasting impact on Jewish attitudes toward unfair gossip and slander. The book became so popular among traditional Jews that Rabbi Kagan himself is usually referred to, not by his own name, but by the name of his monumental work.

When it comes to appropriate speech, no one wants to promote more *lashon hara* or slander. However, I suggest, against today's accepted opinion, that our focus, and even, our obsession with *lashon hara* in Jewish life may now be doing more harm than good.

Ours is a society that depends on open dialogue and ethical criticism. The lifeblood of democracy and a vibrant community, be it here or in Israel, is the ability to communicate and express oneself without the fear of intimidation or retaliation. Political and organizational leaders, and even military leaders, must be accountable to citizens. Powerful institutions owe stakeholders legitimizing explanations about their behavior and its effects.

Appropriate speech demands, as a first principle, (in Hebrew, *lechatchila*) that we participate actively in conversations centered on ethical, political, aesthetic, scientific, spiritual, and social concerns. We must learn to listen to one another with increased openness. We must learn how to give voice responsibly to our opinions in an honest and nonstrategic manner. Just as the Bible warns us against talebearing and slander, so too, does it command us to engage in moral rebuke or *tochacha*. Finally, the kinds of dialogues that

I am imagining require a deep respect for one another. This implies concern and care for others, but it also demands a heightened toleration and appreciation of differences. Although the commandment to love the stranger has been on the books in Judaism from time immemorial, its salience and urgency has never been greater.

In promoting dialogue, I am not encouraging the kinds of shrill and shallow gamelike debates that fill the airwaves, but I am suggesting that we learn how to sit down and reason with each other in new and more mature ways. This requires an openness to one another, and a willingness to learn and to change. The goal is not only a change in action, but a growth in consciousness, a new way of looking at ourselves. This means that we must expand and sharpen the vocabulary of Torah. In order to equip the next generation to meet the demands they will inevitably be facing, we need to pass on to them a living and breathing tradition responsive to the real world.

In the Shema prayer, we are bidden to diligently teach our children the words of Torah and to "*speak* of them when you sit down and when you walk, and when you lie down and when you rise" (Deuteronomy 6:7, emphasis added). Such positive speech is at the heart of the Jewish ethical vision. But the subjects of these dialogues, grounded in Torah values, must move beyond parochial concerns, and be opened up to include a broad array of perspectives on today's most salient issues and problems, like the meaning of sustainability, the risks of global warming, unfairness of income and wealth inequalities, ethical limits of science, availability of healthcare, rampant ethical failures in business, and what it means to live a spiritual life, a life of integrity and community (to name just a few).

In every class I have attended or in every book on the topic of *lashon hara* that I have read, the topic of appropriate speech is always introduced with a long list of thou shalt nots. Toward the end of the class or the book, the speaker or author adds on, seemingly almost as an afterthought, "of course, there are exceptions when *lashon hara* is permitted and perhaps even required. In such situations always consult with a rabbi." While this approach may have been appropriate at other times in Jewish history, it is now anachronistic. What happens, for example, when it is the rabbi him or herself who is the problem?

Imagine for a moment those optical illusions like the old woman and the young girl. When looked at from one perspective, the drawing looks like an old hag with a wart on her nose. The identical drawing, however, when looked at from a second perspective looks like a young, attractive woman with her face tilted away from the viewer. Our perceptions depend on how our minds interpret and distinguish the figure from the ground.

I am calling for a similar, but self-conscious kind of mind-shift when it comes to our understanding of appropriate language. Appropriate language is first and foremost a positive mitzvah. We have an obligation and a responsibility to one another to engage in dialogue, to learn from everyone (as the Ethics of the Fathers teaches us), to report facts as we see them, and not to muddle truth for personal gain.

"And God said, 'Let there be light,' and there was light." It is through language that God and we create worlds together. Language is the way we express our deepest thoughts and desires to one another. It is with words that we study and learn. Speech is the bridge that connects us to each other. It is finally time to cut *lashon hara* down to size, and to reconceive it merely as a side-constraint on the more fundamental obligation of positive communication, and not as a central aim of Jewish ethics.

Our Jewish Day schools, if they are to remain relevant, should aim to give students the skills to communicate precisely and to express themselves creatively as a foundational goal. A day school I am familiar with threatened to expel a student if he did not remove his Youtube video that was critical of his school's Chanukah play. This sixth grader should have been lauded and praised for his creativity, and his ability to express himself with honesty and humor. Do you know how to make and upload a coherent and compelling video on to Youtube? This student, though, was harassed by teachers, publicly reprimanded in front of the entire school, threatened, and reminded about the laws of *lashon hara*. (And, the intended lesson to the student was what again?)

While this is a simple example, it is a poignant one that does demonstrate one of the most unfortunate aspects of our obsession with *lashon hara*. It is a principle of law that can be invoked inappropriately by those in power and with authority, just as easily as it can be used appropriately. When it comes to *lashon hara*, authorities often self-select in a way that promotes their own interests, and not necessarily the interests of the Jewish community at large. There is as much hypocrisy surrounding *lashon hara* as there is real soul-searching.

Do newspapers in Israel and Jewish newspapers in the United States have a responsibility to investigate and report on allegations made against the Israeli army? Can we as a community tolerate dissension even in times of war? When we call such reporters self-hating Jews, do we strengthen community and enhance democracy, or do we squash real and legitimate communication? I was told by a former Israeli soldier that when it comes to survival, we must always trust those in charge. Might not this be a recipe for disaster?

When leaders do not report sexual abuse in their organizations to the appropriate authorities for fear of what the non-Jews will do and say, should we invoke the *lashon hara* card again? And, more importantly, should the rest of us tolerate such obfuscation? We are taught that we are all responsible for one another (*kol yisroel arevim ze la ze*). This is a deeply democratic sentiment, but one that demands open channels of communication, and the courage to blow the whistle when appropriate.

Last year, a spokesperson for the *Agudas Yisroel*, complained publicly at Yeshiva University that anyone raising questions about Agriprocessors business practices is engaging in slander or *motzi shem ra* in Hebrew (*lashon hara's* more notorious first cousin). I would suggest that this is a knee-jerk reaction and not a defensible ethical position under the circumstances, given the evidence that was publicly available at the time. Similarly, when a Rabbinical Council of America (RCA) rabbi called for an independent investigation of the Orthodox Union's handling of the Agriprocessor affair, publishing his comments in the *New York Times*, he was vilified online, and at least one well-known rabbinic colleague of his openly and publicly questioned this rabbi's character.

These criticisms are intimidation tactics meant to protect the powerful, wrapped in the cloak of false sincerity and pious platitudes. The elephant is in the room, and we are ordered in so many different ways to keep our eyes and ears closed and our mouths shut.

Today, religious and secular ethicists recognize the importance of transparency. If we are to err here, it is on the side of more and better disclosure. Advocating ever higher standards for *lashon hara* is often a reactionary form of passive-aggressive behavior. Warnings against *lashon hara* play on our deepest fears surrounding the almost magical power of words. In the guise of ethical propriety, those who demand silence in the face of wrongdoing become accessories to the crime.

My suggestion here to shift our focus away from *lashon hara*, no doubt, entails some risk. If we choose to give each other more latitude to voice our real opinions, and to speak truth to power, we will necessary have to develop thicker skins and a greater ability to forgive one another when we inevitably exaggerate and make false claims. Those advocating a zero tolerance policy for *lashon hara* seem to think that we are the most delicate of creatures, incapable of surviving mere whispers, and unable to tolerate criticisms aimed against us. For the sake of the long term benefit of open dialogue, we need to challenge and carefully test these assumptions.

Lashon hara is wrong when it is merely hurtful gossip with no positive function. This holds even when the content is true. Slander, the purposeful communication of false information intended to damage is even worse. But to use these ancient Jewish values to promote the interests of the powerful and well-placed against the needs of the least well-off members of society is a common, contemporary sin with far more allure and worldly returns. It is precisely here that we should keep our focus and avoid letting others, even our leaders, teachers, and rabbis, change the subject.

Chofetz Chayim literally means a lover of life. Would the *Chofetz Chayim* have written the same book if he were alive today? As a lover of life with all of its sacred messiness, I think not. His was a very different historical period, with its unique problems and shortcomings. Our task today is not to echo nineteenth century wisdom, but it is to return to the deepest strands in our tradition to help us understand and solve our own contemporary ethical crises.

There is both a need and deep hunger for authentic Jewish ethics. We fool ourselves, however, if we think ethics comes prepackaged. "Read this book, speak with this rabbi, go to this lecture." In the real world, it doesn't work this way. It is time to start speaking, teaching, and doing Jewish ethics in a new key.

Ethics is not a spectator sport. Jewish ethics comes alive only when together we begin to openly discuss those issues that matter most to us. It is deeply ironic that an important Jewish value like *lashon hara* is misused (and in some cases, knowingly misused) by so many to hamper this important work so crucial to our community's long term health and survival. The elephant is already in the room and the call of the hour is to learn how to say so with unapologetic force, precision, and respect.

CHAPTER 6

THE ART OF MORAL CRITICISM

> You shall not hate your brother in your heart; you shall surely rebuke your fellow and not bear sin on his account.
> Leviticus 19:17

> True unity between people can arise only in a form of action and thinking that does not attempt to fragment the whole of reality.
> David Bohm

> Listen, I'm an f***ing steamroller, and I'll roll over you and anyone else.
> Eliot Spitzer to Jim Tedisco, minority leader of the State Assembly, during Spitzer's first month as governor

Moral criticism, or as the Bible puts it *rebuke* (*tokhehah* in Hebrew), is a necessary activity for social learning and improvement.[1] Moral criticism is part of a give and take among individuals who must necessarily share, at least, a minimal set of core values, including most importantly respect for one another, a common ethical vocabulary, and a basic moral grammar. For moral criticism to take hold and to have any possibility of truly being effective there must *already* exist meaningful channels of communication. As the philosopher Michael Walzer has noted, "We do not have to discover the moral world because we have always lived there. We do not have to invent it because it has already been invented" (1987, p. 20).

Each one of us, simply by virtue of being human, inherits a moral tradition. As we grow and mature we slowly become its spokespersons. We begin to make claims about fairness and justice for ourselves. Next, we begin to feel sympathy for others. We want to live in a world where our own needs and the needs of our close family members are being adequately satisfied.

But we also want to be part of a larger community where not only are our own personal needs being met but everyone's essential needs are satisfied. We begin, over time, to choose to take on additional moral responsibilities. As we mature further, it may dawn upon us, that we should and do care not only about the members of our own communities, but also about every human being.

As the rabbis of the ancient Talmud put it:

> Anyone for whom it is possible to protest the wrongdoing of a member of his or her household and does not protest, is held accountable for the wrongdoing of the members of his household. So too in relation to the members of his city; so too in relation to the whole world. (Shabbat 54b)

As we grow, the circle of moral concern broadens. It need not stop with human beings and we begin to factor in the welfare of all sentient beings, even those yet to be born. As Princeton University philosopher Peter Singer has noted "in suffering, animals are our equals."

Rebuke or moral criticism is one of the many moral responsibilities that come with advancing maturity and wisdom. It can take on many different forms. It might be as simple as a private conversation between two friends, an email, or a letter to the editor. It might include giving a formal speech, writing an article, engaging in a dialogue, or even writing a book on moral criticism. At its deepest and perhaps most penetrating and useful level, moral criticism may not even look like moral criticism at all. Literature, film, poetry, the visual arts, and even humor—by showing the familiar and everyday in unfamiliar and strange ways—can convey a kind of criticism that direct methods can not. (See, for example, Rorty, 1989.)

Moral criticism, however, can easily backfire. Rather than contributing to a better world, moral criticism can become part of the problem. Is this not the "sin" that the Bible itself is warning us about in Leviticus—"you shall surely rebuke your fellow and not bear sin on his account?" (19:17). The New Testament famously takes this idea further and notes, "Do not judge so that you will not be judged. For in the way you judge, you will be judged; and by your standard of measure, it will be measured to you. Why, then, do you look at the speck in your brother's eye and pay no attention to the log in your own eye?" (Matthew 7:1–3). Rebuke can make things worse rather than better. I believe that there is a profound truth to James P. Carse's insight that the attempt to eradicate evil completely is itself evil (1986).

Others may see us as competitors, misinformed, old-fashioned, too liberal, too conservative, too postmodern, holier-than-thou, angry, ugly, too religious, not religious enough, jealous, fearful, hypocritical, irreverent, irrelevant, or just plain flat-out wrong. Not only might others not listen to us, worse case, they may seek out revenge and try to hurt us. Thus, moral criticism may end up provoking a negative cycle culminating in violence.

Today, in the age of what some have dubbed "the cheating culture," it seems as if there are fewer and fewer shared core values (Callahan, 2004). Moral vocabulary has thinned. And, each one of us possesses a unique moral grammar. Is it still possible to engage in an authentic moral dialogue? Is moral criticism simply an anachronism? Just consider the word *rebuke* for a moment. When was the last time you heard anyone use this word?

Still, I want to suggest that society's health depends upon moral criticism properly pursued. Creativity, imagination, and even genius (on rare occasions) reside in each one of us as individuals. Ralph Waldo Emerson's nineteenth century teaching, from his famous essay "Self-Reliance," is just as true today as it was when he first wrote it:

> Whoso would be a man must be a nonconformist. He who would gather immortal palms must not be hindered by the name of goodness, but must explore if it be goodness. Nothing is at last sacred but the integrity of your own mind.

It is true that we are products of our own culture and society, but it is also true that culture and society are accountable to the individual no matter how unique or idiosyncratic we may be. Every voice counts and every voice is crucial. In speaking from our own perspectives, inside our own histories, and experiences, each of us possesses an irreplaceable and infinitely valuable point of view. You are the only one with your exact set of values, desires, goals, and skills. *You* are the only one that has lived *your* life, experienced *your* experiences, and seen and heard what *you* have seen and heard. As the great philosopher Immanuel Kant noted you are not only a means to the ends of others you are an end unto yourself.

But, how can one find an appropriate voice in today's fractured and broken world to express moral criticism? A voice that is not too loud nor too soft, a voice that is not too shrill nor too easy, a voice that is neither accusing nor blind to what is going on around you, a voice of both strength and humility. Is not all rebuke by definition harsh and unfair? In criticizing others, aren't we always being hypocritical? I do not think that these are easy questions, nor do I think that we have given them sufficient attention.

Rebuke, at its best, according to the ancient rabbis, "leads to love" (Genesis Rabbah 54:3). They also noted, however, that "just as it is a *mitzvah* (commandment) to say something which will be listened to, so too is it a *mitzvah* (commandment) to refrain from saying something which will not be listened to" (Yevamot 65b). So, where and how do we draw the line?

I suggest here that the process of moral criticism or rebuke, if it is to be effective at all, must always begin as a form of self-criticism. Before we attempt to encounter the other, we must come face to face with the stranger that is ourselves. Are we indeed "masters of our own house"? as Sigmund Freud wondered. The remainder of this chapter outlines a set of open-ended questions as to what this prescription of moral rebuke entails.

Is My Behavior Consistent with My Rhetoric?

At its simplest and most basic level, self-examination demands that each one of us look critically at our own behavior and actions. Before one criticizes his neighbor one must make sure his own house is in order. Joseph Telushkin, in *A Code of Jewish Ethics*, writes:

> Before rebuking someone for an offense, be sure that you yourself are not guilty of the same wrongdoing. The Talmud tells us that Rabbi Yannai had a tree whose branches extended beyond his private property onto a public road. Another man in the town had a similar tree that interfered with traffic, and some local townspeople, whose passage was obstructed by it, came to Rabbi Yannai to complain. He told them, "Go away now, and come back tomorrow." That night he hired workers to cut down his tree. The next day he ordered the man to have his own tree cut down. The man responded, "But you also have such a tree." Rabbi Yannai replied, "Go and see. If mine is cut down, then cut yours down, and if mine is not cut down, you need not cut yours down." (2006, p. 385)

A careful reading of this story shows that even though Rabbi Yannai's tree "extended beyond his private property," his tree presumably did not interfere with public traffic. Nevertheless, Rabbi Yannai correctly anticipated the response he would elicit if he ordered the man to cut down his tree without cutting down his own tree first.

The near tragic story of the former attorney general and governor of New York, Elliot Spitzer, provides a dramatic and contemporary example of what can go wrong in moral criticism of others if it is completely divorced from self-examination. For years, Spitzer served as a powerful, necessary, and effective critic of corporate greed and excess. He castigated and challenged chief executive officers for their outrageous pay and compensations packages. He took on the largest and most successful investment banks on Wall Street for unfairly inflating their stock prices. Spitzer opposed mutual funds that provided special privileges to selected clients. In the seemingly anything goes world of corporate business practices, Elliot Spitzer was often a lone voice of restraint and common sense.

His inaugural address, after his successful bid for governor with its record margin of victory, provides an eloquent example of moral criticism. With its inspirational message and tone, it is *still* worth quoting at length:

> To return to policies of opportunity and prosperity, we must change the *ethics of Albany* and end the politics of cynicism and division in our state. If ever there was a time that called out for *introspection* by those in government, it is now. Lincoln spoke of listening to "the better angels of our nature." Indeed, those of us who work in the great building behind me must *hear and heed the serious responsibility* that public service demands and rise to this moment and show the public in words and in deeds that we understand that *our responsibility is to the people of New York.*
>
> The reform we seek is substantial in size and historic in scope. It will require a new brand of politics—a break from the days when progress was measured by the partisan points scored or the opponents defeated. No longer can we afford merely to tinker at the margins of the status quo or play the politics of pitting one group against another. We must replace delay and diversion with energy and purpose in the halls of our capital. What we need now more than ever is *a politics that binds us together*, a politics that looks to the future, a politics that asks not what is in it for me, but always *what is in it for us*...And so, together, we must strive to build One New York through a politics that operates on the principle that we rise or fall as one people and one state. (Spitzer Inaugural Address, emphasis added, January 1, 2007 as quoted in the *New York Times*.)

Unfortunately, I believe for all of us, Spitzer did not heed his own words. While correctly calling for the "introspection" of others, he failed to look inside of himself first. Just months before his downfall, he boasted to a reporter, "I'm not great at the self-reflecting type of answers" (Margolick, 2008, p. 52). He failed the first principle of moral criticism, what we might dub the Rabbi Yannai principle: *Cut down your own tree before you order others to cut theirs down.*

Less than 15 months after Spitzer delivered his inaugural address, he resigned in shame and ignominy as governor of New York after being taped making arrangements to visit a prostitute who worked for a prostitution ring called the Emperor's Club VIP. Among the saddest sidebars to this story was the report that inside the New York Stock Exchange, traders spontaneously broke into applause upon hearing the news of Spitzer's speedy and unforeseen resignation. Although it is understandable why those who felt unjustly accused by Spitzer might celebrate his downfall, should we not also pause, if just for a moment, to wonder about what such applause really says about our culture and our future.

What exactly is it that we are celebrating when one of our best and brightest falls so hard? Perhaps it is a momentary relief to know that no one can really live up to the high rhetoric and aspirations of Spitzer's inaugural address. Perhaps there is a strange kind of satisfaction and even a camaraderie to learn that we are all hypocrites (as we most certainly are) of one sort or another.

As we celebrate Elliot Spizter's sudden moral and political collapse, however, at some point it must surely dawn upon us that just as we are applauding *his* downfall we are applauding *our own* downfall, as well. Is it really true that any of us are better off now than we were before Spitzer's fall? To the extent that our moral language has been corrupted and our jointly shared moral capital has been depleted, as it has, I suggest that we are all worse off now than we were before. This is hardly something worth applauding.

WHAT ARE MY MOTIVES?

In addition to asking ourselves about our own behavior and actions, this is really the easy question, we must also ask ourselves about our own motivations. Why do I choose to engage in moral criticism? This, is not an easy question to answer. Steven Mitchell is surely correct when he writes:

> Our conscious experience is merely the tip of an immense iceberg of unconscious mental processes that really shape, unbeknownst to us, silently, impenetrably, and inexorably, our motives, our values, our actions. (Mitchell, 2002, p. 22)

In engaging in moral criticism, then, we have to ask ourselves questions that go beyond the merely surface reasons we might give to ourselves and to others. Given the fact that moral criticism is such dangerous business (think of even the most successful moral critics in history like Lincoln, Gandhi, and King) why would anyone ever risk it?

The art of moral criticism is like walking a tight rope pulled taught between the poles of self-interest and a regard for others. The first-century rabbinic sage, Hillel, put this insight in the form of a question. "If I am not for myself, who will be for me? And, being only for myself, what am I?"

Would-be contemporary moral critics are well-advised to always identify and own up to their own mixed-motives. One wonders, for example, whether Elliot Spitzer would have engaged in many of the hardball tactics he often used to intimidate (and anger) his opponents if he had understood better his own motives and needs for personal gain and political power.

My point here is *not* to suggest that such motives are always fatal to an effective criticism, rather, to the contrary, such motives are usually necessary to provide sufficient fuel for an ongoing engagement with others (the reason we celebrate Saints so much is that there are so few of them). Rather, my point is that by better identifying and taking responsibility for such motives one can consciously examine them and, attempt, at least, to balance them with a fair regard for the interest of others. Spitzer, in his inaugural address, correctly spoke about listening to the "better angels of our nature." Perhaps he should have openly noted and acknowledged our baser instincts, as well.

Martin Buber, the great twentieth century Jewish philosopher, quotes a famous Hasidic Jewish Master, Rabbi Bunam, as follows:

> Everyone must have two pockets, so that he can reach into the one or the other, according to his needs. In his right pocket are to be the words: "For my sake was the world created," and in his left: "I am earth and ashes."

We are a bundle of motives and interests, some high and some low. It is true that the world was created for "my sake," but it is just as true that "I am earth and ashes." Mature moral criticism, a kind of rebuke that will effectively improve our world and not tear it apart further, must necessarily be grounded in a realistic assessment of human complexities and contradictions. The opportunity for human improvement is great but not infinitely so. It is bounded by the environment in which we live and by our own natures and limitations. Moral criticism must grow out of a deep respect for such boundaries and not a disregard for them.

FOR WHOM AM I SPEAKING? TO WHOM AM I SPEAKING?

> Once, when Rabbi Mordecai was in the great town of Minsk expounding the Torah to a number of men hostile to his way, they laughed at him. "What you say does not explain the verse in the least," they cried. "Do you really think," he replied, "that I was trying to explain the verse in the book? That doesn't need an explanation! I want to explain the verse that is within me."
>
> Martin Buber

Parents and teachers criticize children. Lawyers and doctors criticize clients. Conservatives criticize liberals and liberals criticize conservatives. Americans criticize other nations and other nations criticize Americans. Jews criticize Jews, Christians and Muslims criticize themselves. And, everyone criticizes each other.

When we offer moral criticism we speak *out of* a particular role (spouse, parent, teacher, doctor, social worker, etc.). We speak *for a* particular ideology, tribe, or tradition (liberal, conservative, Republican, Democrat, capitalist, socialist, white, African American, Spanish, Jew, Christian, Muslim, Kantian, utilitarian, secular humanist, gay, straight, man, woman, etc.). We *quote others*, but offer the words up as our own.

Authentic moral criticism, however, must go beyond this kind of abstract and theatrical rehearsing. We must learn to speak not only from inside of an inherited ideology and a given point of view, but as one who can also move beyond a fixed ideology and a predetermined set of beliefs. Our own ideology can itself become the object of critical self-reflection (Kegan, 1994).

Effective criticism is concrete and personal. It derives from one's own history and experiences, but is always oriented toward the future. It is relevant and in the moment. One must patiently seek and find one's own voice and words and one's own opportunity and appropriate time. In confronting another with a script in hand, we absent ourselves and substitute our own authentic being for that of an abstract other. We remove ourselves from the space of dialogue and protect ourselves from having to reveal our own self, our own ideas, values, desires, uncertainties, and weaknesses. Moral criticism is useful for a society precisely because it can access and benefit from everyone's point of view. In speaking for a prepackaged ideology this great benefit is forfeited and the possibility of social advancement is lost.

For whom am I speaking? One should always strive to answer this question in the same spirit that Rabbi Mordecai answers his detractors in the above quote, "I want to explain the verse that is within me." James P. Carse puts this same point as follows:

> To enter a culture is not to do what the others do, but to do whatever one does with the others. This is why every new participant in a culture both enters into an existing context and simultaneously changes that context. Each new speaker of its language both learns the language and alters it. Each new adoption of a tradition makes it a new tradition—just as the family into which a child is born existed prior to that birth, but is nonetheless a new family after the birth. (1986, p. 71)

For sure, we need to fulfill the specific roles that we have taken on or have been assigned as others are counting on us, and certainly we choose ideologies that make sense to us. At our best, however, we learn to infuse these roles with our own personal contributions and meanings. We master an ideology only by emerging from it intact with an ability to value both its strengths and weaknesses. Responsible moral criticism means that *I* am speaking directly to *you*.

The effectiveness of moral criticism hinges on my ability to articulate my own point of view, to speak for myself, to voice. Equally important, however, is the ability *to listen*. "The heart of dialogue is a simple but profound capacity to listen. Listening requires we not only hear the words, but also embrace, accept, and gradually let go of our own inner clamoring. As we explore it, we discover that listening is an expansive activity" (Isaacs, 1999, p. 83). In truth, voicing and listening are two aspects of a single activity.

Moral criticism, if it is merely a monologue, is no moral criticism at all. To be effective, moral criticism must be part of an ongoing dialogue founded upon mutual respect and tolerance. Moral rebuke, when necessary, is not directed to an anonymous *other* nor is it directed to society in general. At its best, it is an encounter, a turning toward one another, a meeting of equals. Embedded in every authentic critique is an invitation for response and further give and take.

In truth, the *other* to whom I am speaking is unknowable, a kind of mystery. Just as I am an unfinished product so too he or she is growing and developing over time. Moral criticism must be informed by history, but it is always targeted toward an open and undecided future. Both the content and tone of moral rebuke reflect these inherent uncertainties.

WHAT AM I TRYING TO ACCOMPLISH?

Am I speaking merely to hear my own voice or am I trying to better the world? And, if it is the latter, precisely how do I intend to accomplish this task? The contemporary Yale University philosopher Seyla Benhabib describes the kind of "communicative ethics" I have been calling for here as follows:

> When we shift the burden of the moral test in communicative ethics from consensus to the idea of an ongoing moral conversation, we begin to ask not what all would or could agree to as a result of practical discourses to be morally permissible or impermissible, but what would be allowed and perhaps even necessary from the standpoint of continuing and sustaining the practice of moral conversation among us. The emphasis now is less on *rational agreement,* but more on sustaining those normative practices and moral relationships within which reasoned agreement *as a way of life* can flourish and continue. (Benhabib, 1992, p. 38, emphasis in original).

In other words, in engaging in moral dialogues, we are not necessarily looking for a final agreement, but we are searching together for ways to keep the conversations going. The point of moral criticism is not to force you to change your behavior against your will but to work together with you to establish and maintain "ongoing moral conversation."

James P. Carse distinguishes between two types of games; finite and infinite. "A finite game is played for the purpose of winning, an infinite game for the purpose of continuing the play" (1986, p. 3). Finite games are about borders; infinite games are about horizons. Finite games are displays of power; infinite games demand strength. Finite games are always theatrical; infinite games are always open and dramatic. *Moral criticism can be played as either a finite game or an infinite one.* When it is played as a finite game, there are always winners and losers, the tone is always self-confident and knowing, the purpose is to get you to do what I want you to do. I am stingy with forgiveness both for myself and for you. When it is played as an infinite game, by contrast, there are never winners and losers (if any one of us loses, we all lose), the tone is hesitant, halting, and uncertain. During the course of play, I allow myself room to grow just as I allow you to grow. The point of moral criticism when it is viewed as an infinite game is not to force you into submission, but it is to surrender jointly and playfully to an emergent covenant to which we are both heirs and contributors.

"Whoever plays, plays freely. Whoever *must* play, cannot *play*" (Carse, 1986, p. 4). If I feel that I *must* rebuke you, I almost certainly *should not* rebuke you. Paradoxically, moral criticism is most appropriate only when I recognize that I have a choice to make and when I am willing to assume responsibility for my own words. I rebuke best not in my role as teacher or father nor as a member of this or that religion. I rebuke, moment to moment, spontaneously, face to face; one person to another.

In the Jewish thought, there is a deep and abiding tradition that each person is responsible for the other. It is out of this mutual and shared responsibility that moral criticism grows. In the age of terrorism, nuclear capabilities, globalization, and environmental degradation, we must urgently find new and better ways to extend the felt experience of mutuality beyond the members of any one tribe, religion, or nationality. This is a tall order. It represents not just a change in outer behavior but a deep change in consciousness. It is a movement toward a new kind of this-worldly spirituality (Rosenthal and Buchholz, 2004).

Is Anyone Listening to Me?

The probability of moral criticism actually taking hold is slight. Most moral criticism is only partially heard and usually misunderstood. It is generally viewed as just another self-interested move in a finite game. If it is heard at all, it is probably interpreted in strategic rather than spiritual terms.

In the biblical verse with which this chapter began, the Hebrew word for rebuke—*tokhehah*—is repeated twice. To the ancient rabbis this repetition is meaningful. "If one sees his fellow engage in offensive behavior and rebukes him, but his friend does not accept it from him, from where do we learn he must go back and rebuke him again? From our verse in Leviticus 19:17, you shall *surely rebuke*—as many times as necessary" (Arakhin 16b). Moral criticism thus requires patience, a sense of timing, and persistence.

When no one listens, the first instinct is to speak louder. This is almost always counterproductive. If I am using the wrong vocabulary in the first place, what use is there in repeating the same words over again at a higher volume? If we are operating out of two distinct sets of values, how can I hope to convince you that my values are better than yours? In the context of a moral dialogue, it is far better to remain silent and to listen more carefully. There is a rhythm, however slight, to every conversation. To participate in the dialogue you must discover its rhythm.

Moral criticism demands an active kind of listening rather than a passive one. One must learn to listen and accept what can not be changed. It requires imagination and creativity. Rebuke only works if one has an open-mind and is willing to first hear and tolerate the rebuke of others.

Ask yourself, is my behavior consistent with my moral aspirations? What are my motives? For whom am I speaking? To whom am I speaking? And, what am I trying to accomplish? In the end, perhaps the best we can do is to become the change we are trying to accomplish in others. The goal in moral criticism is not to control others, but it is to build together a permanent bridge of dialogue as we walk on it (Quinn, 2004). It is a kind of search to find shared values and invent a common moral vocabulary.

Is anyone listening to me? Perhaps this is not the most important question, at all. A self-reflective attitude demands that we finally muster the courage to look deeply into the mirror and question ourselves. Am I listening to myself? For sure, I hear the words I use, but do I really understand them? I form the sentences I write, but do I allow the sentences to reform me? I polish my rhetoric, but do I really practice it? I listen to you, but do I let it affect me?

CONCLUSION

The great American philosopher John Dewey stated his ethical postulate at the beginning of his long career as follows:

> In the realization of individuality there is found also the needed realization of some community of persons of which the individual is a member: and, conversely, the agent who duly satisfies the community in which he shares, by that same conduct satisfies himself (quoted in Garrison, 2004).

This is a high standard, rarely achieved in practice. I think of this not only as an ethical postulate but as a spiritual achievement, as well. Spirituality, of the sort I am speaking about, is the wholly natural and human experience of blending integrity and integration through acceptance of the past, commitment to the future, reasonable choice, mindful action, and dialogue (Pava, 2007).

Moral criticism, or rebuke, I suggest is, at times, a necessary part of this kind of spirituality. Nevertheless, *it is an extremely dangerous activity.* It is more likely to go wrong than right. The thesis of this chapter has been that moral criticism, if it is to make any sense at all, must first and foremost be a form of self-criticism. Despite his own personal shortcomings, Elliot Spitzer was surely correct when he stated in his inaugural address, the question is never "what is in it for me, but always *what is in it for us.*"

Effective moral criticism is a rare art. In the Jewish tradition, King David's confidante and advisor Nathan provides a precious example of an effective rebuke. It is an example that had an important effect upon David himself, but it has, perhaps even more importantly, through the ages become a permanent part of our moral understanding of what it means to be a fair and just leader.

King David, in an act of amazing hubris, goes to bed with Bathsheba and then subsequently and conveniently arranges to have her husband Uriah killed in battle. "Put Uriah in the fiercest part of the battle, and then withdraw from him so that he will fight the enemy alone." After Uriah's death, David marries Bathsheba. Here's how the prophet Nathan rebukes David:

> And Nathan came unto David, and said unto him, There were two men in one city; the one rich, and the other poor. The rich man had exceeding many flocks and herds: But the poor man had nothing, save one little ewe lamb, which he had bought and nourished up: and it grew up together with him, and with his children; it did eat of his own meat, and drank of his own cup, and lay in his bosom, and was unto him as a daughter. And there came a traveller unto the rich man, and he spared to take of his own flock and of his own herd, to dress for the wayfaring man that was come unto him; but took the poor man's lamb, and dressed it for the man that was come to him. And David's anger was greatly kindled against the man; and he said to Nathan, As the Lord liveth, the man that hath done this thing shall surely die: And he shall restore the lamb fourfold, because he did this thing, and because he had no pity. And Nathan said to David, Thou art the man. (II Samuel 12:1–7)

This was an artful rebuke that was not designed to eradicate evil nor to stop the conversation. It is a rebuke that honors acceptance of the past, commitment to the future, mindfulness, reasonableness, and dialogue. In fact, David did not turn around and challenge Nathan or argue with him but he calmly accepted responsibility for his sin.

To conclude, moral criticism is rare but not extinct. It can be wise and learned as it is in the case of Henry David Thoreau's essay on civil disobedience. It can be short and penetrating as in Abraham Lincoln's second inaugural address delivered in 1865. Moral criticism can be inspiring, healing, and uplifting as in Martin Luther King's "I have a dream" speech. It can represent a life's work as in the case of Rabbi Abraham Joshua Heschel's grand opus.

Or, it can be as wordless, nameless, and unforgettable as the Unknown Rebel standing defiantly in front of a line of army tanks in Tianmen Square in 1989. Effective moral criticism (*tokhehah*) is rare but it is as necessary now as ever.

NOTE

1. The Oxford Handbook of Judaism and Economics edited by Aaron Levine (Oxford Handbooks in Economics) (2010), Chapter 15: "The Art of Moral Criticism: Rebuke in the Jewish Tradition and Beyond," by Moses L. Pava, pp. 295–297. By permission of Oxford University Press, Inc.

REFERENCES

Benhabib, Seyla, *Situating the Self: Gender, Community and Postmodernism in Contemporary Ethics* (New York: Routledge, 1992).
Buber, Martin, *Tales of the Hasidim,* downloaded on June 12, 2008 from http://members.tripod.com/-chippit/jewish.html.
Callahan, David, *The Cheating Culture: Why More Americans are Doing Wrong to Get Ahead* (New York: Harcourt Inc., 2004).
Carse, James P., *Finite and Infinite Games: A Vision of Life as Play and Possibility* (New York: Random House, 1986).
Emerson, Ralph Waldo, "Self-Reliance," downloaded on June 12, 2008 from http://www.emersoncentral.com/selfreliance.htm.
Garrison, Jim, "Dewey and the Education of Eros: A Critique of the Ideal of Self-Creation," *Journal of Curriculum Theorizing*, 2004, Vol. 20, No. 4, pp. 147–161.
Iaacs, William, *Dialogue and the Art of Thinking Together* (New York: Doubleday, 1999).
Kegan, Robert, *In Over Our Heads: The Mental Demands of Modern Life* (Cambridge: Harvard University Press, 1994).
Margolick, David, "The Year of Governing Dangerously," *Vanity Fair*, 2008.
Mitchell, Steven, *Can Love Last? The Fate of Romance Over Time* (New York: W.W. Norton & Company, 2002).
Pava, Moses L., "Spirituality In (and Out) of the Classroom: A Pragmatic Approach," *Journal of Business Ethics*, 2007, Vol. 73, No. 3, pp. 287–299.
Quinn, Robert E., *Building the Bridge as You Walk On It: A Guide for Leading Change* (San Francisco: Jossey-Bass, 2004).
Rorty, Richard, *Contingency, Irony, and Solidarity* (Cambridge: Cambridge University Press, 1989).
Rosenthal, Sandra and Rogene Buchholz, "The Spiritual Corporation: A Pragmatic Perspective," *Research in Ethical Issues in Organizations*, Vol. 5 (Stamford, CT: Jai Press, 2003) pp. 55–62.

Telushkin, Joseph, *A Code of Jewish Law, Volume 1: You Shall Be Holy* (New York: Bell Tower, 2006).

Walzer, Michael, *Interpretation and Social Criticism* (Cambridge, MA: Harvard University Press, 1987).

CHAPTER 7

DEAL BREAKER AND THE MONEY-LAUNDERING RABBIS

> Fantasy, abandoned by reason, produces impossible monsters; united with it, she is the mother of the arts and the origin of marvels.
>
> Francisco Goya

The use of imagination can improve the quality of ethical dialogues in several distinct ways. It is imagination that allows us to empathize with those with whom we disagree, and, as we identify with and understand someone else's feelings, the emotional distance between us is presumably shortened. Further, at a cognitive level, imagination helps us to understand and to see the world, not only from our own point of view, but from the perspectives of others. Each of us has our own beliefs, ideas, and history, and we know that it is these beliefs, ideas, and the accidents of history that color our perceptions of the environment and impact the information we take in and filter out.

With imagination, though, we can ask ourselves all kinds of "what if" questions: What if I believed x instead of y? What if I was born Christian or Muslim instead of Jewish? What if I was poor instead of middle class? By asking these questions, and many other similar ones, and honestly entertaining various answers, we open ourselves up to new ways of thinking. We begin to actively seek out new sources of information and to appreciate new forms of art. Strange arguments suddenly become more tolerable to hear, and foreign viewpoints come into sharper focus.

Through moral imagination we broaden the space of dialogue, unlock seemingly closed-off areas of discussion, and learn how to search together for new compromises and alternative solutions. At its best, imagination generates new images of what we might become and nurtures more encompassing ideals than those we have inherited from our past.

One of the single most important questions facing advocates of reasonable dialogue is: Is it really possible for us to overcome our own inherent self-interest? Can the individual human mind begin to reimagine itself as part of a more inclusive identity? Or, are we doomed to conceive of ourselves as forever locked in a struggle of competing and mutually exclusive interests?

The contemporary philosopher Daniel Dennett raises these questions in his recent book *Breaking the Spell* as follows:

> Whenever an agent makes a decision about the best course of action, all things considered, we can ask from whose perspective this optimality is being judged. A more or less standard default assumption, at least in the Western world, and especially among economists, is to treat each human agent as a sort of isolated and individualistic locus of well-being. What's in it for *me*? But although there has to be something in the role of the self—something that answers the *cui bono* question for the decision-maker under examination—there is no necessity in this default treatment, common as it is. (2006, p. 176)

This is an adventure of the imagination being described here by Dennett. In his words, "there is no *necessity* in this default treatment." But if Dennett is right and the "self" is not necessarily "me" or "I" than what is it? Here is Dennett's answer:

> I can care for others, or for a larger social structure, for instance. There is nothing that restricts me to a *me* as contrasted to an *us*. I can still take my task to be looking out for Number One while including, under Number One, not just myself, and not just my family, but also Islam, or Oxfam, or the Chicago Bulls! The possibility, opened up by cultural evolution, of installing such novel perspectives in our brains is what gives our species, and only our species, the capacity for moral—and immoral thinking. (2006, p. 176)

There is a level of consciousness, a way of being in the world, Dennett promises, that allows us to overcome narcissism, to jettison individual self-interest, to reexperience ourselves as interconnected beings and not as atomistic, isolated, individuals. There is a genuine and authentic state of mind beyond our "default" condition of always asking "what's in it for me?" (see also Pava, 2009).

It is hard for me to imagine that anyone can live in this place permanently, nor would we necessarily want to, but to strengthen our faith in dialogue, it is useful to remind ourselves that many of us can, at least, temporarily find refuge in an alternative worldscape. Hardened assumptions of me versus you (or us versus them) can melt away almost immediately through the kind of imaginative mind-shift Daniel Dennett is talking about.

FANTASY AS THE DARK SIDE OF IMAGINATION

Imagination serves as a sturdy bridge linking us up to one another in positive ways. Imagination promotes the interests of open dialogue, and dialogue, in turn, provides the content and is the source of legitimacy for contemporary ethics. There is, however, another side to imagination. The psychoanalyst Carlo Strenger describes these two poles of imagination as follows:

> On the one hand the imagination is our tool to transcend the existing, to envisage the nonexisting, and thus to create something new. On the other hand the imagination can be used under the aegis of the pleasure principle, and then it is generally called fantasy. In fantasy we imagine a desired state of affairs. But we do not imagine it as a possibility to be realized in the future. Instead we imagine that what we desire occurs *now*. We want to feel that we actually have what is not ours in reality. The function of fantasy is not to enable us to experiment with other views of the world, with possible elaborations of the future. Its goal is to relieve pain immediately by generating the feeling of what it would be like if a desire were fulfilled. (1998, p. 178, emphasis in original).

Fantasy, rather than serving as a sturdy bridge between us, in this view, is more like a wall separating us from one another. If it is true that through an act of fantasy we can "feel that we actually have what is not ours in reality," there is a literal withdrawal from our everyday interactions with one another. Now, there is no reason to remain in the give and take space of dialogue. "I have used my imagination not in order to imagine what is absent, but in order to give myself the experience as if it were present" (p. 178).

The reduction of pain through fantasy is not free. In fact, it is a high cost luxury item. In Strenger's words "The...price paid for the habitual use of fantasy is the denigration of the real" (p. 178). The overuse of fantasy can cause us to lose track of our real lives as responsible and accountable members of a larger community. Strenger explains further. "The point is that the more an individual relies on fantasy as a means to reduce the pain of absence, the more fantasized realities achieve a status close to that of the actual world. The result is that the individual's actual life comes to feel unreal (pp. 178–179)."

Although Strenger does not examine the ethical implications of fantasy directly, I believe that the extreme fantasies, of the type he is describing, erode the possibility and hope of real dialogue. Reduced dialogue means that the back and forth of ethical criticism is stunted, the exchange of new ideas and ideals from one person to another (and one culture to another culture) is halted, and moral growth becomes an impossibility. Whether fantasy is consciously or unconsciously embraced, its effects isolate the fantasist in a static, lonely, backward-looking, and make-believe world. New experiences are blocked. Information is ignored, and communication grinds to a halt. It is granted that fantasy, on occasion, can serve as a needed respite, a kind of personal holiday from reality. As a preferred way of life, however, institutionalized fantasy can turn into a self-imposed private prison from which it is nearly impossible to escape. The inability to communicate with one another is devastating to those who aspire, or who once aspired, to live ethical lives of meaning and purpose in community.

A call of the hour is the need to become more self-conscious about how we use the gift of imagination. Do we use it as a tool to deepen life's experiences, to enrich our shared lives, and to tear down self-imposed fences? Do we use it to become more intertwined and more involved with one another? Or, rather, do we use it as a protective shield, and as a way of building a private and impenetrable enclave to keep others out? At the moment, it is not always obvious which way we are heading toward here.

Strenger's psychological analysis is helpful to navigate this dangerous terrain. The symptoms of self-destructive fantasy, he writes, include:

- a self "experienced as not quite real" (p. 179),
- change anticipated as a result of "effortless movement" in a "frictionless reality" (p. 179),
- a "contemptuous rejection of real-life options which could provide a step toward authorship" (p. 180),
- endless repetition "of the same patterns" despite the lack of effectiveness in accomplishing ones goals (p. 180),
- a "state of bitterness" (p. 176), and, finally,
- a "constant accusation of others who are taken to be responsible for the subject's failure to live her own life" (p. 176).

Strenger's main interest, in his work, is on tracing the corrosive aspects of fantasy in the life of his clinical patients. What I find both useful and worrisome from a moral point of view, however, is the possibility that the negative aspects of fantasy life that he describes and documents so well may also be shared (although never openly recognized explicitly as fantasy) among members of a community to the detriment of the community's moral health and viability.

THE CASE OF THE MONEY-LAUNDERING RABBIS

The communal response and reaction to the arrest of several prominent Syrian Jewish rabbis on federal charges of international money laundering on July 23, 2009 (as part of a massive sting operation), following an intensive ten-year FBI investigation, suggest a shared denial of reality among many in the Jewish community in favor of a fantasy-tinged view of the world. The arrested rabbis include Rabbi Saul Kassin 87, of Brooklyn, New York (NY), and spiritual head of the Sephardic community in the United States, Rabbi Eliahu Ben Haim, 58, of Long Branch, New Jersey (NJ), and Rabbi Edmund Nahum of Deal, NJ. According to the prosecutors, more than 3 million dollars were laundered by the rabbis. Hundreds of hours of video and audio recordings document the illegal transactions.

To start the money laundering, FBI cooperating witness, Solomon Dwek, also of Deal, NJ, and the son of Rabbi Isaac Dwek, founder of the Deal Yeshiva, gave checks made out to religious charities run by the rabbis. Dwek told the rabbis that the money came from profits from his illegal sales of counterfeit handbags including knockoff versions of Prada, Gucci, and Canali products. A newspaper report, based on court documents, summarizes the allegations against the rabbis:

> Three of the rabbis had connections to cash sources in Israel, and for a fee, those men in Israel made money available through "cash houses" run out of Brooklyn homes, offices and a bakery. The men who ran those cash houses obtained the money at the direction of the co-conspirators in Israel, then gave the funds to the rabbis in Deal and Brooklyn. The religious leaders took their cut, generally 10 percent, then turned over the remainder to the FBI [cooperating] witness. During one meeting in Brooklyn, Eliahu Ben Haim, the principal rabbi of Congregation Ohel Yaacob in Deal who is accused of laundering $1.5 million, spoke with the witness about his cash source in Israel. Ben Haim said he talked to the man every day or every other day, and said in the past four years, the Israeli man had the rabbis send out wires, under different names, all over the world, from Australia to New Zealand to Uganda. "It's unbelievable. I never saw anything like it," Ben Haim said. "I mean every country imaginable. Turkey, you can't believe it... All different names. It's never the same name... Switzerland, everywhere, France, everywhere, Spain... China, Japan." In another method, the [cooperating] witness would bring a check to two other rabbis, Saul Kassin and Edmund Nahum, principal rabbi at the Synagogue of Deal. Kassin is the spiritual leader of 75,000 Syrian Jews in Brooklyn. Prosecutors said the rabbis would write the witness checks from a charity bank account for a slightly smaller amount, payable to the entity of his choice. The witness then cashed the Kassin checks through Ben Haim, authorities said. Criminal complaints say Kassin laundered more than $200,000 and Nahum laundered about $185,000. (www.app.com, July 23, 2009)

US Attorney Ralph J. Marra Jr. stated that those arrested on July 23 were, for all intents and purposes, "crimes bosses." Further, Marra stated that this money-laundering case was "unprecedented" in the "number and prominence of the individuals involved." In an almost surrealistic footnote to this story, prosecutors stated that rabbis referred to the illegal money being exchanged using the term *gemorah*—in their convoluted accounting one *gemorah* was equal to 1,000 dollars—and set up meetings by impiously asking one another "when do you want to learn [Torah]?"

The alleged crimes, of course, raise many questions about Jewish leadership, materialism in the Jewish community, Israel's participation in the alleged crimes, and the values-in-use—as opposed to the stated values—of Jewish communal leaders. These allegations also raise questions about the role of enablers in this process—that is, those of us who are not directly involved in crimes, but who create an environment conducive to criminal and other unethical behavior. Obviously, the most important questions we can raise concern our shared future as a Jewish community: How can we prevent or, at least, reduce the likelihood of these kinds of scandals in the future? Do we need to alter long-held educational philosophies and structures? Do we need to offer students greater professional options? To what extent is religious Judaism consistent with democratic principles of government both in the United States and Israel?

These questions, as critical as they are to our long-term health, are rarely raised in public dialogues among Jewish leaders and their followers. Rather than talking about these broad but crucial questions and trying to answer them in reasonable, open, and transparent ways, ethical dialogues are commandeered by fantasy and illusion. We attempt to relieve the almost unbearable psychic pain by jointly imagining that "we actually have what is not ours in reality" and we pretend together that our desired state of affairs actually exists now (Strenger, 1998, p. 178)

FANTASY ISLAND

Consider some of the various reactions to the money-laundering accusations. Israel's Yitzhak Kakun, editor-in-chief of the Shas weekly *Yom Le'Yom*, states without reservation and "regardless of the details of the case" that this is a clear example of anti-Semitism:

> There is a feeling here that the FBI purposely attempted to arrest as many rabbis as possible at once in an attempt to humiliate them. Regardless of the details of the case—I am not familiar with the precise charges and the evidence—you would never see the FBI and police behaving that way with Muslim sheikhs or Christian priests. It is so obvious that the whole thing is motivated by anti-Semitism. (as quoted at http://www.jpost.com/JewishWorld/JewishNews/Article.aspx?id=149936, 2009).

Others in the Jewish community note the timing of the arrests, about six months after Obama's inauguration, and explain with due solemnity and dire forecasts:

> The fact that this big bust is happening now, presents a worrisome picture of what could be in store for Jewish communities in America in the coming months, as more efforts may be made by "zealous" US governmental agencies, under the ultimate control of the US Department of Justice—and of course the White House—to uncover activities which may have been even accepted as being commonplace among many communities... But for the moment anyway, this subject appears to be under wraps, while the media and US legal authorities appear to be having a field day in "nailing the Jews." The bottom line to this entire scenario is that things have changed for the American Jewish Community, and for Israel, since the new US Administration has taken over in Washington—and definitely not for the better. (http://www.onejerusalem.com/2009/07/28/why-now/)

The Jewish Press, self-described as the largest, independent Jewish weekly in the United States, is careful not to ascribe anti-Semitic motives to the government. "We do not for a second suggest that every time Jews are accused of crimes we should play the anti-Semitism card and deny any possibility of wrongdoing." Nevertheless, they do believe that biased media coverage is a salient enough issue here to merit its own editorial and musings:

> We cannot be indifferent to the packaging of the New Jersey arrests. Reporters were not present at the "perp walk" by some quirk of fate. They were alerted by the U.S. attorney as to what was coming. And the U.S. attorney could not have been unmindful of the public relations value of individuals identified as rabbis being part of that walk... But can there be any doubt that the U.S. attorney wished to exploit the arrests to the greatest extent possible and was prepared to trade on the public relations value of the rabbinic element? Doubtless he wanted to make a point about lawbreakers and knew how the media usually treat any news about rabbis being arrested. And therein lies the rub.
>
> (http://www.jewishpress.com/pageroute.do/40309)

As one reads through these quotes it is almost impossible not to recall some of Carlo Strenger's symptoms identified above: endless repetition of the same patterns despite their ineffectiveness, a feeling of bitterness, and accusations against others for being responsible for one's own failures.

The fantasies illustrated in the above quotes serve a positive function in temporarily relieving some of the felt communal pain and humiliation, but at what long-term cost to the community? In changing the subject from what we can do together to improve our situation to what *they* (the FBI, the Justice Department, the president, the media) have done to us, we squander the opportunity for improvement that this crisis offers us. While fantasies can be shared, as we see here, they are impervious to rational critique and resistant to reasonable dialogue, and thus isolate us from one another, and make real communication between us almost impossible.

In addition to launching claims of anti-Semitism and media-bias, others have gone even further. Rabbi David Bibi, spiritual leader of the Synagogue of Long Beach, writes in the *Long Island Jewish Star* that not only must we presume these accused rabbis as innocent, but what we must recognize that what these leaders did is a fulfillment of a mitzvah. Here is his rationale:

> Three Sephardic rabbis are accused of succumbing to compassion. Was there personal gain for any of them? I highly doubt it. Did they succumb to a young man who was ostracized by others? Did they succumb to a young man who came to them again and again pleading that his children had no food on the table? Did they succumb to the suffering son of a trusted scholar? They did. They fulfilled the verse, Ve'ahavta LeReacha Kamocha [Love your neighbor as you love yourself], even though they were duped, and my sense of judging favorably tells me that Hashem [God] is with them.
>
> (http://thejewishstar.wordpress.com/2009/08/06/in-my-view-don%E2%80%99t-point-fingers/)

Through a simple shift of perspective and an extreme looseness of interpretation of what it means to love one's neighbor, rabbis Kassin, Ben Haim, and Nahum, are magically converted from accused felons arranging "learning" dates with each other in order to exchange thousands of *gemorahs* into Jewish heroes and champions of what is best in our community! Should the Long Island *Jewish Star* have published this? Absolutely. As a newspaper, it is their responsibility to provide its readers with a fair and accurate representation of what is happening in the world around us. But, I suggest, rather than taking Bibi's words literally that what see here is an egregious example of how fantasy operates and its potentially pernicious effects.

Fantasy isolates the fantasist in a static, lonely, backward-looking, and make-believe world of one's own invention. Real information is completely ignored, and useful communication grinds to a halt. Is it really relevant, for example, for readers interested in reasonable debate, to learn from Bibi that God is with the accused rabbis? The fact that the FBI has sufficient evidence to arrest such prominent rabbis suggests to me, at the absolute minimum, a need for communal soul-searching. This process, however, is made infinitely more difficult to achieve because of the almost total detachment from reality the illustrated in Bibi's article. Whether done with intention or not, the free-floating fantasy of Rabbi Bibi is a kind of verbal pollution that will surely erode the social and moral capital of the Jewish community over time. He should be called to accountability on this, and not just by outsiders, but by communal insiders, as well.

Is Solomon Dwek a *Moser*?

Sandi Shapiro, a real estate agent and Long Branch resident, is more concerned about the FBI informant, Solomon Dwek, than about the underlying charges brought against the rabbinic leaders of the Syrian Jewish community. She stated in an interview:

> This is something that is really bothersome to me. Not only did these people believe him and believe in him in his own community, they trusted him. I don't believe in corruption, especially when it comes to government, but for him to go to these people, with taxpayers' money, he gives it to them, he bribes them; it's entrapment. [Solomon Dwek is] a filthy snitch. (http://failedmessiah.typepad.com/failed_messiahcom/2009/08/dwek-faces-shunning-if-not-death.html)

Labeling a fellow Jew as a *moser* (or snitch in Schapiro's description) is an extreme charge in Jewish life. Here's how one rabbinic authority has described this concept:

> A moser is one who informs against his fellow Jews or hands over Jews or Jewish land to non-Jews. In the Middle Ages, Jews were often at the mercy of gentile rulers. When a Jew informed against his fellow Jew or handed him over to the authorities, this was considered a heinous crime because it frequently endangered not only the direct victim of the slander but the entire Jewish community. The Talmud records two cases where an informer was killed by one of the Sages (Berakhot 58a and Bava Kamma 117a), and these stories were codified by Maimonides (Laws of Wounding 8:10). Yet this was the exception to the rule, as is made clear in Maimonides' code (ibid., 8:11). In actuality, Jews throughout the Middle Ages did not execute informers. In Germany they simply excommunicated them, while in Spain such an informer was judged by a court of rabbis who would pass sentence and hand the informer over to the gentile authorities for punishment.
>
> (http://www.shalomctr.org/node/1063)

Since the arrests of the rabbis, there have been several anonymous postings on the Web describing Dwek as a *moser*. "He is a filthy snitch and should be dealt with accordingly," is a typical comment that appeared on the website Voz IS Neias (www.vosizneias.com).

In one of the most inflammatory remarks to date, Sam Hirsch, an attorney and a former New York state assemblyman from Brooklyn, was recorded on a Jewish radio program stating that Dwek "should have been killed" for informing on other Jews. The Jewish Week website has subsequently reported that Hirsch has now backtracked from this comment stating that "he was referring to a concept of traditional Jewish law that called for informers to be killed but that no longer applies today" (www.app.com/article/20090801/NEWS/908010320/1070/NEWS02&source=rss).

Dwek's father, Rabbi Isaac Dwek, himself a prominent rabbi in the Syrian Jewish community, has been silent on the corruption charges brought against his colleagues (although he continues to share his pulpit with one of the accused rabbis), but has spoken publicly and with great emotion about the grave sin of disloyalty to the Jewish community. In fact, in the immediate aftermath of the arrests, he pronounced the traditional blessing—*baruch dayan emet*—that one usually recites upon hearing news about the death of someone. Further, he no longer refers to his son by name, but now describes him as a "former member of my family."

There is no question that Solomon Dwek is a fascinating and complex character with seemingly obvious and self-interested motives to turn FBI informant, as he himself is under arrest for massive fraud. Focusing communal attention primarily on Dwek, flirting with calls for his murder, and pretending that he is no longer your son, however, are just more self-indulgent fantasies. These actions represent "the denigration of the real," as Strenger stated above, and lead us around in perpetual circles going nowhere.

As we debate whether or not Dwek is a hero or a goat, the real and continuing crisis in Jewish leadership goes unmentioned and unexamined. Fantasists expect change as a result of "effortless movement in a frictionless reality." They reject real-life options which might actually improve their situations. Spending our time talking about the "heinous" crimes of the informant and "former" son of Deal, Solomon Dwek, will never get us to where we ought to be going now. Dwek, if anything, is more of a symptom of a much deeper problem, than the cause of our ethical meltdown. In the thrall of fantasy, Jewish ethics itself becomes unreal.

THE HIJACKING OF JEWISH ETHICS

> Besides the fact that [the Patriarchs] were righteous, pious and lovers of God to the greatest extent possible, they were also straight. They dealt with the nations of the world, even immoral idolaters, with love, and they cared about their welfare because they understood that such behavior sustains the world.
>
> Netziv, Ha'amek Davar, Introduction to Genesis

There is a sad and poignant character in Charles Dickens's novel *Great Expectations* named Miss Havisham. In the book, we meet her more than 30 years after her fiancé left her at the altar on their planned wedding day. She remains in the room where she first heard the shocking news, mourning, stuck in time, spectral, accusatory, bitter, and still wearing her once magnificent wedding dress, but now faded, brittle, and turning to dust. "Her life is the symbolic rejection of a fact she has never come to terms with. She just freezes in a state of protest, essentially denying that her life has continued... Protest is kept alive not as a motivator for change but as a goal in its own right" (Strenger, 1998, p. 176).

The Jewish community cannot turn into a Miss Havisham, mourning forever lost and stolen opportunities and hateful and rejecting of others. Nor can we allow Jewish ethics to fade, become brittle, and turn to dust. The tighter we hold onto a fixed and never-changing conception of Jewish ethics, the faster we will kill it. Jewish values are not fixed propositions embedded in written form that can be easily handed off from one generation to the next. Jewish values are necessarily the hard-won product of contemporary and creative Jewish minds. If they are embedded anywhere, they are embedded in our daily actions and in the institutions we help to create through continuous dialogue, leadership, and active participation (Pava, 2009).

Gershom Gorenberg correctly describes Jewish ethics, at its best, as alive, vibrant, and multivocal. He writes:

> Historically, debate over the truth is basic to Judaism. Religious texts are ambiguous and contradictory; they evade a single authoritative reading. Rabbinic tradition rejects reading the Biblical text without the chorus of arguing interpreters who came afterward. Interpretations necessarily stress one part of the text and read others in its light. If there is a common denominator in rabbinic ethics, it's that God created human beings in the divine image, from one set of parents, and that all human life is therefore sacred. (2009, p. 16)

This "chorus of arguing interpreters" does not appear out of nowhere, however. It is dependent upon a rejection of extreme fantasy and an openness to other points of view, absent (for the most part) in the reactions to the arrests cited above.

At the heart of a reinvigorated Jewish ethics is the biblical commandment (repeated twice) to love the stranger. Who else is there but the stranger to challenge us and to wake us up from our dreams of omnipotence? Who else will tell us to stop blaming everyone else and look inside ourselves?

The Syrian Jewish community in the United States is notorious for it rabbinic ban prohibiting its members from marrying converts to Judaism. This blatant ruling is so at odds with traditional Jewish ethics that it can only be understood as an unholy fantasy of purity and perfection. It represents nothing short of a hijacking of Jewish ethics.

It is true as *The Jewish Press* and other defenders have pointed out that the accused rabbis were individuals acting on their own initiative. It is also true, no doubt, that the vast majority of Syrian Jews are honest and hardworking Americans. Nevertheless, there is a shocking insularity to this community. Inside this protected enclave, too many of its members have become oblivious to even the most minimal demands of law and ethics. Like Miss Havisham, in *Great Expectations,* they operate ghostly, sadly, without real challenge or opposition from the outside.

THE OPPOSITE OF FANTASY IS ACCEPTANCE

The flip side of fantasy is acceptance. Acceptance, in this view, is not a passive resignation, but it is an active turning toward the complexities of the world. Acceptance does not arrive immediately, but it is a slow and painstaking process. It means that even when we cannot understand things as they are—they simply don't make sense from our point of view (rabbis don't act this way!)—we don't turn away and ignore them. Acceptance is a psychological process. It involves patience, the overcoming of fear, a willingness to change, and the toleration of differences. But it has important ethical implications. It is a first step toward dialogue and a mature opening up of ourselves to deeper levels of reality. The irony of acceptance is that it is the most direct route toward real and lasting change.

Through a constructive use of imagination, the philosopher Daniel Dennett suggested that we can move beyond a sense of ourselves as isolated and solely self-interested individuals. In his words, "There is nothing that restricts me to a *me* as contrasted to an *us.*" It through embracing this kind of imaginative leap, that we can finally extricate ourselves from the many fantasies that imprison us.

To one degree or another we are all fantasists. The case of the money-laundering rabbis is hardly unique in Jewish history or in contemporary Jewish life. It does remind us, however, of our own responsibilities as enablers. Do we have the courage to challenge one another's illusions or do we take the path of least resistance and remain silent? Changes in technology like the advent of the internet are helpful in drastically reducing the cost of communication, but mechanical solutions alone are not sufficient. Technology, and the ease of communication it allows, may just as easily cheapen language and undercut civil discourse as readers of many blogs quickly discover. The ethical crises our community faces today demand not only external changes, but internal ones, as well. I agree with Karen E. Starr when she concludes in her recent book, *Repair of the Soul* that "cultivating open channels between foreground and background, union and separateness, imagination and reality makes the creation of new meaning possible, and potentiates the experience of the sacred" (2008, p. 117).

CONCLUSION

I keep a newspaper article from the *Jerusalem Post* on my desk at school so that every student who comes into my office can read it. The article appeared in 1996, about a month before Yigal Amir's murder of Yitzhak Rabin. The title of the article is "They Will Share the Guilt." The article, written by two Jewish writers associated with the Hartman Institute in Jerusalem, hints about the possibility of Rabin's assassination. In the article, the authors document the harsh and incendiary public statements of a prominent Jewish rabbi attacking Rabin's political policies, implying that Rabin, a military hero of Israel, was now a traitor (a *moser*) to the state.

The author suggested, with deadly accuracy, that if and when Rabin is assassinated, it is precisely these leaders—who are undercutting the most basic premises of Israeli democracy—who will be to blame. Rereading this article with the advantage of 20–20 hindsight is chilling, but it also provides a powerful argument in favor of recognizing our responsibility to strengthen society's fragile democratic institutions and values. These values include respecting others, non-coercion, transparency, equal rights, freedom of expression, pluralism, compromise, individual and communal responsibility, and many others.

For those who still insist that Yigal Amir was a crazy young man acting alone, this article provides a powerful wake-up call. Amir did murder Rabin, but he did so in order to realize his teachers' antidemocratic ideals. These ideals, grounded in fantasy and protected from challenge by illusion, are still very much alive, as the case of the money-laundering rabbis illustrates. As the artist, Francisco Goya noted many years ago, "Fantasy, abandoned by reason, produces impossible monsters…"

REFERENCES

Dennett, Daniel, *Breaking the Spell: Religion as a Natural Phenomenon* (New York: Viking Press, 2006).
Gorenberg, Gershom, "The Jewish Way: Killing in God's Name?" *Moment Magazine* (July/August 2009).
Pava, Moses L., *Jewish Ethics as Dialogue: Using Spiritual Language to Reimagine a Better World* (New York: Palgrave, 2009).
Starr, Karen E., *Repair of the Soul: Metaphors of Transformation in Jewish Mysticism and Psychoanalysis* (New York and London: Routledge, 2008).
Strenger, Carlo, *Individuality, The Impossible Project* (New York: Other Press, 1998).

CHAPTER 8

LOVING THE STRANGER AND THE FALL OF AGRIPROCESSORS

> Imagination over dogma, vulnerability over serenity, aspiration over obligation, comedy over tragedy, hope over experience, prophecy over memory, surprise over repetition, the personal over the impersonal, time over eternity, life over everything.
> Roberto Mangabeira Unger, 2007, p. 237

> The dignity of difference is at the heart of the Bible's command to love the stranger.
> Rabbi Jonathan Sacks, 2001

In Leviticus, the Bible directs us to "love your neighbor as yourself" (19:18) This is a difficult principle to achieve. It is useful to conceive of this more as an aspiration and a promise about human potential than as a specific rule of behavior. It points us in the right direction, but it does not necessarily tell us how to get there. Accomplishing this mitzvah is a life's task rather than a finite project. The Bible expects us over time to move beyond our own self-interests, narrowly defined, and to incorporate the interests, needs, and desires of others into our decision making.

Loving one's neighbor also implies not just a change in behavior, but a change in attitude, as well. To love someone is to respect and to trust them, to care and feel compassion for them, and to open oneself up to them. Loving one's neighbor deepens the experience of community beyond a merely utilitarian calculus. It is a kind of glue that holds the community together. In the Jewish tradition, it is understood by some as the single most encompassing principle of the entire Torah. As the great sage Hillel famously summarized this 2,000 years ago, "That which is hateful to you, do not do to your neighbor. That is the whole Torah; the rest is commentary. Go and study it."

Just a few verses later, however, the Bible points us in a different direction. "The stranger that sojourns with you shall be unto you as the homeborn among you, and you shall love him as yourself; for you were strangers in the land of Egypt" (Leviticus 19:34).[1] This principle, too, is better thought of as an aspiration rather than as a simple rule of behavior. But this mitzvah is considerably more radical and demanding than the first one. Through loving one's neighbor community is strengthened as existing interpersonal relationships become more deeply felt. Loving the stranger, however, challenges the very notion of a static and unchanging community. Who is this stranger who is neither friend nor enemy? To love the stranger requires an imaginative leap of faith into unknown and uncharted territories.

As we contemplate the meaning of loving the stranger perhaps it strikes us as an odd and paradoxical call. How can one love a stranger who by definition is unknown to us? It asks us to cross an ambiguous and mysterious boundary that most of us, most of the time, are not especially comfortable or inclined to traverse. It demands not just a thickening of already familiar community ties, but it promises the possibility of a broadening and an enlarging of community. It is not simply context-preserving, but it is context-transforming (Unger, 2007). We are asked to bring the outsider inside and thus to transform and to transcend our current conceptions of who "we" are. If loving your neighbor is the glue that keeps community together, then loving the stranger is the fuel that pushes community forward. If loving the neighbor is backward-looking, then loving the stranger is oriented toward the future. "The importance of the present lies in carrying the responsibility of honoring both past and future—that is, knowing how to compromise in our commitments toward preservation and betrayal" (Bonder, 2001, p. 13).

Loving the stranger demands acceptance, appreciation, patience, tolerance, curiosity, and imagination in the face of mystery and the kind of infinite difference celebrated in the following rabbinic insight. "Humans stamp many coins with one seal and they are all the same; but God has stamped every human with the seal of the first man, yet not one of them are like another" (Sanhedrin Chapter 4, Mishna 5).

To love the stranger is to recall one's own status as an outsider (for you were strangers in the land of Egypt) and to actively seek out what is strange and new both in ourselves and in the world around us rather than to withdraw and to hide. As Julia Kristeva has perceptively noted, "Our ability to live *with* others requires that we must live *as* others, recognizing the strangeness within ourselves" (Marcano, 2003, p. 161, emphasis added). The mitzvah of loving the stranger represents the aspiration to become more complex and to grow over time. Or, as Jim Garrison, has put it, "To grow we must be vulnerable and risk ourselves in relationships of care and concern" (1997, p. 38). It is a dynamic principle that seeks to propel the community forward and not a static one holding the community still.

SACRED MESSINESS

Loving the stranger is to transgress the status quo in the exact same way that the patriarch Abraham transgressed when he left behind his country, birthplace, and father's house in search of a better life "to the land that I will show you" (Genesis 7:1). It is to invite three unknown travelers into your modest, desert tent, and to treat them with the dignity of good and ample food and quiet and cool rest as Abraham and Sarah did. To love the stranger is to break with Pharaoh and Egypt once and for all and to begin the unknown journey into a distant promised land. Loving the stranger is possible but not easy. In short, ethics is like a circle, and loving the stranger represents a permanent call to broaden this circle.

We experience a constant tension between the centrifugal pull of loving one's neighbor and the centripetal push of learning to love the stranger. This is the contemporary condition in which we sooner or later discover ourselves. It is precisely in between this push and pull that today we live our lives on a daily basis. This chapter suggests that although it once made sense to think of the love of one's neighbor as a nearly all-encompassing view of ethics, as Hillel did, the call of contemporary life and its complexities demand a tilt in our perception toward an enhanced appreciation of our differences. An important goal today of ethics is not to overcome difference or to simply ignore it, but to learn to accept difference and even (at our best) to love it.

The contemporary Rabbi, Irwin Kula, puts this newly emerging view of ethics as follows. We need to:

> see as many sparks as possible, to sink into the messiness, to fall in love with multiplicity. We need to tune in to the conversation that is always going on among our many selves, and the dialogue, the contradictions, the harmony, and the dissonance that fills the world" (2006, p. 303).

He calls this evolving attitude "sacred messiness." And the call of this hour, more often than not, is to immerse ourselves in this sacred messiness and not to run away from it, Jonah-like, toward safety prematurely.[2]

MOVING BEYOND THE TRADITIONAL INTERPRETATION OF LOVING THE STRANGER

The mitzvah of loving the stranger has been officially on the books in Judaism from time immemorial, however, its traditional meaning has been (perhaps not surprisingly) limited dramatically. From a traditional Jewish point of view, the term for stranger used in this biblical verse (*ger* in Hebrew) has been almost universally translated as a proselyte or convert to Judaism. The mitzvah has therefore historically been understood as a special case of the broader principle of loving ones neighbor and not as a separately identifiable push into uncharted territories.

The ancient rabbis understood this verse as a special obligation to treat newcomers to Judaism in a favorable way. Maimonides summarized the typical rabbinic view as follows:

> How great is the duty which the Torah imposes on us with regard to proselytes. Our parents we are commanded to honor and fear; to the prophets we are ordered to hearken. A man may honor and fear and obey without loving. But in the case of "strangers," we are bidden to love them with the whole force of our heart's affection. (as quoted in Hertz, 1969, p. 790)

Although converts in Judaism possess nearly the exact same rights and obligations as born Jews, the rabbis of the Talmudic period were nevertheless especially concerned about the process of assimilation, warning explicitly, for example, that you should not remind the convert about his "idolatrous background."

My point in this chapter is not that this traditional interpretation is wrong. It remains a creative, appropriate, and timely understanding of the biblical material given the cultural demands of antiquity and the middle ages.[3] The point here is that we should not let the heavy weight of this authoritative insight obscure our own contemporary ability to create meaning with this text. For those who are most familiar with the biblical text and its traditional interpretations there is a particularly strong need to make the words themselves strange. They will need to learn how to purposely bracket what they already "know" in order to read the text with a kind fresh or second naivete'. There is a need to self-consciously rediscover the original inspiration locked tightly away in these ancient phrases. Traditionalists might begin this process by asking themselves the rather obvious question of how the term stranger can possibly refer to converts when the verse itself states that the Jews themselves were strangers in Egypt?

Rabbi Jonathan Sacks, the current Chief Rabbi of Great Britain, admits that he used to think that loving your neighbor was the greatest command in the Bible. Now he writes, however,

> I was wrong. It isn't hard to love our neighbors because by and large our neighbors are people like us. What's tough is to love the stranger, the person who isn't like us, who has a different skin color, or a different faith, or a different background. That's the real challenge. It was in ancient times. It still is today. (2001, p. 1)[4]

Loving the stranger is not a special case of loving ones neighbor but it is a unique and distinct ethical principle stretching us beyond our comfort zones. The great nineteenth century Jewish philosopher Hermann Cohen was not exaggerating when he wrote that "The alien [stranger] was to be protected, not because he was a member of one's family, clan, religious community, or people; but because he was a human being. *In the alien [stranger], therefore, man discovered the idea of humanity*" (as quoted in Hertz, 1969, p. 313, emphasis in original).

BALANCING THE NEEDS OF NEIGHBORS AND STRANGERS IN THE REAL WORLD: THE CASE OF AARON FEUERSTEIN

It is relatively easy to make the theoretical point that we need to balance the needs of our own community against the needs of others outside of our community. But how does one proceed in practice? To where can we turn for a real-world example of what it means to put into practice the aspiration of loving the stranger in the contemporary world? Consider the case of Aaron Feuerstein.[5]

By anyone's definition, Aaron Feuerstein has spent most of his life as a successful entrepreneur. In 1995, his company, Malden Mills, employed 3,100 union workers and generated 400 million dollars in revenue. Malden Mills owned the patent on Polartec Fleece, a an extremely lightweight synthetic fiber, made primarily from recycled products, that keeps wearers warm and dry. This product was so innovative that *Time* magazine named Polartec one of the greatest inventions of the twentieth century.

Malden Mills served as a supplier to such well-known companies as L.L. Bean, Eddie Bauer, and Patagoinia. In addition, Malden Mills manufactured Polartec Fleece for military use by the United States (US) Army. At the same time that General Electric (GE) and other well-known companies were terminating employees and relocating overseas in search of cheap labor, Malden Mills was increasing its workforce in Lawrence, MA, one of the most depressed areas of the country, and paying its employees above average wages. While "Chainsaw Al" Dunlap was the poster boy for sensible and aggressive business practices, Aaron Feuerstein quietly and methodically created a socially responsible and profitable business. "He extended credit to struggling local businesses, sponsored English classes for immigrant workers, and offered training for textile workers. He took special care of his own workers, making sure that they had a safe and comfortable work environment. Even union leaders praised him" (Massmoments.org).

Tragedy struck on very same night he was joyously celebrating his seventieth birthday with relatives and friends. On December 11, 1995 the worst industrial fire in Massachusetts history almost completely destroyed his manufacturing facilities. Feuerstein now faced one of the most excruciatingly difficult decisions of his long business career. He could pocket the 300 million dollars in insurance and retire. He could use the insurance money and relocate the business overseas. Or, he could recommit himself to Lawrence, MA, and to the guiding principles of his long and successful business career.

Less than a week after the fire, Feuerstein publicly committed himself to remaining in Lawrence and rebuilding the factory. Feuerstein went even further than this. At a company-wide meeting, Aaron Feuerstein stated, "I will get right to my announcement. For the next 30 days, our employees will be paid their full salaries. But over and above the money, the most important thing Malden Mills can do is to get you back to work. We're going to continue to operate in Lawrence. We had the opportunity to run south many years ago. We didn't do it then, and we're not going to do it now." The auditorium erupted with relief, applause, and tears. Later, explaining his actions, he quoted the Talmud, "when all is moral chaos, this is the time for you to be a *mensch* [honorable, descent person]."

Within a few months, however, business experts began to question Aaron Feuerstein's dramatic decision. He parted ways with two of his key employees who strongly disagreed with him. In the end, it cost Feuerstein 25 million dollars to keep his employees on the payroll. He invested 400 million dollars to build a state-of-the-art factory, the first new textile mill in New England in more than 100 years. But by 2001, Feuerstein could not make the payments on his borrowed funds and he was forced into bankruptcy.

For several years, Feuerstein struggled gallantly to keep family control of the business. Unfortunately, he was not able to raise the 92 million dollars he needed to satisfy his creditors. In July of 2004, Malden Mills Industries, now controlled by creditors, replaced Aaron Feuerstein as CEO of the company.

Looking back at the recent history of Malden Mills and Aaron Feuerstein, one is at pains to draw an easy lesson from all of this. What does it mean when we read and reread Feuerstein's words in the midst of the battle. "We insist the business must be profitable...But we also insist a business must have responsibility for it workers, for the community. It has a social obligation to figure out a strategy, which will be able to permit workers to make a living wage. There's a responsibility to the workforce, to this community."

Some have argued that Feuerstein abandoned his own entrepreneurial instincts. He failed to view business decision making "solely on a perception of market opportunities" (Formaini, 2001, p. 2). He allowed emotions and sentiment to determine his actions. He invoked an ancient but outmoded set of religious values when he should have been maximizing profits. From this point of view, Feuerstein is a cultural dinosaur who abandoned the entrepreneurial spirit precisely when he needed it most.

I suggest, however, an altogether different interpretation. Feuerstein, in deciding to keep the factory open—continued to rely upon his imagination, playfulness, creativity, risk-taking, alertness to new opportunities, realism, efficiency, singleness of purpose, and independence of thought—all those essential values that constitute the spirit of entrepreneurship. But he exploited these characteristics in an attempt to deconstruct our conception of business success and failure. He tried to balance and integrate his traditional business acumen with other important social values. In doing so he provided us with a deeper, messier, and more complex model of entrepreneurship, one that emphasizes social responsibility, community, compassion, interconnectedness, and a sense of wholeness. Aaron Feuerstein is not a rabbinic scholar interpreting texts for academic purposes. He is, however, an entrepreneur who has internalized the singular importance and timeliness of the biblical mitzvah of loving the stranger.

In his seventieth year, Feuerstein was not invoking an ancient but outmoded set of religious values—*in fact I know of no Jewish source or rabbinic authorities that demand the kind of superogatory actions he chose to engage in.* Rather, Feuerstein is as much an innovator and an iconoclast in ethical life as he is in business life. It is ironic that business magazines like Forbes and others that have criticized Feuerstein have not applauded the risk-taking, creativity, and independence of mind that he demonstrated in an attempt to create a unique kind of business.

Aaron Feuerstein clearly sees the long-term dangers that injustice, poverty, and inequity pose to our economy and our country. He has identified the failure of traditional business answers and he is searching, in the most noble spirit of entrepreneurship, for new and alternative solutions. His is a quest to respect difference and to honor the humanity of the other, including the stranger. He surely has not succeeded completely in his self-chosen task, but to the extent that he has alerted us to problems we might otherwise not want to face, he has left us a legacy too important to ignore. Feuerstein's failure is certainly one of those entrepreneurial failures "that are desirable and even necessary" (Sarasvathy, 2001, p. 7) In this sense, Aaron Feuerstein represents the best of the spirit of Jewish entrepreneurship.

AGRIPROCESSORS AND THE TRAGEDY OF MORAL MYOPIA: THE CASE OF AARON RUBASHKIN

Aaron Feuerstein's case provides an example of ethical heroism. It is proof that, at least on occasion, business men and women can rise above their own self-interests and can imaginatively experience what it is like to be an Other. Aaron Feuerstein's decision shows what it means to implement the biblical mitzvah of loving the stranger in the contemporary world. Feuerstein's example shatters our conventional understanding of morality and raises the bar for the rest of us. This second case, about another and very different Aaron, demonstrates what happens when sympathy and concern for strangers is completely missing.

Aaron Rubashkin was born into a Lubavitch Hasidic family in the Russian town of Nevel. When the Germans invaded during World War II, Rubashkin and his family fled to Central Asia. After the war, Rubashkin and his wife made their way to Vienna and then to Paris, where he became a butcher.

In a recent interview with reporter Nathaniel Popper, the elder Rubashkin reminisced, "Listen, I'm a person like everybody else, even though I look to you with a beard—a white beard. Mine English is poor. I haven't got no college degree. I working since 14, 15. I don't complain. I'm trying to survive."

Not only did Rubashkin survive, but by all outward appearances, until very recently, he and his family have thrived economically. After seven years in Paris, Aaron Rubashkin moved to Brooklyn, New York, in 1952, and he opened a butcher shop on Fourteenth Avenue in the heart of Boro Park. Sholom Rubashkin, Aaron's second son recalls those early years. "He worked hard labor. He worked 18 hours a day. He picked up the meat, he cut the meat, he sold the meat, he delivered the meat. Oh, did he work hard—six days a week."

With his hard work, competitive spirit, help from nearly everyone in his family, dedication, skill, friendly demeanor, charm, and good luck, the shop prospered and grew into a Boro Park institution. As the business grew and diversified, the Rubashkin family became one of the most respected and honored Chabad Lubavitch families in Boro Park. Among their Hasidic neighbors, they are well known for their community leadership, outsized generosity and amazing hospitality. In 2005, Moshe Rubashkin, Aaron's son, was elected chairman of the Crown Heights Jewish Community Council, a group that receives about 2 million dollars per year in government funds.

In 1987, Aaron Rubashkin purchased an abandoned meat processing plant in Postville, Iowa. Under Rubashkin's direction and encouragement and his son Sholom's management, business grew exponentially. The Rubashkins introduced modern, industrial practices and a new business model to a traditional and sleepy industry that had until then little or no apparent concern for efficiency and technology improvements. Under the aptly named business, Agriprocessors, they developed new ways for packaging meat to keep it fresh for longer periods of time. They introduced new and innovative ways of marketing and distributing their products. And, they used a new technology for streamlining and speeding up the kosher slaughtering process. Agriprocessors kept overhead and costs low and began to benefit from its growing size and market share. Agriprocessors was able to pass on some of its cost savings to the kosher consumer and brought high-quality kosher meat and poultry to small Jewish communities that had, until then, not been able to get kosher meat. Interestingly, the majority of their output was sold as nonkosher.

Until recently, sales rose consistently. According to *Cattle Buyers Weekly*, in 1997 Agriprocessors generated 80 million dollars in sales. By 2002, this figure had jumped to 180 million dollars in annual sales. While sales figures for the most recent years are disputed, Nathaniel Popper cites a report published by the state of Nebraska that Agriprocessors' yearly sales were 250 million dollars. The *New York Times* reported annual sales of 300 million dollars (November 6, 2008).

While the kosher beef and poultry industry remains relatively small it has been growing fast in recent years. At its height, Agriprocessors provided 60 percent of all US kosher beef and 40 percent of kosher poultry.

TROUBLE IN IOWA

Troubling reports about Agriprocessors' business practices first surfaced in 2000 with the publication of Stephen Bloom's *Postville: A Clash of Cultures in Heartland America*. In response to these early criticisms, Sholom Rubashkin explained to the author tersely, "We have stayed on this planet longer than anyone else because we believe our way is the right way. You start slipping, making changes here and there, and then you have nothing. We live by our rules here and they've got to understand that."

Agriprocessors, however, did learn an important lesson from this episode and to counteract negative publicity, it began to actively manage its reputation and its business environment in a serious and purposeful way. The Rubashkins became large campaign donors to many politicians and befriended Postville town council members. They hired public relations experts and high-priced and well-placed attorneys. In addition, they were the beneficiaries of sophisticated lobbying tactics which resulted in the Bush Administration issuing new directives concerning ritual slaughter, "making it almost impossible for on site FSIS [USDA Food Safety and Inspection Service] inspectors to stop a glatt kosher production line" (http://failedmessiah.typepad.com/failed_messiahcom/2008/01/exclusive-usda.html).

As Agriprocessors continued to grow, however, it began to make news again. This time it was accused by PETA (People for the Ethical Treatment of Animals) for its inhuman slaughtering practices. PETA's 2004 accusations were buttressed by hours of videotapes documenting a highly unusual method of ritual slaughter and showing animals surviving for several minutes after the slaughter took place. In some cases, the animals got up and walked around while bleeding profusely with torn tracheas dangling from their necks.

According to Dr. Lester Friedlander a former USDA (US Department of Agriculture) slaughter inspector, "The footage captured by PETA represents the most egregious violation of USDA Humane Methods of Slaughter Act I have ever witnessed." According to Dr. Bernard Rollin, an animal expert at Colorado State University, "what was depicted on this video tape is one of the most atrocious incidents I have ever witnessed." According to Rabbi David Rosen, former chief rabbi of Ireland, "I've been in many slaughterhouses in my time, and I've never seen anything like that."

Rabbi Ezra Raful of Israel's Chief Rabbinate stated, "You see there, it looks like he ripped out the trachea and esophagus. We do not allow the animal to be touched after the shehita [ritual slaughter] until the main part of the bleeding stops."

Even according to Rabbi Tzvi Hersh Weinreb, the executive vice president of the Orthodox Union, the kashrut agency in charge of assuring kosher standards are being strictly enforced (they currently oversee over a half a million products), Agriprocessors slaughtering practices were "especially inhumane" and "generally unacceptable."

More Trouble in Iowa

The accusations of inhumane slaughtering practices, as startling to kosher consumers and others as they were, receded into the background, as new allegations concerning the company's unfair treatment of foreign workers gained force. In May of 2006, the *Forward*, a weekly Jewish newspaper, first broke the new story. The long list of allegations against Agriprocessors and Rubashkins include:

- the lowest hourly wages of any slaughterhouse in the nation,
- workers' pay being shortchanged three or fours hours per week on a regular basis,
- exploitive rental agreements,
- several OSHA violations,
- environmental pollution,
- a supervisor alleged to be demanding bribes from workers,
- no pay to workers for preparation and clean-up time as required by an earlier Supreme Court decision,
- little or no safety instructions,
- widespread fear among the approximately 800 undocumented immigrant workers, mostly Hispanic, of being fired or reported to authorities, and financial fraud.

Executives at Agriprocessors denied any wrongdoing and claimed that the failure of the workers to join a union was evidence of workers' satisfaction with the status quo (employees at Hebrew National and Empire, Agriprocessors two main competitors, are unionized). Further, the company argued that it offers workers health insurance (for those employees willing to contribute 50 dollars per week) and the company set up an emergency fund for employee use.

Citing his own family's immigrant background, Sholom Rubashkin admitted that work at a slaughterhouse may not be pleasant, but the company never mistreated its employees. Rubashkin summarized his philosophy as follows, "America has always been built by people who are coming to try to better their economic position and are willing to do jobs that other people are not willing to do. That's how this country is growing."

In May of 2008, US immigration agents entered the Postville plant and arrested more than 300 Agriprocessor workers (about one third of the workforce at the time) on charges of using false social security numbers in what was described by the Des Moines Register (May 12, 2008) as the "largest workplace raid in Iowa history." "As two law enforcement helicopters hovered overhead, dozens of federal agents descended on Agriprocessors Inc., the nation's largest kosher slaughterhouse."

Despite this major setback and a slight fallback in demand on the part of kosher consumers, Agriprocessors continued its production for the next several months, finding and hiring new workers to replace those who were arrested.

Kosher Communities Respond

In response to growing allegations against Agriprocessors, several groups in the Jewish community have responded. On April 16, 2008, *K'hal Adath Jeshurun*, with no explanation, discontinued its certification on all of Agrirprocessors products. Intense debates about the appropriate relationship between ritual law and ethics have re-emerged.

Rabbi Morris Allen of the Conservative Movement developed what he calls the *Hechser Tzedek*, a kind of justice certification that would appear on kosher products to ensure fair working conditions. In New York, an Orthodox group, *Uri L'Tzedek*, announced plans to certify kosher restaurants that treat its employees in a fair and just way. A group of Los Angeles rabbis are planning to issue similar certifications.

The Rabbinical Council of America (RCA) announced plans to set up a task force to publish Jewish Principles and Ethical Guidelines for Business and Industry to adopt on a voluntary basis (possibly offering a certifying label). Rabbi Shmuel Herzfeld, an Orthodox Rabbi in Washington DC and a member of the RCA, has called for an "independent commission whose members have not in the past been paid by either the Orthodox Union or

Agriprocessors" to investigate and make sure that in the future "basic standards of kashrut and worker and animal treatment" are being maintained (*New York Times*, August 6, 2008).

Agudath Israel, a Haredi Jewish communal organization in the United States loosely affiliated with the international World Agudath Israel, does not agree with any of the above approaches. It maintains that Agriprocessors, as a matter of objective Jewish law and ethics, should be given the benefit of the doubt. Rabbi Avi Safran, spokesperson for the organization, stated at a symposium held at Yeshiva University on December 9, 2008:

> I don't know if they mistreated animals as PETA says—I don't know; I don't know if they ran a meth amphetamine lab as a government affidavit said, I don't know if they harassed employees, I don't know if they hired underage employees, I don't know. Neither does anyone, no matter what anyone thinks. What I do know and what all of us should know is that it is Jewishly wrong to assume guilt on the basis of accusations. It is, to put it clearly and simple, unethical—Jewishly unethical. And to create and to herald a new effort as a result of the accusations against people disregards a clear Torah law called *hotzaas sheim rah* [slander].

Agriprocessors and Rubashkins' legal and ethical troubles, however, did not end with the May workplace raid and arrests, nor are they limited to the accusations against the Midwest slaughter houses. Similar worker complaints have been lodged by Agriprocessor workers at a Brooklyn warehouse where the company eventually fired employees who voted to join the United Food and Commercial Workers Union. (*Forward*, August 14, 2008).

In the past, the National Labor Relations Board found that the Rubashkins had a "proclilvity" for violating its rules. In 2002, Moshe Rubashkin, Sholom's brother, was arrested for bank fraud and pleaded guilty. More recently, Moshe Rubashkin and his son were indicted on federal charges related to an abandoned textile mill in Allentown, Pennsylvania. Both have now pleaded guilty according to a document released by the US Environmental Protection Agency. In 2006, the USDA issued a letter of warning to Agriprocessors stating the agency was concerned about the company's "ability to maintain sanitary conditions, and to produce a safe and wholesome product."

On September 9, 2008, Iowa's Attorney General charged Aaron and Sholom Rubashkin and several other executives with more than 9,000 child labor law violations. The complaint stated that not only did the company knowingly hire illegal immigrant workers but also knowingly hired minors to operate conveyor belts, meat grinders, circular saws, power washers, and power shears. They were 32 children under the age of 18 working at the plant and 7 of these were younger than 16 years of age.

On October 30, 2008, Aaron and Sholom Rubashkin were arrested on federal charges of immigration-related offenses. On November 14, 2008, Sholom Rubashkin was arrested again on charges of a multimillion dollar bank fraud and was subsequently found guilty. He was sentenced to 27 years in prison.

"A Slaughterhouse is Not Pleasant Work"

This case is a complex ethical maze. It raises a host of difficult issues and questions with no obvious answers. There are conflicting versions of the story, many different interests among the various stakeholders (economic and otherwise), and several questions about the significance of ritual observance and its relation to ethical behavior. It raises deep questions about immigration policy and the appropriate role of business in society. Each of these questions and problems can be dealt with separately, one at a time, but my sense is that our difficulties are compounded because how we answer one question will undoubtedly affect our answers to others.

As quoted above, Sholom Rubashkin noted that working in a slaughterhouse is not pleasant work. If one watches the PETA videos (readily available online), one quickly understands (at least partially) what Rubashkin is saying. If anything, he is understating the case here. It is not coincidental that this is an industry that attracts a high percentage of immigrant workers and is seen as less attractive work for US citizens who often have other employment opportunities.

In analyzing this case, I think we need to ask ourselves at the outset, how much of our emotional reactions and intuitive ethical responses are based on our uneasiness regarding our own consumption of meat and our own responsibility as consumers, always demanding the lowest possible prices, in supporting the entire production process? The Orthodox Union has taken the position consistently that its most important goal is to ensure low-cost, high-quality meat for the kosher consumer. This seems to be a relatively straightforward mission and an appropriate one for a certifying agency, but perhaps its taken-for-granted status covers up an ambivalence and uncertainty among (at least) some kosher consumers. (See *New York Times* for a discussion of this topic.)

Aaron Rubashkin is himself an immigrant, and his experiences should not be ignored in our attempt to grapple with this case and the broader social issues it raises. His son Sholom states, "America has always been built by people who are coming to try to better their economic position and are willing to do jobs that other people are not willing to do. That's how this country is growing." Certainly, in the context in which this statement was offered, one cannot help but recognize its self-serving nature, nevertheless this should not cause us to lose sight of the truth it holds. The United States has been a country that has been relatively welcoming to newcomers. The immigrant experience is an important and integral part of the American heritage and culture.

Rubashkin talks about how his family has worked and how devoted Aaron Rubashkin was to his business and to his customers. This is a family possessing extreme entrepreneurial instincts. They saw an opportunity in the kosher beef industry and they seized it. One can challenge their many excesses and significant ethical failures (as I will shortly), but still appreciate the energy, enthusiasm, intelligence, creativity, and desire to achieve.

When Rubashkin defenders tell us that Agriprocessors is not the only company in the United States who knowingly hired illegal immigrant workers, my initial instinct is to say, so what? This does not lessen Rubashkin's alleged guilt in any way. For legal purposes, I believe this kind of logic is perfectly sound. From a broader and more inclusive ethical point of view, however, perhaps we need to reconsider. In fact, the Rubashkins are not alone. How many of us, for example, hire foreign workers to clean our houses or to take care of our children? Do we always withhold social security taxes as required by law?

The fact is that the Rubashkins are part of a larger culture that is today uncertain about the best way to deal with immigrants. Should we adopt stricter immigration controls as many political conservatives and political liberals suggest? Should we adopt easier immigration policies and tightly monitor and control immigrant workers while they are here? What kind of rights should we grant to the temporary workers who live among us? How extensive should these rights be?

None of these questions will be answered satisfactorily by expressing indignation and throwing the book at a single company. The point in analyzing and discussing this case, from an ethical perspective, should be less about assigning blame to specific individuals or groups and should focus more on understanding the interconnections among us and attempting—through real dialogue—to figure how to move forward together.

Rabbi Shafran, of the Agudath Israel, is concerned about slandering innocent people. While his quest for perfect certainty is an impossible one, his point about proceeding with caution, even extreme caution, should not be ignored as the discussion unfolds.

"We have stayed on this planet longer than anyone else because we believe our way is the right way. You start slipping, making changes here and there, and then you have nothing. We live by our rules here and they've got to understand that." So says Sholom Rubashkin. Undoubtedly, we can all agree, with Rubashkin, that continuity is *a* value among *other* values. His statement, however, raises important questions. Are all changes radical changes? And, do radical changes always disrupt continuity? Further, when Rubashkin states that "we live by our rules here," he seemingly fails to consider what happens when *our* rules conflict with *their* rules. Is it possible to compromise on occasion?

Other voices must be brought into this discussion. Let's listen to one of the workers, Juana from Guatemala (not her real name), who has complained about her swollen and deformed cutting hand and the lack of medical attention. "Being here, you see a lot of injustice. But it's a small town. It's the only factory here. We have no choice" (*Forward*, May 26, 2006).

Father Floyd Paul Ouderkirk, a Roman Catholic priest who celebrates Mass with many of the workers, has stated, "If you're not treated well at work, you tend to keep your mouth shut and go deeper until it becomes, well, unbearable." Pointing a finger directly at the Rubashkin family, Ouderkirk complained, "They leave so much to be desired in the moral and ethical treatment of workers" (*Forward*, May 26, 2006).

CONCLUSION

The Jewish tradition recognizes the need for both the pull of loving your neighbor and the push of loving the stranger. Jewish ethics is about the ability to balance these forces against one another to create the energy to live meaningful and holy lives in the present moment. This was, no doubt, the aspiration of Aaron Feuerstein and Malden Mills. In striving to live an ethical life, we are like the captain of a yacht playing off the power of the wind against the opposite power of the keel to keep the boat moving in a straight line.

Most of us easily recognize that there is a kind of absurdity in loving the stranger but not loving one's neighbor. What kind of love would this really be? This chapter suggests, through the use of the Agriprocessor case, that there is another kind of absurdity, one more difficult to recognize, but equally impossible. In the end, it is not possible to truly love one's neighbor (in the deepest sense) in the absence of loving the stranger. While the Rubashkin family, on the surface, was seemingly a model for loving one's coreligionists, in the long run, their love of neighbor was itself tainted.

Just as there can be too little love, there can be too much love. If love is only directed to those already in one's closest orbit, it is a deficient and dangerous kind of love. The Rubashkin family, in this instance, has brought shame not only to themselves but to the Jewish people, whom they profess to love with such abundance. It does make sense to talk of love of one's neighbor as distinct from the love of the stranger, but we should never forget that these two kinds of love are really two sides of the same coin.

Shalom Rubashkin's behavior demonstrates a profound moral myopia. Not only does he fail to "love the stranger," he seemingly doesn't even see the stranger. The philosopher John Dewey was surely correct when he noted that "it is sympathy which carries thought out beyond the self and which extends its scope till it approaches the universal as its limit. It is sympathy which saves consideration of consequences from degenerating into mere calculation, by rendering vivid the interest of others and urging us to give them the same weight as those which touch our own" (as quoted by Garrison, 1997, p. 38). Where was this kind of sympathy demonstrated at Agriprocessors?

The case of Sholom Rubashkin demonstrates what can go wrong when there is a lack of moral imagination, too much love turned inward, little self-awareness, a good dose of greed, poor public policy, and a complete insensitivity to the needs of those members of society who are least well off. In their initial alleged mistreatment of animals, perhaps louder alarm bells should have been raised by the Jewish community. The Jewish tradition prohibits causing pain to animals for no reason, and perhaps those that break this commandment are already in more danger to cut corners in other domains, as well.

Loving the stranger is not a panacea nor is it a substitute for good federal regulations, but is a necessary ingredient to help build a just and caring society in a world of increasing mobility and interconnection. In a world of increasing migration and a broken public policy, Jewish ethical sources remind us of our inherent responsibility to continually broaden the circle of ethics, even as we continue to strive to love our neighbor.

NOTES

1. This mitzvah is reiterated in the Bible in slightly different language as "Love you therefore the stranger; for you were strangers in the land of Egypt" (Deuteronomy 10:19).
2. For an extended and insightful literary and psychological analysis of Jonah's flight see Zornberg, 2008.
3. Unfortunately, even today this highly constrained reading of the text is particularly apt in some situations. For example, the National Council of Young Israel, an organization whose goal is "to foster and maintain a program of spiritual, cultural, social and communal activity towards the advancement and perpetuation of traditional Torah-true Judaism" (www.youngisrael.org) issued a memorandum on August 1, 2007 to its member synagogues banning converts from serving as synagogue presidents (see yucommentator.com). Such a ban is an unfortunate but explicit violation of the traditional understanding of loving the stranger despite the organization's professed goal of perpetuating "traditional" Judaism.

4. For similar views see also Hartman (1999) and Riskin (2007).
5. The material on Aaron Feuerstein has been adopted from Pava (forthcoming).

REFERENCES

Bonder, Nilton, *Our Immoral Soul: A Manifesto of Spiritual Disobedience* (Boston: Shambhala, 2001).

Formaini, Robert I., "The Engine of Capitalist Process: Entrepreneurs in Economic Theory," *Economic and Financial Review,* Fourth Quarter, 2001, pp 2–11.

Garrison, Jim, *Dewey and Eros* (New York and London: Teachers College Press, 1997).

Hartman, David, "Religious Diversity and the Millennium," *Jerusalem Post,* December 3, 1999, p. 8.

Hertz, J.H., editor, *The Pentateuch and Haftorahs* (London: Soncino Press, 1969).

Kula, Irwin, with Linda Lowenthal, *Yearnings: Embracing the Sacred Messiness of Life* (New York: Hyperion, 2006).

Marcano, Donna-Dale, "The Strangeness of the Racialized Subject: Confronting Kristeva's Foreigner," *Philosophy Today,* Vol.47, 2003, pp. 161–167.

Pava, Moses L., forthcoming, "The Spirit of Jewish Entrepreneurship," in *Entrepreneurship: Values and Responsibility,* Vol. 17 International Journal of Practical Philosophy and Methodology, edited by Gasparski, W. and L. Ryan.

Riskin, Shlomo, "Love the Stranger," *Jewish News,* Vol. 61, No. 7, 2007, p. 53.

Sacks, Jonathan, "The Chief Rabbi's New Year Message BBC Online Religion and Ethics," 2001, downloaded on November 11, 2008 from www.chiefrabbi.org. articles/otehr/rhbbc.html.

Sarasvathy, Saras D, "Entrepreneurship as Economics with Imagination," *Business Ethics Quarterly,* Vol. 11, 2001, pp. 10–25.

Unger, Roberto Mangabeira, *The Self Awakened: Pragmatism Unbound* (Cambridge: Harvard University Press, 2007).

Zornberg, Avivah Gottlieb, "Jonah: A Fantasy of Flight," *Psychoanalytic Dialogues,* Vol. 18, 2008, pp. 271–299.

CHAPTER 9

THE PROBLEM WITH INCOME AND WEALTH INEQUALITIES

Should religion inform "public policy" discussions? Mixing religion and politics can produce volatile results. Religion can lead to coercion, authoritarianism, a lack of tolerance, and little appreciation for the benefits of pluralism and freedom of expression. In addition, mixing religion and politics can be harmful to religion, as Yale law professor Steven L. Carter reminds us. Subjecting religion to the compromises necessary in political debate can undermine and distort authentic religious values (Carter, 1994). Despite these important concerns, invoking religion in the public sphere can also produce positive results by reminding us that there is a deep connection between shared material prosperity and a spiritually fulfilling life. In fact, the sharp division between the material and spiritual is a human invention—at times quite useful. But, in the end, there is no real discontinuity between the two.

This chapter suggests, from the point of view of Jewish ethics in a new key, that there is a workable and good enough solution to the dilemma of how best to benefit from religious wisdom in the context of a diverse and multicultural population. *The goal of a religiously grounded ethics should be to critique, enhance, and strengthen the democratic values and institutions of society.* These values include noncoercion, transparency, equal rights, compromise, equality of opportunity, individual and communal responsibility, and many others. To the extent that religious institutions are dedicated to promoting and enlarging democracy, religion can take an open and very active role in the public sphere. By contrast, to the extent that religion exploits the public domain to promote its own particular agenda and parochial needs, it is overreaching and harmful to both society and itself. While this might seem, to some, to be too limited a role for religion to play, I disagree. In fact, I think that abiding by the simple rule that religion must support democracy opens up the political debates and allows them to take place in a more honest and forthright way than ever before. Given this framework, this chapter specifically raises the following question: What role can the Jewish tradition play with regard to the contemporary question of income and wealth inequality?

FRAMING THE ISSUE

Let me begin this discussion with just a few economic statistics:

1. As of 2006, the United States had one of the highest levels of income inequality among developed countries. It is one of only a few countries where income inequality has increased since 1980. (CIA World FactBook)
2. In 2007, according to US government statistics, 37.3 million people lived in poverty, about 13 percent of the total population. (www.census.gov)
3. In 2007, among African-Americans, about one fourth of the population lived in poverty and among Hispanics just over one fifth fell below the poverty line. (www.census.gov)
4. Children are particularly vulnerable. More than one third of black children under 18 and about 31 percent of Hispanic children under 18 lived in poverty in 2007. (www.census.gov)
5. With respect to wealth, at the end of 2001, 10 percent of the population owned 71 percent of the wealth, and the top 1 percent controlled 38 percent. On the other hand, the bottom 40 percent owned less than 1 percent of the nation's wealth. (Phillips, 2006)
6. Perhaps, most troubling of all from a Jewish perspective, Israel now has greater income inequality that all OECD (Organisation for Economic Co-operation and Development) countries except the US, Turkey, and Mexico. (Jerusalem Post, June 23, 2008)

Consider, as a stark contrast to the above statistics, the ideals and aspirations inherent in the Jewish institution of the Jubilee year. According to the Torah's original plan every 50 years, or about once in a lifetime, there was supposed to be a radical redistribution of wealth.

> And you shall hallow the fiftieth year, and proclaim liberty throughout the land unto all the inhabitants thereof; it shall be a jubilee unto you; and you shall return every man unto his possession... You shall not wrong one another but you shall fear your God (Leviticus: Chapter 25).

Nechama Lebowitz believed that the purpose of both the Jubilee and the Sabbatical laws was to prevent "the concentration of power and property in the hands of the few." While it may be hard to imagine that this law was ever fully operative, the quote does provides a clear statement of the Jewish pull toward economic equality and the Jewish sensitivity toward the least well-off members of society.

David Hartman is one of the most articulate spokespersons for the contemporary meaning of the biblical vision of the Jubilee. He writes that we cannot simply reduce these principles to dietary food laws. "If we want to treat the State of Israel as an opportunity to reinstitute the laws of the Sabbatical and Jubilee years, we must try to uncover the spirit and goals of these mitzvot."

According to Rabbi Hartman, the "spirit and goals" include a fundamental concern with "distributive justice, with social equality, and with preventing permanent economic helplessness." He continues:

> The prophetic warning that exile is due to the nonobservance of the Sabbatical and Jubilee laws should stimulate our halakhic leadership to recommend ways of avoiding such problems as long-term indebtedness, the economic exploitation of local and foreign workers, and unjust labor-management relations. (1999, p 243)

My only disagreement with Hartman's statement is the fact that he limits his discussion to an Israeli audience. The Jubilee-vision applies especially in the United States as indicated by the fact that these famous biblical verses appear on the Liberty Bell in Philadelphia, one of the central icons of the American democracy.

It is impossible, of course, to derive specific policy prescriptions from these ancient laws, nevertheless, the power and attraction of the biblical worldview undercuts those contemporary conservative view-points that are based solely on the "sanctity of private-property." From the Bible's point of view, there is nothing sacred about it. To the extent that one argues in favor of the status quo distribution of wealth, one would be hard put to turn this into a "religious" imperative. Rather, it would seem that question of wealth distribution should be viewed in terms of overall social welfare. And, if we are to make a mistake here, we should err on the side of the poor and disenfranchised, and not the rich.

A Historical Perspective

In Judaism, wealth distribution *is* framed as an ethical question. In noting that a "Sabbath consciousness" should not be restricted to Jewish home life, but should also be expressed in a political way, Hartman helps jumpstart this discussion. The Jewish tradition can also provide a much needed historical perspective. The experiences of the Jewish people throughout the millennia provide a vast reservoir of practical knowledge and know-how. To ignore this history would be a type of willful ignorance.

Poverty is not a new problem. As Deuteronomy states, "the poor shall never cease out of your land." But, it is precisely because of this fact of life that Judaism requires us to "open our hands to the poor and needy." Perhaps one of Judaism's most important lessons to us is that *when it come to economics, if the rules of the game are not fair, we've got to fix them.* We see this principle in operation in many situations. For example, the Mishna (Kritut 8a) relates how Rabbi Shimon ben Gamliel changed the sacrificial laws in order to promote economic equity. When the price of pigeons shot up to a golden dinar because of high demand, Rabbi Shimon ben Gamliel promised, "I will not go to sleep tonight until the price comes down." As head of the Sanhedrin, he stepped in and reduced the number of birds required for sacrifice by women after childbirth. This dramatically lowered the demand and the price of the birds fell almost instantly. Rashi, the preeminent Talmudic commentator, explains that this case provides an example of changing the law for the "sake of God."

Another famous example, of creative interpretation in the interests of economic equity is Hillel's innovation of the *prozbul,* a legal document that allowed the lender and borrower to circumvent the cancellation of debt in the Sabbatical year. Hillel's creative reading of the biblical text removed a tremendous barrier to the free flow of funds and is correctly seen as a boost to economic development and communal equity and welfare (see Gittin 36a–36b). Jewish thought is deeply conservative in the special sense that it is concerned with conserving the Jewish people over time. Judaism also recognizes the reality of changing circumstances. Its survival has often depended on the appropriate balance between respect for the status quo and respect for appropriate and measured change.

One of the most pernicious effects of income and wealth inequality is its effect on access to education. Simply put, the likelihood of graduating from a four year college if you are at the bottom of the economic ladder is much lower than if you are at the top. About half of all students from the top quarter of the economic hierarchy graduate from college while only 7 percent of those from the lowest quarter will graduate. These statistics are particularly disturbing when it is recognized that future economic success is highly dependent on education levels.

Judaism, of course, has much to teach the world on the topic of education. Interestingly, the very same Hillel who invented the *prozbul* and who contributed so much to Judaism's progressive tendencies, was at one time himself barred from the house of study because of his own abject poverty. As the Talmud tells it at Yoma 35b:

> Everyday Hillel used to work and earn one tropaik, half of which he would give to the guard at the house of learning, the other half being spent on food. One day he found nothing to earn and the guard at the House of Learning would not permit him to enter. He climbed up and sat upon the window to hear the words of the living God... They say, that day was the eve of Sabbath in the winter solstice and snow fell down upon him from heaven. When the dawn rose, Shemayah said to Abtalion: "Brother, on every day this house is light and today it is dark, is it perhaps a cloudy day."
>
> They looked up and saw the figure of a man in the window. He was covered by three cubits of snow. They removed him, bathed and anointed him, and placed him opposite the fire. They said, "This man deserves that the Sabbath be profaned on his behalf."

To the extent that poverty is a bar to education, think how much poorer society is in the long run. How many contemporary Hillels are out there? We don't know, but even if it's just one, the outcome of barring him or her from obtaining an education is truly staggering.

This, of course, is just a story, and, as before, drawing specific policy prescriptions from it would be irresponsible at best. Nevertheless, it does demonstrate a deep practical wisdom earned through thousands of years of a single community attempting to live out biblical ideals in a real world of scarce resources.

CHESED IN THE CONTEMPORARY WORLD

In addition to the important historical perspective that Judaism offers, Judaism's highly refined notion of *chesed* [usually translated as loving kindness or acts of loving kindness] is a useful and usable paradigm for contemporary democratic thought. *Chesed* is active and optimistic. It must go beyond the letter of the law. It requires imagination. *Chesed* is so essential to Judaism that Isadore Twersky once wrote in an important paper titled "The Jewish Attitude Toward the Welfare State," that it is the "distinctive function which legitimatizes our worldly existence." (published in Lamm and Wurzburger, 1967, p. 224).

At its best, *chesed* is about *bringing the outsiders inside*. All of this is emphasized in the following beautiful midrash comparing Job and Abraham:

> Now when that great calamity came upon Job, he said unto the Holy One, blessed be He: "Master of the Universe, did I not feed the hungry and give the thirsty to drink? And did I not clothe the naked?

Nevertheless the Holy One, blessed be He, said to Job: "Job, thou has not yet reached half the measure of Abraham. Thou sittest and tarriest within thy house and the wayfarers come in to thee. To him who is accustomed to eat wheat bread, thou givest wheat bread to eat; to him who is accustomed to eat meat, thou givest meat to eat; to him who is accustomed to drink wine, thou givest wine to drink. But Abraham did not act in this way. Instead he would go forth and make the rounds everywhere, and when he found wayfarers *he brought them into his house*. To him who was unaccustomed to eat wheat bread, he gave wheat bread to eat; to him who was unaccustomed to eat meat, he gave them meat to eat; to him who was unaccustomed to drink wine, he gave wine to drink. Moreover he arose and built stately mansions on the highways and left there food and drink, and every passerby ate and drank and blessed Heaven. (Abot de R. Natan, 7 as translated by J. Goldin).

I believe that it is precisely this idea of bringing the wayfarer into the house that Judaism's idea of *chesed* is most useful to the contemporary debate about wealth and income inequalities. Ethics is ultimately about seeing our own humanity in the other, and seeing the other's humanity in ourselves. On Passover, we invite the poor to join us at our festive meals. This is not just an act of charity, this is an act of self-preservation. Treating everyone with equal human dignity may not be the sole aim of community, but it is certainly a necessary means for every other aim.

The huge and increasing gap between the haves and the have-nots is not compatible with a world in which true *chesed* is even possible. To "bring the wayfarer into the house" does not mean merely providing for subsistence, although surely it must include the basic necessities of life such as food, shelter, and healthcare.

From and Abrahamic point of view, it also means providing decent education, safe streets, hope for the future, and equal opportunities for every single citizen. To "bring the wayfarer into the house" requires us to open our eyes and see the economic conditions in which such a large fraction of our population is seemingly trapped.

Statistically it has been demonstrated that increases in income and wealth inequality leads to greater unemployment, less spending on education, more babies born with low birth weights, higher rates of incarceration, and higher rates of homicide. These findings hold even when the researchers controlled for absolute levels of wealth. What this means is that it is the inequality itself and not the amount of wealth or poverty that leads to a deterioration in all of these social indicators.

Chesed is active caring in the context of community. It may very well be true that in the end all of us are merely "strangers and settlers" (see Leviticus 25:23) in God's eyes. But in Jewish thought, it is the preeminent human job to lessen and soften this felt strangeness. This is exactly what we are here for!

Maimonides put it perfectly when he warned that "he who locks the doors to his courtyard and eats and drinks with his wife and family without feeding the poor and bitter of soul—his meal is not a rejoicing in a divine commandment but a rejoicing in his own stomach."

THE ISSUE OF WEALTH INEQUALITY IS NOT A PURELY ECONOMIC QUESTION

Bringing the outsider inside is an economic goal. That 37.3 million human being are living in poverty in the United States today would seem to prove that we have not achieved anything close to economic stability or sustainability. But wealth inequality is not just an economic issue. In Jewish thought, the question of how wealth is allocated is linked to human dignity and self-worth. Unlike other religious systems, from a Torah perspective, poverty is not considered to be a "blessed state." (published in Lamm and Wurzburger, 1967, p. 239).

One of the amazing facts about the Maimonides's famous "Eight Levels of Charity," is that there is no mention of the amount of tzedakah [charity] required. The focus is solely on the manner in which tzedakah is given. "We are required to take more care about the mitzvah of tzedakah than any other positive mitzvah." This is because the Maimonides recognizes how profoundly wealth, power, and dignity are interrelated. This emphasis on providing jobs for the poor is obviously still a timely insight. In addition, his concern for anonymity in the process and his emphasis on a central collection and distribution agency are also still extremely urgent lessons. Furthermore, from a more conservative political perspective, his warning that one should "not put into the box unless he knows that the one responsible for the box is faithful" is pregnant with meaning.

JUDAISM IS A FORM OF PRACTICAL IDEALISM

Judaism's standards are consistently high but they are not of another world. Judaism has a realistic view of human nature. It is not naive, for example, about the "cunning rogue" who gives a poor man a single dinar in order to give him just enough money to make him technically ineligible for "the gleanings, forgotten sheaves, the produce of the corner of the field, or the poor tithe." Given Judaism's penchant for practical idealism, from a traditional perspective there are two types of errors we can make when it comes to ethics. On the one hand, we can view Judaism as merely a set of rules and we can distance ourselves from the very purposes of those rules. On the other hand, we can get so carried away with an imagined prophetic passion that we can forget the facts on the ground.

"My esteemed mentor and colleague, the late Aaron Levine states flatly that Judaism "does not subscribe to the notion of income redistribution." (1987, p. 135.) I will state just as flatly that he is making the first kind of error. He can't find a Talmudic passage that says that in the year 2011 the United States shall adopt a program of income redistribution and draws his conclusion from the Talmud's silence. In focusing on the rule book, he has lost sight of Judaism's basic ethos. By contrast, Michael Lerner's passionate call for a constitutional amendment to ensure greater income equality becomes so unhinged from reality that he does more harm than good (2002). He is making the second kind of mistake.

CONCLUSION

So where does this leave the rest of us? In the end Judaism will not magically produce a Solomon-like solution to the problem of income and wealth inequality. Any proposed solution must begin with an examination of the root causes for the increasing disparity between the haves and the have nots. Further, policy prescriptions must be based on economic data and rigorous empirical analysis.

In the end, though I do not think that a Jewish approach to this question can provide the one solution. But, it certainly can rule out proposals based on ideological ideas like the sanctity of private property or the elimination of private property. And, second, and more important, it can help us identify and recognize some interesting proposals that are worth looking into. Robert Frank's call for a progressive consumption tax to replace the current income tax is one of the most thoughtful and carefully constructed economic arguments in this area (1999). Similarly, Anne Alstott and Bruce Ackerman's idea of a Stakeholder Society in which every citizen enters adult life with 80,000 dollars, although seemingly radical, would satisfy many of Judaism's own aspirations (2000).

From a Jewish perspective, there has always been a communal aspect to tzedakah and it is wrong to think of it as a purely individual responsibility. To support this I merely cite the laws of Jubilee one last time and also note Maimonides's useful distinction in his *Guide to the Perplexed* between *tzedek* and *tzedakah*. The former is legally prescribed and regulated and the latter stems from one's own moral conscience. (Twersky, p. 240).

Is Judaism conservative or liberal in its political philosophy? I don't think that this is the right question. Judaism's contribution to democracy is in helping us frame the debate, in its historical experience, in its getting us to see beyond the economics, and in its practical idealism. In other words, Judaism, among other religious traditions, provides a critical morality to help us all bring the outsiders inside and to thus strengthen democratic societies.

REFERENCES

Alstott, Anne, and Bruce Ackerman, *The Stakeholder Society* (New Haven: Yale University Press, 2000).

Carter, Stephen L., *The Culture of Disbelief: How American Law and Politics Trivialize Religious Devotion* (New York: Anchor Books, 1994).

Frank, Robert, *Luxury Fever: Money and Happiness in an Era of Excess* (Princeton: Princeton University Press, 1999).

Hartman, David, *A Heart of Many Rooms: Celebrating the Many Voices Within Judaism* (Woodstock, VT: Jewish Lights Publishing, 1999).

Lamm, Norman, and Walter Wurzburger, editors, *A Treasury of Tradition* (New York: Rabbinical Council of America, 1967).

Lerner, Michael, *Spirit Matter* (Hampton Roads Publishing, 2002).

Levine, Aaron, *Economics and Jewish Law* (New York: Yeshiva University Press, 1987).

Phillips, Peter, *Censored 2007: The Top 25 Censored Stories* (New York: Seven Stories Press, 2006).

PART 3

FRONTIERS

CHAPTER 10

"THE EXALTATION OF THE POSSIBLE": ETHICS AND PLAY

> It is essential to understand that a constant tension between two diametrically opposed concerns—preserving and betraying—is intrinsic to spiritual life.
>
> Rabbi Nilton Bonder

> The best way is that you grasp one thing, yet you must not let go of the other.
>
> Ecclesiastes

Although there is always a great temptation to do so, it is impossible to think of ethics as complete and perfect. *Even as we surrender to an ethical system, as we always must, we do so playfully.*[1]

We view ethics as both real and not real, and in doing so, we temporarily give up the rationalistic demand for consistency. Ideals are always imperfect ideals. In embracing playfulness, we experience new pleasures and freedoms. We seamlessly move from the world of play to the world of the player (and back again).

In play, we grant ourselves and others the needed liberty to experience the world from different perspectives. Normal constraints are relaxed. Everyday points of view are challenged. New values, beliefs, and desires emerge. Responses become varied, paradoxical, and complicated. We stay with our emotions and stop hiding from them. We tolerate and welcome differences. We develop more sophisticated tastes, nuanced sensitivities, and mature emotions.

Over time, we discover that play is a way of being in the world more lightly and less permanently, yet more profoundly and comfortably. In play, we discover new purposes, choices, modes of being, and new opportunities.

More open ways of interacting with others suddenly become available to us. More honest communication is possible. According to the psychoanalyst D.W. Winnicott, one of play's all-time greatest advocates, "Playing has a place and a time. It is not inside...Nor is it outside...Playing facilitates growth and therefore health; playing leads into group relationships; play can be a form of communication..." (1971, p. 41). Dialogue and dialectical thinking become a way of life. Creativity is enhanced. Imagination is embraced. Deeper layers of meaning are revealed.

In play, we hold on to our old selves less tightly. We take more risks. We move to the edge of our own capabilities and consciousness. We enter what one psychologist has dubbed a state of "flow" (Csikszentmihalyi, 2003). We push and challenge ourselves and each other. We begin to experiment more and we realize that in order to take ourselves *more* seriously we have to take ourselves *less* seriously first. A tiny gap between the past and the future opens. Identities loosen. Transitions become possible. The promise of growth and transcendence is strengthened.

It is through play that we evolve. New and challenging ways of interpreting and making meaning in the world are adopted. Perceptions are widened. New connections are made and old ones are seen as obsolete.

More complex, identities emerge to subsume older and more simple ones. We are still who we always were, only better. Play is evocative and transformative:

> Through play we learn that all perspectives and behaviors belong to categories and that these categories can be manipulated. They can support each other (science and discovery), transform each other (art), or cancel each other out (comedy)...When we are able to step back from one categorical level to see and play with it from another, we begin the process of transformation. (Gordon and Esbjorn-Hargens, 2007)

The content and authority of ethics derives from legitimate and open dialogue. It is a process that one chooses (or not) to participate in. Such a process—to work effectively—must recognize its own limitations and imperfections. Paradoxically, it must come to recognize that its own ideals are only imperfect ideals. Whatever we agree to today will become outdated and constraining over time. However brilliant and insightful we are now, no one can anticipate what the future will bring.

It is because of all of this that no matter how important ethics are to the quality of our lives and no matter how permanent we think our ethics to be now, we must learn to approach and embrace our own ethics in a playful and tentative way; as simultaneously real and unreal.

Beyond the Traditional Perspective

This is *not* how we traditionally think and talk about ethics in personal or organizational life nor how we teach ethics in the classroom (and beyond). Typically we think of ethics as a fixed and complete system of rules and/or principles. Rules that we are bound to follow regardless of the circumstances, categorical imperatives. Our attitude toward ethics is usually not playful but obedient, serious, and reverent. It is we who serve ethics and not the other way around.

We are taught that there is always a right and wrong answer to every ethical quandary and such answers are not dependent on the context or the circumstances in which we find ourselves. They are not contingent on our mode of interpretation and understanding. The answers to ethical questions do not rely on own consciousness but are somehow free-floating, part of the furniture of the universe. "If I don't know what to do, I can always ask an authority figure and he or she will tell me what to do." We are taught to serve ethics with complete devotion and an unusual singleness of mind.

Play, in sharp contrast to ethics, is seen as a juvenile activity. It is something we outgrow over time. Children and adolescents are allowed and even encouraged to play, but as we mature, culture becomes more constraining and less tolerant of its playful deviants. Over time, one is expected to make permanent choices and final commitments. For sure, recreation is still seen as a necessary form of relaxation and fun, but one must draw a sharp line between her vocation and avocation, between work (reality) and play (imagination).

From this traditional perspective, mixing ethics and play creates a strange and dangerous hybrid. To traditionalists of every bent, approaching ethics playfully sounds suspiciously more like conveniently abandoning them altogether than deepening our attachment to them. Those who raise questions with regard to conventional ethics are generally not viewed as trying to repair and improve upon ethics but as weird outliers, out of touch with reality.

In fact, it is true that those who raise questions *may turn out* to be weird outliers or worse, but they may *also* turn out to be scientists, poets, artists, philosophers, business men and women, musicians, engineers of renown who have much to contribute to the world and to our own understanding of ourselves and what we together might become. They often turn out to be the catalysts for a kind of growth that benefits everyone. If we can tolerate and accept them long enough, they may provide us with new paradigms and valuable ways of looking at the world. Every ethical system is imperfect and therefore *demands* on occasion, at least, that we violate it.

DEFINING PLAY

James March, one of the word's leading experts on decision-making, defines play as follows:

> Playfulness is the deliberate, temporary relaxation of rules in order to explore the possibility of alternative rules. When we are playful, we challenge the necessity of consistency. In effect, we announce—in advance—our rejection of the usual objections to behavior that does not fit the standard model of intelligence. (1988, p. 261)[2]

According to March's definition, play is not antithetical to reason and law, rather play and reason stand in a *complementary* relationship to each other. In March's view, play is essential to a full understanding of intelligence broadly conceived.

It is true that in order to get where we want to go, where we *already* have good reasons to go, a technology of rational decision-making is sufficient and play is unnecessary. However, it is when we *don't* know what we really want, when our future is open, that play becomes essential to the decision-making process.

It is only when we come to recognize and admit a kind of existential ignorance concerning our values and ideals, what the philosopher James Carse has called a "learned ignorance" (2008, p. 16), that we can adopt a more experimental and tentative approach to our own selves. We temporarily relax rules in order to explore a new and higher-order set of rules.

In adopting a technology of rational decision-making we assume a set of stable, fixed, and well-ordered preferences. The relevant question is: Which of several possible known paths is the most efficient one to get to this fixed destination? In other words, a technology of rational decisions-making asks: What is the cheapest way of satisfying current desires? This is often the correct question to ask but not always. March's point is that decision-making can be alternatively framed in an altogether different way as an opportunity for testing and experimenting with these very preferences and desires. Regardless of cost and efficiencies, What kinds of desires and end-states are really worth pursing in the first place? That is, which of my several desires—upon experimenting with them—are really desirable? Which values *does experience teach us* are truly valuable? March's view represents a dramatically radical (even if underappreciated) expansion of how decision-making is theorized and thought about.

Here is how James March summarizes his view:

> Playfulness is a natural outgrowth of our standard view of reason. A strict insistence on purpose, consistency, and rationality limits our ability to find new purposes. Play relaxes that insistence to allow us to act 'unintelligently' or 'irrationally', or 'foolish' to explore alternative ideas of possible purposes and alternative concepts of behavioral consistency. And it does this while maintaining our basic commitment to the necessity of intelligence. (1988, p. 261)

Decision-making is no longer imagined solely as a one-way street in which we economically pursue pre-determined goals. March insists on a much broader conception of human intelligence. According to his enlarged vision, decision-making might also come to be seen as an opportunity to explore, test, and expand goals. In this way, decision-making can become a profound learning experience and a significant opportunity for ethical growth and moral development, carrying us gracefully beyond the status quo of our currently held beliefs, actions, values, habits, and identities. As the great Jewish philosopher and theologian Martin Buber has aptly stated, "play is the exaltation of the possible."

AN ETHICS OF PLAY

Emphasizing the central role of play for human development, the psychologist Jean Piaget once wrote, "Play is the answer to the question, How does anything *new* ever come about? (as quoted by Elkind, 2007, p. 3, emphasis added). But, if we are to begin to play with ethics and to hold on to inherited ethical systems more lightly in the hope of joyfully discovering new possibilities, as this chapter suggests we ought to, it is useful to begin to think more carefully and systematically about how to proceed. In other words, if we are to *play with ethics*, Is there not also a need for an *ethics of play*? And, if so, What might such an ethics include? In this section, we examine these questions in detail.

RESPECT THE PAST

Novel responses and playful tactics make sense only against a backdrop of meaning and purpose. In embracing play, the very first principle is a respect for traditions, rules, and rituals of the past. No matter how playful one becomes it is impossible to tear oneself away from one's own history. Everyone is a product of the past and will always remain so.

The political philosopher Michael Walzer is dead-on when he warns, "There is no such thing as choosing from scratch; there are no absolute beginnings" (2004, p. 13). We are born into a particular family, place, epoch, nation, and religion. We are born male or female, white or black, rich or poor. We inherit an ethical tradition (or traditions) through birthright. We learn to speak a specific language with its own vocabulary and grammar.

Our first responsibility then is to protect the accumulated moral and social capital, the hardware and software that we ourselves exploit on a daily basis but to which we have made no contributions. Just as the first ethical rule for medical doctors is "do no harm," so too for everyone. This entails reviving many traditional values in a very literal way such as honoring parents and the elderly, accepting what is, appreciating the gifts we have received, and adopting a learned patience toward the accumulated wisdom of our forebears. Whatever we grow into tomorrow, we will always remain creatures rooted in and dependent upon a particular past and a unique history.

Acknowledge Contingency

Even as we respect the past, we must never idolize it. History is a happenstance. It all could have happened differently. While at some level everyone knows this, it is difficult to acknowledge contingency on a regular basis. It is hard, nearly impossible, for me, as a born Jew, to imagine that I could have been born as a Christian or Muslim, just as for many others it is inconceivable that they might have been born into a Jewish family. Nevertheless, this is exactly what an ethics of play entails. Acknowledge contingency. Imagine what it might be like to be someone else, to have been born into the world at another time and in a strange place with a different body-shape, skin color, and an alternative history, perspective, and set of values.

In this vein, the late Richard Rorty, has noted, "moral consciousness [is] historically conditioned, a product as much of time and chance as of political or aesthetic consciousness" (1989, p. 30). Acknowledging this kind of pervasive contingency, however, is psychologically demanding. It is almost as if we are abandoning not only our tribes, but ourselves, too. Identity and integrity are put into play and there is a perceived loss of control.

It is as if we are pulling up anchor only to drift aimlessly with the prevailing currents across a vast and indifferent ocean. Yet, the acknowledgment that even moral consciousness is merely a product of time and chance, historically conditioned, if it can be tolerated at all, can be experienced as liberating too. Integrity is not only fidelity to a past but it demands openness to a future (Torbert and Associates, 2004). It makes it easier to accept and celebrate differences. It is a path to greater understanding and sympathy for the plight of others. It allows us to broaden generously the circle of ethical concern beyond our own families, co-religionists, and citizens to honor everyone. If *anyone* can play, *everyone* must play.

EMBRACE AMBIGUITY

What does it mean to embrace ambiguity? It is to realize that our understanding is never immediate, automatic, and pure; it is always filtered through ongoing social and historical processes of interpretation and reinterpretation. It is to understand with Richard Rorty that we must give up the "hope that objects will constrain us to believe the truth about them, if only they are approached with an unclouded mental eye" (1982, p. 165). In short, embracing ambiguity entails *sacrificing certainty* once and for all.

Psychologically, it is no easier to embrace ambiguity than it is to accept contingency. At a certain level, all of us seek and crave certainty, conjuring it up and then believing in it. In ethics and religion we create creeds that we repeat over and over again to convince ourselves—against ourselves—that what is, at best, a probable and likely outcome is definite and sure ("I believe with perfect faith..."). We ourselves draw strict and high boundaries around the edges of our own beliefs and then pretend that it was not us who drew the boundaries in the first place. Even when it comes to science there is a strong tendency to choose to forget that in order for a theory to be "true" it must also be falsifiable (i.e., potentially false).

A "playful" but profound example of embracing and institutionalizing ambiguity when it comes to issues of the highest ethical concern is found in a seemingly strange Jewish law concerning capital punishment. According to the rabbis of the Talmud in the Tractate of Sanhedrin, 23 judges are required to try a capital case. If all 23 judges find the defendant guilty, however, the judges are disqualified and the verdict is thrown out. There is a deep suspicion in Jewish law toward such "perfect" unanimity.

What does such conformity, after the fact, tell us about the processes of dialogue and deliberation? Suspicions are raised about whether or not there was ample opportunity for everyone to state their positions. Perhaps perfect unanimity is a signal that some of the more powerful judges silenced and bullied the less powerful ones? Unanimity suggests an impossible kind of certainty and ignores the ambiguity inherent in every human judgment. Rabbi Nilton Bonder adds the following instructive commentary and extension:

> This law—an expression of the soul and obviously subversive—is leery of any case that is so well presented that every shadow of doubt is eliminated. Unanimity reflects accommodation to an absolute truth, and absolute truth, which has tremendous destructive potential, is inimical to life. It is the soul that detects this, for it is the soul's interests that are jeopardized by such unanimity. Public opinion, dogmas, conventions, morality, and traditions can often represent a kind of unanimity that disqualifies their capacity to judge what is fair, healthy, or constructive. (2001, p. 16)

Of the many lessons one can derive from this seemingly odd and ancient law, the most important and enduring one for present purposes is its explicit recognition that every system of law, even one that might claim divine authorship, is inherently flawed, incomplete, and imperfect in our hands.

EXPERIMENT WITH VALUES

The values we inherit from tradition and the values we adopt in school and at work help to define who we are. They provide us with a fixed and historically-tested framework within which we can make important decisions. Sticking with old values is a way of respecting the past and tolerating the stress of ambiguity. Nevertheless, through play we learn to test and challenge ethics and experiment with values in an attempt to learn and grow.

Play reduces (but does not eliminate) the risks associated with such experiments. The central paradox in play is expressed well in the following quote from contemporary psychologists Gwen Gordon and Sean Esbjorn-Hargens:

> Holding the paradox that something is simultaneously what it represents and not what it represents enables the player to engage an obstacle to play, however terrifying it may be, without risking a full loss of control. The implicit or explicit limits that bind play in space and time make it safe for the player to surrender to the playful urge, take chances, try on new roles, and attempt tasks that, under normal circumstances, might be avoided as too difficult or unpleasant. It is a place where the novelty and risk of new situation or experience only add to the intensity and pleasure of play. The player is able to be in control of being out of control and so enjoy a sense both of risk and of mastery simultaneously. (2007)

In play there are self-imposed and jointly-shared psychological limits to the meaning of our actions. Outside the frame of play, actions and expressions are intended to be understood in their traditional, literal, and typical ways (both by ourselves and others). Within the frame of play, however, we devise a safe "container" where the usual meaning of actions is temporarily suspended and meaning is purposely left open and undecided (Kegan and Lahey, 2001). The seeming magic of play is that it opens up a tiny gap between the past and future—an intermediate space between us—where we can "be in control of being out of control." In this in-between space, temporary and exceedingly fragile, we discover the freedom to explore alternative values, mysterious and even disturbing experiences, and all kinds of strange and imaginary worlds.

INVENT NEW MEANINGS

One of the many purposes of play is to invent new meanings that challenge and subsume old and familiar "images" (Boulding, 1961). To play well is not just to follow the rules of the old games but it is to alter the rules subtly and thereby invent new games. It is to think of games not as finite but as infinite (Carse, 1986). This requires imagination and a light touch:

> One can seek meanings without assuming they are rational, context-free, or fixed "forever" or that meanings can be attained only through or depend on the use of reason. Play, aesthetics, empathy with, or being used by other's feeling states are also sources of meaning and intelligibility. (Flax, 1990, p. 223)

Inventing new meanings opens up new possibilities for the future. James March points out, however, that the power of play affects not only the future but the past, as well. In playing with history, we reconstruct it to fit contemporary needs. In play, he writes:

> we expose the possibility of experimenting with alternative histories. The usual strictures against 'self-deception' in experience need occasionally to be tempered with an awareness of the extent to which *all experience is an interpretation subject to conscious revision*. Personal histories, and national histories, need to be rewritten rather continuously as a base for retrospective learning of new self-conceptions. (1988, p. 263, emphasis added)

Most attempts to playfully invent new meanings will probably have little or no impact on anyone (except perhaps the author him or herself).[3]

A good example in business, however, of a recent reconstruction of meaning that almost certainly has important implications for everyone is the notion of corporate sustainability (Porritt, 2008). Until very recently it has been taken as self-evident that the sole purpose of a modern business entity is to maximize profits for corporate shareholders.

This view, however, has now lost its taken-for-granted status and has been put into play by several large and small corporations that have officially recognized sustainability as a fundamental and primary business goal through triple-bottom line reports and other company pronouncements.

It is interesting to note, in line with the thesis of this chapter, that what started as off-beat and strange business practices not too long ago (for example, Ben & Jerry's, The Body Shop, Tom's of Maine, Herman Miller, and a handful of others) have now become mainstream. I would suggest, however, that there is still a playful quality to almost all discussions concerning sustainability including the triple bottom line reports themselves. There continues to be a sense that behind closed doors, corporate executives have still not "really" bought into it. Business critics, however, should understand that a radical change in business philosophy of the kind we are talking about here, is a slow process with progress starting and stopping on a continual basis. A play ethic requires that such critics learn to temper their understandable suspicion of corporations with a tolerance for what seems as slow progress here. Critics will need to remind themselves of the paradox inherent in play "that something is simultaneously what it represents and not what it represents." This brings us to the next topic.

Suspend Judgments

During play we learn to suspend judgments. The more complex the play, the more difficult this task becomes. Although suspending judgments becomes more important in a post-modern age, it is an ability already assumed in ancient and traditional social acts such as apologizing, repenting, rebuking, and forgiving (Pava, 2008).

Today, the ability to suspend judgments must take us even further. It demands an increased tolerance for hypocrisy. "A bad man with good intentions may be a man experimenting with the possibility of becoming good. Somehow it seems to me more sensible to encourage experimentation than to insult it" (March, 1988, p. 263).

Further, a play ethic also calls into question certain well-accepted ideas and prescriptions concerning both evaluation and accountability. The notion that evaluation must be based on a set of criteria determined *before* action is taken assumes the traditional "rational model" of behavior where preferences are known, fixed, and stable. In play, however, it may turn out, that it is more "intelligent" to act first and then to develop evaluation criteria. As James March points out "there is nothing in a formal theory of evaluation that requires that the criterion function for evaluation be specified in advance." (1988, p. 264) Although, at first hearing, this has a strange sound to it, it is one of the most profound implications of a play ethic.

Second, and related to this point, the notion of accountability—how we explain ourselves to each other—needs to be broadened and tempered with a greater ability to suspend judgments. As it becomes more accepted that novel goals evolve out of action, accountability no longer implies that an individuals and organizations must always know what it is that they are doing before they do it. We must begin to build a play ethic into the very notion of accountability. This is especially important for teachers and all professionals working in complex, ambiguous, and constantly changing environments. It is also relevant for helping to nurture experimental values like corporate sustainability discussed above.

Traditional notions of evaluation and accountability can have perverse outcomes if they reinforce individuals and organizations into following routine and standard procedures when such procedures have become outdated and ineffective. "Experience should be used explicitly as an occasion for evaluating our values as well as our actions" (March, 1988, p. 259). More complex methods of evaluation and accountability must allow for learning, growth, and change.

INSTITUTIONALIZE PLAY BUT CONTINUE PLAYING WITH PLAY

Authentic play always possesses a quality of serendipity. It is accidental and lucky. Nevertheless there are several ways that play can be institutionalized both at the individual level and at the organizational level. Time can be set aside for playful activities such as reading, viewing movies, and trips to the museum. Decisions, including business decisions, can be based on intuition and gut feelings rather than logic and intellect. One can engage in brainstorming, mindfulness exercises, and meditation practices. Organizations set up separate divisions especially designed to take on high risk research and development projects. They hire multi-cultural work forces with diverse backgrounds and experiences. Compensation schedules are re-negotiated to allow for failures as well as successes.

James March who has taught us so much about play spoke of the possibility of developing a "technology" of play. He raised questions (perhaps playfully) about "optimizing" play (see p. 261). In this vision, play itself becomes subject to a set of rules and comes perilously close to returning to a mechanistic worldview from which it seems March has been trying to escape. A technology of play, however, forgets James Carse's first principle that he or she who *must* play, *cannot* play (1988).

The hope of a set of fixed rules to determine play reminds me of a famous Hasidic tale retold by Martin Buber:

> There once was a man who was very stupid. When he got up in the morning, it was so hard for him to find his clothes that at night he almost hesitated to go to bed when he thought about the trouble he would have on waking. One evening, he finally made a great effort, took paper and pencil, and as he undressed noted exactly where he put everything he had on.
>
> The next morning, very pleased with himself, he took the slip of paper in hand and read: "Hat"—there it was, he sat it on his head; "pants—there they lay, he got into them; and so it went until he was finally dressed. "that's all very well, but where am I myself?" he asked in great consternation. "Where in the world am I?" He looked and looked, but it was a vain search; he could not find himself.
>
> "And that is how it is with us," said the rabbi. (As quoted by Bonder, 2001.)

There is no slip of paper from which we can hope to read off the answer to the question "Where in the world am I?" So too, in the end, there can be no set of rules to guide us on how to play better. A technology of play is a contradiction in terms. It is like a painter using a paint-by-numbers set or a poet stealing metaphors from poets of the past and claiming them as his own. And, even if a technology of play *did* exist, it would quickly become the subject of another round of even more creative and complex play.

To sum up: Finding the good-enough balance between work and play is less a technology or a kind of science and more of a spiritual quest. A kind of uncertain and dangerous play that challenges and provokes the ethical status quo must be respectful, trusting, pragmatic, imaginative, original, stimulating, grounded in the realities of the situation, and developmentally appropriate. Like all spiritual acts it must strengthen integrity and interconnections simultaneously (Pava, 2007). Once one has accepted play as transformative—there is no retreating to a full embrace of the rational model of decision making as March hints at nor is there a return to the (false) security it promises.

The biblical poet, Ecclesiastes noted long ago:
Everything has its season; there is a time for every matter under heaven:

A time to be born, and a time to die;
A time to plant, and a time to uproot,
A time to kill, and a time to heal;
A time to break down, and a time to build up;
A time to weep, and a time to laugh... (Ecclesiastes, Chapter 3 as quoted in Birnbaum, 1973)

This is the playful attitude we necessarily bring to ethics. What Ecclesiastes did not mention, however, is that there does not necessarily have to be separate and distinct times for each of these activities. In fact, as we reject dualism we come to notice that we are *always* being born and *always* dying, *continuously* planting and *continuously* uprooting, *forever* killing and *forever* healing, *constantly* breaking down and *constantly* building up, *eternally* laughing and *eternally* weeping. This is the paradox of play.

CONCLUSION

It is impossible to think of ourselves as completed beings. So too it is impossible to conceive of our own ethical systems as perfect. We must surely know that we hold many beliefs that are simply flat-out wrong. So too, we know that we are driven by undesirable desires. Because of all this we necessarily treat ourselves and our ethical systems playfully. We need to co-create a space neither here nor there; a space that provides room to explore and experiment, a gap between the past and the future.

Adam and Eve in paradise had but one prohibition. "But of the tree of the knowledge of good and evil thou shalt not eat...(Genesis 2:17) Playfully, I imagine, Eve fed Adam the forbidden fruit and history—as we experience it—begins.

NOTES

1. This is the author's version of the work. It is reprinted here by permission of Blackwell Publishing. The definitive version was originally published in *CrossCurrents, Association for Religion and Intellectual Life*, Vol. 61, Issue 1, pages 88–103.
2. March's definition is similar to that of Gregory Bateson who wrote that play "is a name for contexts in which the constituent acts have a different sort of relevance...from that which they would have had in non-play...The essence of play lies in a partial denial of the meanings that the actions would have had in other situations" (as quoted in Zerubavel, 1991, p. 11). See also Sutton-Smith (1997) and Caillois (2001) for extensive and rigorous discussions concerning definitions of play.
3. It is not always clear why some reconstructions have a profound impact and others whither away. Biblical codes, defined by Wikipedia as "the notion that there are information patterns encrypted in the text of the Bible, or, more specifically, in the Torah, the first five books of the Hebrew Bible," for example provides a most novel way of reading a text and certainly has a "playful" quality to it. Nevertheless, biblical experts view it—not as a significant advancement toward understanding—but as a kind of silly and immature game.

REFERENCES

Birnbaum, Philip, *Five Megilloth* (New York: Hebrew Publishing Company, 1973).

Bonder, Nilton, *Our Immoral Soul: A Manifesto of Spiritual Disobedience* (Boston, Shambhala, 2001).

Boulding, Kenneth E., *The Image: Knowledge in Life and Society* (Ann Arbor: the University of Michigan Press, 1961).

Caillois, Roger, *Man, Play, and Games,* translated by Meyer Barash (Urbanna and Chicago: University of Illinois Press, 2001).

Carse, James P., *Finite and Infinite Games: A Vision of Life as Play and Possibility* (New York: Random House, 1986).

Carse, James P., *The Religious Case Against Belief* (New York: The Penguin Press, 2008).

Csikszentmihalyi, Mihaly, *Good Business: Leadership, Flow, and the Making of Meaning* (New York: Viking, 2003).

Elkind, David, *The Power of Play: How Spontaneous, Imaginative Activities Lead to Happier Healthier Children* (Cambridge: De Capo Press, 2007).

Flax, Jane, *Thinking Fragments: Psychoanalysis, Feminism & Postmodernism in the Contemporary West* (Berkeley: University of California Press, 1990).

Gordon, Gwen and Sean Esbjorn-Hargens, "Are We Having Fun Yet? An Exploration of the Transformative Power of Play," *Journal of Humanistic Psychology*, 2007.

Kegan, Robert and Lisa Laskow Lahey, *How the Way We Talk can Change the Way We Work* (San Francisco: Jossey-Bass, 2001).

March, James, "The Technology of Foolishness," reprinted in *Decisions and Organizations* (Oxford: Blackwell, 1988).

Pava, Moses L., "Teaching Spirituality In (and Out) of the Classroom," *Journal of Business Ethics*, 2007, Vol. 73, No. 3,

Pava, Moses L., "The Art of Moral Criticism: Rebuke in the Jewish Tradition and Beyond," 2008, Working Paper.

Porritt, Jonathan, *Capitalism: As If the World Matters* (London: Earthscan, 2008).

Rorty, Richard, *Consequences of Pragmatism* (Minneapolis: University of Minnesota Press, 1982).

Rorty, Richard, *Contingency, Irony, and Solidarity* (Cambridge: Cambridge University Press, 1989).

Sutton-Smith, Brian, *The Ambiguity of Play* (Cambridge: Harvard University Press, 1997).

Torbert, Bill and Associates, *Action Inquiry: The Secret of Timely and Transforming Leadership* (San Francisco: Berrett-Koehler Publishers, Inc., 2004).

Walzer, Michael, *Politics and Passion: Toward a More Egalitarian Liberalism* (New Haven & London: Yale University Press, 2004).

Winnicott, D.W., *Playing and Reality* (New York: Brouner-Routledge, 1971).

Zerubavel, Eviatar, *The Fine Line: Making Distinctions in Everyday Life* (New York: The Free Press, 1991).

CHAPTER 11

AN OPTIMISTIC CASE FOR THE FUTURE OF JEWISH ETHICS IN A POST-MADOFF WORLD

> Pessimism leads to weakness, optimism to power
>
> William James

It is relatively easy to describe the future of Jewish ethics—both its theory and its practice—in pessimistic terms, especially if one expects the near future to be anything like the recent past. What is more difficult and urgent at this particular juncture in our history is to construct an optimistic case for the future of Jewish ethics, one rooted in our tradition, and at the same time, fully-informed of the facts of our current situation. What is less necessary is a utopian thought experiment disengaged from social realities. It is to this urgent and constructive project that I will return and devote most of my attention in this chapter. But before imagining an optimistic and hopeful scenario, a plausible path out of the Escher-like maze we find ourselves lost in today, it is sobering to pause and consider as a backdrop to our discussion the following recent and notorious examples of ethics failures in the Jewish community:

> On January 4th, 2006, Jack Abramoff pleaded guilty to fraud, tax evasion, and conspiracy to bribe public officials. After serving three and a half years in prison, Abramoff is now working at Tov Pizza in Baltimore, MD.
>
> Bernie Madoff languishes in the same prison as Carmine Persico, a former boss of the Colombo crime family. Madoff pleaded guilty in March 2009, after stealing between $18 and $65 billion from his clients.

Rabbi Leib Tropper, founder of a group called the Eternal Jewish Family, established to "fortify the walls of conversion" both in the US and in Israel, was caught on tape talking to 32 year-old Shannon Orand of Houston, Texas. According to the recorded conversation, Rabbi Tropper demanded that "the woman perform a number of sexual services for himself and his friends in exchange for granting her a conversion certificate" (www.Haaretz.com, December 24, 2009).

Rabbi Saul Kassin, 87, of the Sharee Zion synagogue in Brooklyn, N.Y.; Eliahu Ben Haim, 58, the principal rabbi of Congregation Ohel Yaacob in Deal; Edmond Nahum, 56, of the Deal Synagogue; Mordchai Fish, 56, of Congregation Sheves Achim in Brooklyn; and Lavel Schwartz, 57, Fish's brother were charged with money laundering on July 23, 2009 as part of a public corruption and international money laundering investigation in New Jersey.

In February 2010, Takana, a religious Zionist organization, accused Rabbi Mordechai Elon, former head of Yeshivat Hakotel located in the Old City of Jerusalem and a beloved and popular leader of the religious Zionist movement in Israel, of maintaining ongoing sexual relationships with a number of his male students. "The affair was made public now because we had become increasingly concerned that we had no other way to protect the public from the possibility of more harm," according to a Takana document. The rabbis further explained, "Rabbi Elon did not follow the restrictions imposed on him, particularly in the area of personal relationships."

On June 21, 2010, Sholom Rubashkin, former executive at Agriprocessors, once the largest kosher meat producer in the US, was sentenced to 27 years in prison under federal financial fraud charges.

My Jewish students at the Sy Syms School of Business of Yeshiva University are appalled at the perceived high incidence of cheating in their classes, but the students themselves do not take or want responsibility for the situation. Rather most students maintain that it is the primary responsibility of the faculty and the administration to reduce cheating in the classroom. One student told the college newspaper, point blank, that given a chance to cheat on an important exam, students will cheat.

I believe that my students are highly intelligent, extremely motivated, and fully committed to living meaningful Jewish lives. Most of these students have been educated in Jewish Day Schools since kindergarten, and many of them have attended Yeshivot in Israel for one or two years. These are ambitious students with high aspirations for their professional and family lives. Nevertheless, even among the best and the brightest, those who identify most strongly and proudly with their Jewish heritage, when it comes to raising the Jewish ethical bar for themselves and for the broader Jewish community, there exists a deep and pervasive pessimism. In light of recent events, can we really blame them?

The weight of the status quo feels thick, heavy, and overwhelming to this next generation of Jewish leaders. It is like these students are moored to an anchor sunk deeply into the ancient sands of the ocean's floor. The felt pressure among these young 20-somethings to succeed and flourish on a personal level is widespread and tangible, even as economic conditions and competitive pressures worsen. At the same time, though, they hear the call for Jewish ethics as an unreal and naïve demand. Students do usually rhapsodize about Jewish ethics during graduation speeches, but the lofty and impractical rhetoric is designed to be ceremonial and self-congratulatory rather than challenging, real, and demanding of fellow students.

My students read and hear about the Abramoffs, Madoffs, Troppers, Kassins, Elons, and Rubashkins, and they draw no connections or profound moral lessons from them (I'm not sure there are any profound lessons be learned here), other than the obvious ones of "everyone's doing it" and "don't get caught." "These are just the bad apples," they will argue. Some of my students, influenced by parents, unimaginative teachers, and cynical op-ed writers will defend some on this list as the unfortunate and wholly innocent targets of anti-Semitism.

Listening to the Apathy and Pessimism

I do not, even for a moment, blame my students for their bland attitudes. There do exist profound and deep-seated reasons for pessimism and apathy when it comes to the future of Jewish ethics, reasons not only external to the Jewish tradition, but internal ones, as well. First, the call of Jewish ethics in the early part of the twenty-first century is often vague and peripheral to the Jewish community's real concerns and obsessions. Jewish institutional leaders are seemingly always fighting a never-ending battle to keep their organizations financially afloat. Given this reality, Jewish ethics almost always takes a back seat to more real world, mundane, and quantifiable concerns. At the same time, those who do speak up loudest for Jewish ethics often simplify the tradition and amputate its necessary complexities and nuances, precisely those aspects of the tradition that might arguably serve the contemporary Jewish people most helpfully and deeply.

Second, Jewish newspapers around the country, with a few notable exceptions, celebrate and mourn the material, financial, and professional successes and failures of the Jewish community (careful not to rattle the powers that be) rather than adopting the habits of objective and critically mature reporting. Further, Jewish scholars carefully and painstakingly examine ancient Jewish texts in minute details, searching for linguistic irregularities, historical patterns and causes, and textual inconsistencies, but rarely, if ever, risk academic neutrality by explicitly drawing normative and prescriptive conclusions for contemporary Jewish life. It is these most-informed and deeply committed voices, currently on the sidelines, that are needed now more than ever.

Third, it often seems that tangible power in the Jewish community belongs to the good-hearted and not-so-good-hearted mega-donors who rule haphazardly and arbitrarily, depending on the whims of the moment and whom the rich and well-placed happen to be listening to now. Jewish public schools with a "Hebrew" focus may or may not be a good idea for the Jewish people as a whole, but it is certainly not an idea that bubbled up from the bottom to the top.[1] Given the reality of the top-heavy Jewish communal structure (there has never been a time in Jewish history when the difference between the superrich and the rest of us has been so wide), one is certainly justified in openly wondering whether or not the voice of Jewish ethics really matters to the power of the ruling elite? Jewish ethics requires ongoing, lively, and potentially meaningful and impactful dialogues among all its stakeholders. To the extent that decisions are made only from the top down, or even perceived to be made in this way, there is little reason for anyone other than the superrich to participate in such conversations.

Fourth, the Jewish people are seemingly splintered beyond repair with endless turf battles and arguments among UltraOrthodox, Orthodox, Conservative, and Reform Jews, secularists, atheists, Zionists, anti-Zionists, neo-Hasidic, feminists, and eco-Jews. Everyone is rightfully claiming a piece of the truth for themselves, but how many of us are willing to grant the same rights to others? One does not have to be overly suspicious to challenge those of us who claim to speak in the name of Jewish ethics: For whom are we *really* speaking? In the absence of a more unified Jewish people, it is hard to imagine a truly legitimate and broad-based Jewish ethics to emerge. Like it or not, Jewish ethics stands or falls upon the degree of unity or disunity of the Jewish people.

Fifth, ethical language, when it is finally openly embraced, is often exploited for self-interested reasons. Consider the Orthodox rabbis of the Rabbinical Council of America (RCA) who produced a document entitled "Jewish Principles and Ethical Guidelines for the Kosher Meat Industry" and then turned around and claimed that following the letter of the secular law of the land is all that is necessary to meet one's ethical and social responsibilities. Rather than raising the level and quality of ethical dialogues, the strategic and self-interested use of inherited Jewish ethical language eats away at the shared moral capital accumulated over centuries and longer. Such contemptuous use of our common ethical heritage leaves all of us with fewer collective and tested resources to help resolve moral problems and makes us even more cynical after the fact than before.

Finally, the Jewish tradition itself, or at least one important strand within the tradition, speaks in the name of a profound and nearly all-encompassing pessimism. As Michael Berger, a contemporary Jewish scholar has noted, "a theological assumption of *continually declining generations* is a tenet of Judaism" (as quoted in Kellner, 1996, p. 7). In Hebrew, the decline of the generations is called *yeridat hadorot* (or sometimes *nitkatnu hadorot*, the generations have become diminished). From this perspective—the further we get from the revelation at Sinai, the more spiritually impoverished we become—the Abramoffs, Madoffs, Troppers, Kassins, Elons, and Rubashkins are not so difficult to understand, after all. As the Talmud put it nearly 2,000 years ago, "Just as is the difference between gold and dirt, so is the difference between our generation's and father's." Or, in another poetic burst, the Talmud records the opinion of at least one rabbi, "if the earlier scholars were sons of angels, we are the sons of men: and if the earlier scholars were sons of men, we are like asses, and not even like the asses of Rabbi Hanina ben Dosa...but like ordinary asses."

YERIDAT HADOROT MADE ME DO IT

> On Yom Kippur, the rabbi stops in the middle of the service, prostrates himself beside the bema and cries out, "Oh, God. Before You, I am nothing!"
> Saul Rosenberg, president of the temple is so moved by this demonstration of piety that he immediately throws himself to the floor beside the rabbi and cries, "Oh, God! Before you, I am nothing!"
> Then Chaim Pitkin, a tailor, jumps from his seat, prostrates himself in the aisle and cries, "Oh God! Before You, I am nothing!"
> Rosenberg nudges the rabbi and whispers, "So look who thinks he's nothing."

Jewish pessimism concerning moral progress is nothing new (there *is* nothing new under the sun as Koheleth declared and Woody Allen continues to echo to this day), and my students and others in the Jewish community can certainly justify their moral pessimism as both traditionally authentic and reasonably appropriate. Given contemporary conditions and circumstances, one legitimately wonders, why bother with anything at all?

Rabbi Chaim Luzzato, an eighteenth-century rabbinic scholar and author of one of the most famous ethical treatises in Jewish history, *Mesillat Yesharim* (Path of the Just) was a strong advocate of the no-holds-barred concept of the decline of the generations. Here is how he described the spiritual, moral, and intellectual conditions of his own generation:

> Our faults are so numerous that we do not need much thinking to become aware of how unworthy we are. All of our learning counts for naught. The most learned among us is no greater than the most insignificant disciple of

former generations. We ought to realize this fully, so that we may not become unwarrantably proud. Let us recognize that our mind is unstable, that our intellect is extremely weak, that our ignorance is great, that error is rife among us, and that what we know amounts to very little. Pride hardly becomes us. Rather should we feel abashed and humbled.

And, Rabbi Luzzato wrote this more than 200 years before the shenanigans of Abramoff, Madoff, Tropper, Kassin, Elon, and Rubashkin. What would he think of our own generation? Perhaps, no longer even *ordinary* asses.

According to Menachem Kellner, the doctrine of the decline of the generations, *yeridat hadorot,* is often understood as

> a persistent fact of human (or at least Jewish) experience and that each and every generation is literally inferior to its predecessors. On some views... this decline is qualitative, not just quantitative: according to the Maharal, for example, the Rabbis [of the Mishnaic and Talmudic periods] as individuals were essentially different from and vastly superior to later generations. (p. 7)

Yeridat hadorot to some readers, less familiar with the Jewish tradition than others, may seem like an esoteric doctrine of some historical interest, but of little relevance to today's thinking. Among Orthodox Jews, however, the concept is still widely invoked.

Yeridat hadorot is an ambiguous concept not without some contemporary value. To the extent that the principle is used as a reminder to us of the continued importance of modesty and humility as important human virtues, it can play an important role in our ethical education and decision-making. Especially as the pace of technological progress continues to quicken, we need to learn how to use and apply the new and seemingly magical technologies in more modest and careful ways. As we are debating the extent of the damage to the Gulf of Mexico from the almost unfathomable BP oil spill, we should, no doubt, feel even more "abashed and humbled" than Chaim Luzzato did in the eighteenth century.

A broad application of the doctrine of the decline of the generations, beyond its legitimate use as a reminder to stay modest and humble, however, is a dangerous game to play. What begins with modesty and a deep appreciation for the accomplishments of previous generations—appropriate psychological feelings in many contexts —can easily turn into moral masochism, and, eventually, even into a kind of sadism toward others. It takes only a small step to go from looking backward toward the past in appreciation and gratefulness for the gifts one has inherited to feeling (and even celebrating and enjoying) one's puniness and complete unworthiness in relation to one's forebears. Strangely, one even begins to feel a kind of swelling pride in recognizing and publicly declaring his or her own worthlessness. Next, for those intoxicated with a literal understanding of *yeridat hadorot*, one's gaze eventually turns away from the past and toward the future. For those who truly believe "that each and every generation is literally inferior to its predecessors," it does not take long to realize and embrace the particularly cruel belief that one is *necessarily* superior to his or her own children and students and all *future* generations. Given the inevitable decline in generations, *yeridat hadorot*—parents, teachers, and all true believers will necessarily teach the next generation "you can never be as great as we are!"

Yeridat hadorot can and is used as a handy excuse for poor behavior, as even a cursory google search through today's blogs will show. "*Yeridat hadorot* made me (them) do it." It is often used as a justification for continuing to use the old methods when the old methods aren't working anymore. The following is a typical quote from a contemporary Jewish blogger. I quote it not because it is unusual at all, but because it is illustrative and commonplace:

> However, since then there has been a yeridas hadoros [variant spelling of *yeridat hadorot*], a decline in that perfection and greatness, with each generation on a slightly lower level than the one preceding it. And because we know that the generations before us were better Yidden [Jews] than us, we try our hardest to cling to and emulate the ways of those generations.
>
> We value and revere their piety and the sincere way they lived their lives as servants of Hashem [God], and we try our utmost to live up to those standards. Although the circumstances surrounding us might have improved, with modern technology and labour-saving devices, we believe that human behaviour, rather than improving, has continued to degenerate.
>
> It is for this reason that we are usually fiercely resistant to anyone who tries to change our "old-fashioned, medieval ways" and bring us up-to-date, not just in chinuch [educational methods], but in every other aspect of life. (Moscowitz, no date)

Yeridat hadorot is invoked as a reason to refrain from *tikkun olam* (the repair of the world). It even makes it difficult to draw sensible ethical lessons from biblical narratives. "Whoever says that King David sinned is mistaken," notes the Talmud in a blatant attempt to whitewash what the Bible itself seems to recognize as a heinous crime, and one that everyone might have learned important moral lessons from.

The concept of the decline of the generations is always invoked on an ad hoc basis by its admirers whenever it is convenient, and it is always used as a conversation stopper. Worst of all, *yeridat hadorot* is a self-fulfilling prophecy. If we choose to teach our students and children that our minds are unstable, that our intellects are extremely weak, that ignorance is great, that error is rife among us, and that what we know amounts to very little, as Rabbi Chaim Luzzato once taught, we will create a generation that believes all of this, and worse yet, a generation lost as to how to improve itself. If one perversely set out to create a world where *yeridat hadorot* was truly an inevitable and accurate description of how things work, I can think of no better way to accomplish this task than to teach the concept of the decline of the generations as one of the spiritual laws of the universe. If we are living in a period of moral decay, it is not the inevitable result of the passage of time, but it is a result of thousands of everyday choices we make both consciously and unconsciously. Rejection of the doctrine of the decline of the generations is not a betrayal of the past, but a loyalty to the present moment.

UPWARD, TOWARD ORDER AND PERFECTION

The belief in the inevitable decline of the generations over time in intellectual, spiritual, ethical, and sometimes even physical terms was the mainstream belief in Judaism for more than 1,000 years, although there were probably as many different versions of this theory as there were rabbinic scholars writing about it. Rashi, the preeminent commentator on the Bible and the Talmud, was an unabashed advocate of *yeridat hadorot*. He wrote, "The earlier generation were better and more righteous than the later ones, therefore the former times were better than ours; for it is impossible that the later generations were the equal of the early ones" (as quoted in Lamm, 1990, p. 88). Rabbi Yosef Caro, the author of the *Shulkhan Aruch* and one of the most authoritative voices in the middle ages, determined Jewish Law assuming the reality of this concept. But, even given this widespread and nearly universal acceptance of this view, not all medieval rabbinic authorities embraced the idea.

Not surprisingly to those at all familiar with Jewish philosophy and its history, Maimonides rejected *yeridat hadorot*. Although Maimonides did recognize that he lived in a degraded and corrupted historical period, he understood his contemporary situation as an accident of history, contingent upon particular historical events that could have happened differently, rather than as an inevitable unfolding of history. Menachem Kellner documents and summarizes this view in precise detail:

> Maimonides was convinced that he lived in degenerate times and gave repeated expression to that conviction. This attitude, however, he explained in terms of contingent historical circumstances, not in terms of the doctrine of the decline of the generations. In other instances where he would have been likely to appeal to that doctrine had he held it—the Jews' lack of philosophical sophistication, the destruction of the Temple, the rise of idolatry, the need

for set prayers...he also appealed explicitly to historical circumstances, not some immanent process of decline, be it moral, spiritual, or intellectual...far from seeing history as entropic, moving down as it were towards disorder and dissolution, he actually saw it as moving upwards, towards order and perfection. (1996, p. 54)

In Maimonides's view, the Messianic period will be the eventual result of human intelligence, activity, and initiative, and it will not involve God's "interference" into human affairs.

According to Maimonides, the Messianic era (as opposed to the "world to come"—a wholly spiritual affair), "refers to a time in which sovereignty will revert to Israel and the Jewish people will return to the land of Israel. Their king will be a very great one...all nations will make peace with him...and all countries will serve him out of respect for his great righteousness and the wonders which occur through him (as quoted in Kellner p. 79). Maimonides further clarifies his naturalistic and progressive perspective:

> However, except for the fact that sovereignty will revert to Israel, *nothing will be essentially different from what it is now.* This is what the Rabbis taught: "The only difference between this world and the days of the Messiah is oppression of one kingdom by another." In the days of the Messiah, there will be rich and poor, strong and weak. However, in those days it will be very easy for men to make a living. A minimum of labor will produce great benefits...there will be sowing and reaping even in the Messianic time. (as quoted in Kellner, emphasis added, p. 71)

While Chaim Luzzato believes that all of our learning counts for naught, and, that the most learned among us is no greater than the most insignificant disciple of former generations, Maimonides sees spiritual and ethical growth occurring naturally over time, even in the absence of direct divine intervention.

Like Luzzato's perspective, Maimonides's view is rooted deeply in Talmudic texts and understandings. How did the Talmudic rabbis understand themselves in relation to their own biblical forebears? Consider one of the most famous rabbinic stories concerning the relationship between Moses and Rabbi Akiva:

> Rabbi Judah said the name of Rav: When Moses ascended on high he found the Holy One engaged in affixing coronets to the letters. Said Moses, "Lord of the Universe, who stays thy hand?" He answered, "There will arise a man, many generations from now, Akiva ben Joseph by name, who will extract from every tittle heaps and heaps of laws." Said Moses, "Lord of the Universe, permit me to see him." He replied, "Turn around." Moses went and sat down behind eight rows [of Rabbi Akiva's students] and listened to

the discourses on the law. Unable to follow their arguments, he was ill at ease; but when, coming to a certain subject, the students said to the master, "How do you know this?" And the latter replied, "It is a law given to Moses at Sinai." He regained his composure. Thereupon he returned to the Holy One and said, "Lord of the Universe, you have such a man, and yet you give the Torah through me?" He replied, "Be silent, for that is what occurred to me." (Menahot 9b)

Moses himself, as Menachem Kellner points out, does not accept the thesis of the inevitable decline of the generations, at least according this one rabbinic embellishment. No one was closer to the revelatory moment than Moses, and yet Moses is imagined as being oddly perplexed by Rabbi Akiva's Torah lessons.

Rabbi Norman Lamm, former president of Yeshiva University translates *yeridat hadorot* as the "degeneration of the generations." He concludes his thorough analysis on this topic as follows:

> It is clear that the degeneration theme in talmudic literature refers to sociological facts and historical data of specific kinds, not to some general metaphysical truth or absolute moral norm... They [the rabbis] did not extrapolate from sociology to ontology. Hence, the tendency of our own "later generations" to create an ideology of *nitkatnu hadorot* (a term not mentioned in the talmudic literature), so that examples from the past of intellectual breadth and openness are inapplicable to us, is misplaced. (1990, p. 93)

From the Maimonidean perspective, human progress is not only possible over time, but in view of his central and absolutely certain belief in the coming of the Messiah, it is inevitable. History is not moving down toward disorder and dissolution, but it "moving upwards, towards order and perfection."

Contemporary Example of Moral Progress

In some domains, it seems unquestionable that there has been human progress over time. In science and medicine, new inventions have made food and other necessities cheaper and more plentiful, have increased life expectancies, and have made life easier and less painful for those of us with access to the new technologies. As a simple example, it is noted that for most of human history, tooth decay was a source of almost constant pain for many adults, while today (for many) it is no more than a minor irritation. Improvements in communication now allow loved ones to remain in constant touch with each other no matter where they are on the globe. The internet has made unimaginable quantities of knowledge available immediately at low cost to huge segments of the human population.

Even in the domain of ethics, there are seemingly clear examples of moral progress. Slavery, once openly accepted and justified, is nearly universally condemned (even if it still exists as an institution). Racism, once carelessly endorsed and taught in our homes and schools, in less than a generation, has dramatically declined to the point where in 2008 the United States elected the first ever African-American president. The relationship between men and women has been significantly and permanently (one hopes) altered. Martha Nussbaum, a contemporary philosopher, notes, "Now there are still many cases in which men dominate women—an understatement if there ever was one. But the exposure of their behavior as what it is, the sheer naming of it as oppression, and the existence of widespread public argument about it, changes things for good..." (2007 p. 940). The concept of human rights, including a right to basic healthcare in the United States and elsewhere, is now accepted as a legitimate aspiration. The promotion of and tolerance for gay rights has expanded dramatically. The invention of democratic forms of self-government, including the rights to freedom of religion and freedom of expression, are clear advances that few of us who already benefit from democracy would willingly forfeit. In Israel, the Jewish people who have been the victims of anti-semitism and violence for centuries, have created a vibrant and democratic state. Israel's population is now estimated at more than 7.5 million people, including 6 million Jews. Today, Israel has one of the highest life expectancies in the world, and it ranks first in the Middle East on the UN (United Nations) Human Development Index. According to many, there are more books being published today on Jewish topics than ever before in history.

In the examples cited above, the engine of ethical progress in nearly every case is a potent combination of (1) an increased awareness for the possibility of radical change, (2) moral imagination (Rorty, 2006), (3) an ability to empathize with those who are different from us (loving the stranger), and (4) the establishment of institutions and new norms that allow individuals and groups to question systematically traditional practices and to demand and get answers from those in positions of authority (holding CEOs, government leaders, scientists, doctors, teachers, and even religious leaders accountable to relevant stakeholder groups).

THESE ARE THE BEST OF TIMES, THESE ARE THE WORST OF TIMES...

> A rabbi is asked to settle a dispute. After listening to one side's argument, the rabbi declares, "You're right!" After listening the other side's argument, the rabbi nods and says, "You're right, too." His wife, who is listening, declares, exasperated, "Rabbi, this is absurd! They can't both be right!" The rabbi sighs and replies, "You're also right!"

To my students at Yeshiva University, often paralyzed and confused about the prospects for ethical growth and development, the view of Maimonides and the contemporary examples of moral progress cited above, offer a degree of hope and expectation about the future. But, just as the case for pessimism can be overstated, the optimistic case can be taken to extremes. The danger of Rabbi Chaim Luzzato's ultraconservative position is that it can lead, and often does, to a self-fulfilling prophecy and to an unnatural passivity in the face of changing circumstances. The danger of Maimonides progressive perspective is that it can lead to hubris and much worse. There is an unchecked triumphalism and dangerous certainty inherent in Maimonides's view of progress. From a moral perspective, in a volatile and interconnected world like ours, can we still accept and teach the idea that in the future it is certain ("I believe with perfect faith...") that "all countries will serve him [our Messiah]?" It is time to ask, what are the ethical implications, in the here and now, of such a teaching?

Even as we embrace the progressive view of Maimonides, we cannot completely let go of Rabbi Chaim Luzzato's penetrating insights and wise warning not to "become unwarrantably proud." The twentieth century was arguably the most brutal in human history: two world wars, the Holocaust, Hiroshima, the Stalinist era, Mao Zedong's China, Vietnam, Cambodia, Yugoslavia, and the rise of Sadam Hussein (for a full discussion see Glover, 1999). The twenty-first century, so far, does not look much better with its terrorism (and even the fear of nuclear terrorism), global warming, man-made environmental disasters, unfettered capitalism and financial volatility, alcohol and drug addictions, sexual abuse of children by clergy and others, denials and cover-ups, government mismanagement and corruption, and the unprecedented business frauds in the US, Europe, Israel, and all over the world.

The contemporary philosopher, Michael Walzer, suggests that moral progress is possible but not inevitable. He softens Maimonides's certainty, even as he strengthens the contemporary argument in favor of the future of Jewish ethics. He compares the process of ethical criticism to the continuous building of a family home over many generations. In his words:

> We do not have to discover the moral world because we have always lived there. We do not have to invent it because it has already been invented—though not in accordance with any philosophical method. No design procedure has governed its design, and the result no doubt is disorganized and uncertain. It is also very dense: the moral world has a lived-in quality, like a home occupied by a single family over many generations, with unplanned additions here and there, and all the available space filled with memory-laden

objects and artifacts. The thing, taken as a whole, lends itself less to abstract modeling than to thick description. (1987, p. 20)

Walzer's striking and memorable metaphor—"like a home occupied by a single family over many generations"—and his view of ethical criticism as "thick description" are consistent with some of the most authentic and progressive strands in the Jewish tradition. Anyone who has ever studied a page of Talmud in depth will recognize the accuracy, attraction, and beauty of Walzer's intergenerational model. He avoids the deep pessimism inherent in the concept of *yeridat hadorot,* and at the same time there is no hint of the triumphalism of Maimonides—"the result no doubt is disorganized and uncertain." There is a possibility for progress here, each generation builds its own additions, but it is not a constant progress nor are there any guarantees that we are going in the right direction at any particular point in time.

In a salient contemporary interpretation of the Passover Haggadah's commandment to view yourself as if you are leaving Egypt, Walzer concludes his book *Exodus and Revolution* by noting:

- First, wherever you live it is probably Egypt;
- second, there is a better place, a world more attractive, a promised land;
- and third, that "the way to the land is through the wilderness." There is no way to get from here to there except by joining together and marching. (1985, p. 149)

Walzer's *was* a view that I once endorsed without reservation and it is still one that I recommend highly to my students, desperately in need of an optimistic and balanced case for the future of Jewish ethics. Walzer believes that the resources that we need to progress are already inherent in our own traditions. There is no urgent need to look for a set of universal moral principles generated by philosophers with the view from nowhere because everything we need to engage in practical ethical dialogues among ourselves is already a part of our inherited moral language. It is not to the thin, universal ethical rules that we need to turn, but it is in the thick, inherited practices and conversations of tradition that we must immerse ourselves.

How is moral progress possible? Walzer compares moral and social criticism to the give and take among friends and colleagues:

We often criticize friends and colleagues for not living up to a set of standards that we and they profess to honor. We measure them against their own pretended ideals; we charge them with hypocrisy or bad faith. A critic who holds up a mirror to society as a whole is engaged in a similar enterprise. He means to show us *as we really are*, and what gives this demonstration its moral force, what makes the mirror a critical instrument inspiring dismay and guilt, is a pervasive and profound social idealism...members of any society need to believe that their distributive arrangements and polices are just...the critic tears aside the veil. (Walzer, 1994, emphasis in original, pp. 41–42)

Michael Walzer's view here, and in his other writings, as well, is compelling and hopeful (see especially Walzer, 1983). He combines a practical and real world sensibility to his profound sense of idealism, all the while maintaining a faith in human integrity and goodwill. It is a view consonant with the best of the Jewish tradition. One could do much worse than to stop here.

I now believe, however, what is missing, from Walzer's view is a recognition of the sense of brokenness and incompleteness that many of us now take almost for granted. It turns out that no single philosophical or religious worldview can encompass the hope and faith necessary to keep the project of moral progress going continually and at the same time not blink in the face of human callousness, indifference, misery, and depravity. We now know that the moral world has "a lived-in quality, like a home occupied by a single family over many generations..." as Walzer correctly described it, but only sometimes. There are moments (even long moments) in history, in contemporary life, and in our own lives when the moral world is turned upside down. Rather than feeling at home, comfortable and cozy, we have a feeling of vertigo. We are strangers in a strange land. Even inside the moral world, there exist gaps and discontinuities.

There are times and places that one can rely on Walzer's "pervasive and profound social idealism," but there are other times and other places when such social idealism is completely evacuated ("Given a chance to cheat, I'll cheat"), and we are truly alone. Walzer tells us the "critic tears aside the veil," but in today's world sometimes there are no veils to tear aside. What can a critic have to say to the Abramoffs, Madoffs, Troppers, Kassins, Elons, and Rubashkins, that might be meaningful and make some sort of difference to them? Staring directly into the face of evil, say, for example, the cold and indifferent eyes of a pedophile or an SS officer, the critic can only stand silently and wonder. "Wherever you live it is probably Egypt..." Walzer believes. But, it is slowly beginning to creep into our consciousness that there are places and events in this world even worse than Egypt and its servitude.

HE IS LEFT WOUNDED AND LIMPING, BUT HE IS STILL JACOB

On the day that the Holy Temple was destroyed, a Jew was plowing his field when his cow suddenly called out. An Arab was passing by and heard the low of the cow. Said the Arab to the Jew: "Son of Judah! Unyoke your cow, free the stake of your plow, for your Holy Temple has now been destroyed. The cow then lowed a second time. Said the Arab to the Jew: "Son of Judah! Yoke your cow, reset the stake of your plow, for the Redeemer has now been born..." Jerusalem Talmud, Berachot 2:4

Irving Greenberg, rabbi and theologian, has been writing and speaking tirelessly for decades about the Jewish condition after the Holocaust. It is not easy or comfortable, especially for those who speak in the name of contemporary Jewish denominations (Orthodox, Conservative, Reform, and Reconstructionist), to accept his difficult and nuanced position. Greenberg's teachings demand a change in consciousness, a deep broadening of perspective, and a willingness to sacrifice long-held and seemingly sacrosanct assumptions. Nevertheless, for those who study his writings carefully, it is even harder, if not impossible, to resist embracing his fundamental conclusion, reached only after years of religious, emotional, and intellectual struggles:

> The primary impact of the Shoah [the Holocaust] on the core paradigm of truth and coherence is evident when one recognizes the need to acknowledge the brokenness of all religious worldviews and value systems. Internalizing the implications of the Holocaust inexorably leads to the recognition of the essential fragmented nature of the familiar explanatory models and inescapable limits of normative religious/ethical categories. (2006, p. 215)

Paradoxically, I believe, it is only through an understanding and acceptance of Rabbi Irving Greenberg's emerging and complex position that one can begin to rebuild a mature and optimistic case for the future of Jewish ethics.

For Greenberg, the Holocaust is a "touchstone of theology." Like previous tragedies in Jewish history, including the destruction of the Second Temple, it is an epochal event of such great magnitude, a human experience that necessarily alters our old ways of thinking and living in the world, that it requires us to rethink core beliefs and values. While it is not the first time in Jewish history that human events speak directly to us with such power and directness, it is the first time that our inherited categories and meaning-structures are stretched to the breaking point and beyond. The events of the Holocaust when seen and taken in (to the extent that this is possible) puncture our usual explanations and stories.

> When the Holocaust is recognized as a touchstone, then the test of the validity of theologies is not just the criteria of intellectual and moral coherence but whether the position is credible in the presence of the Holocaust or in light of the implications of the event. (For example, the ideas that religion should

be predicated on the essential goodness of human nature or that sickness and suffering are providentially inflicted on people because they sin are beliefs whose validity would be more difficult to uphold in light of the implications of the Shoah.) (Greenberg, 2006, p.214)

Similarly, extreme and certain beliefs like *yeridat hadorot* or naïve and utopian messianism are much more difficult to defend in the postHolocaust age. In fact, Greenberg himself states explicitly that, "the Shoah...shatters the classic traditional paradigm of rabbinic Orthodox, that faith that instructed its followers to wait patiently for salvation from a miraculous Messiah..." (2006, p. 216). At the same time, "the Holocaust tested and shattered the adequacy of...Western culture and, in particular, liberalism and other movements on the political and cultural Left, with their magnetic promise of redemption of the world and the perfection of human living conditions..." (2006, p. 215).

Greenberg is careful to point out that brokenness does not imply destruction. Brokenness does imply that a tradition can no longer be understood as whole or fully-encompassing. In an illuminating and hopeful metaphor, Greenberg compares our situation to that of Jacob after his struggle with God's angel. "He is left wounded and limping, but he is still Jacob. Indeed, he has been ennobled and become Israel in the very process that has injured him" (Greenberg, 2006, p. 220).

The *Kessef Mishnah* in a commentary on Maimonides's *Mishnah Torah* (Laws of the Holy Temple 1:17) ruled that "to demolish in order to improve is obviously permitted." Greenberg's recognition that in the shadow of the Holocaust, Judaism's core paradigm requires a reinterpretation is an example of such a demolishing "in order to improve." It requires one to stand in relation to his or her tradition in a new and altered way. The moral language and rituals that we inherit are, at best, only fragments. One begins to sense an urgent need to question the "unplanned additions here and there," and critique the meaning of the "memory-laden objects and artifacts" of one's own culture.

Greenberg emphasizes Judaism's traditional idea of limits and boundaries, but now recognizes the need to apply limits not only as one lives *within* the boundaries of one's religious life, but one needs to apply limits to the tradition itself.

> When the fragment—even a good one—expands within a certain space and assumes authority without limit, it cannot sustain the infinity, variety, and uniqueness of life...When humans claim to be God (Absolute), they can only be infinitely more than other humans (the ratio of God to the human) by reducing the other humans to zero. Thus we learn from the Shoah that

all human-implicated Absolutes must be reduced, made partial, in order to make them sources of life and not death. (One way of doing this is to "break" them.) (2006, p. 218).

There is no shame or humiliation in recognizing the limits of one's own identity, but it does demand new relational modes.

NEW RELATIONAL MODES

An appreciation and an acknowledgement of limits entail an opening up of oneself to the reality of the other. The metaphor of domination is replaced with an alternative metaphor of multiple encounters. Martin Buber's conception of the I-Thou relationship ("Through the Thou a man becomes I,") becomes more coherent and urgent (1958, p. 28). Competition, and all of its tangible benefits, is recognized as dependent upon the primacy of cooperation and community. Dialogue replaces debate. "Once the complacency of perceiving one's own truth as whole (i.e., absolutely adequate) is broken, then one can recognize that the opposing view may be on the very same continuum of response and that one position shades into the other... The alternate response is perceived not as an enemy but as the complementary position, or as the corrective movement, or as the challenge that tests and purifies one's own position" (Greenberg, 2006, p. 221).

In recognizing one's own limits and the limits of one's inherited beliefs, one begins to practice self-criticism. The gates of growth and development are unlocked and one can begin the process of *teshuva* (repentance) in earnest. One begins to forgive oneself for past transgressions, and one soon learns to offer the gift of forgiveness to others, as well. Identities are like shields and there is a deep fear and sense of vulnerability in lowering or even temporarily putting down one's shield. In building the optimistic case for the future of Jewish ethics, we must face this fear and vulnerability directly. Learning to forgive others is an important aspect of this process.

It is nearly impossible to believe that real and sustained moral progress across all domains will result only when our worldview finally trumps all of the others. The final goal that we are aiming for should not be a vision where all of the nations of the world acknowledge our story of truth as universal and unchallengeable. Rather we should jettison "final goals" altogether and learn how to work with one another to create and strengthen the conditions of pluralism.

> The most prevalent and effective method of preventing pathological absolutism from rearing it head is to create the conditions of pluralism. Worldwide, after the Shoah, a broad spectrum of movements has drawn

on this insight. The presence of multiple political and economic mechanisms prevents totalitarian concentrations of force. Wider distribution of the levers of power begins to offer potential victims some assurances against their victimization. Because power takes many forms, the breaking up of cultural hegemony and of ethical centralization is also desperately needed" (Greenberg, 2006, pp. 221–222).

Jewish ethics, in the future, must take a leading role in advancing social, corporate, government, and religious responsibilities and accountabilities. This means speaking truth to power, always asking questions, demanding adequate answers, and taking action when such answers are not available or forthcoming. It means recognizing that radical change is possible, moral imagination is a primary source for moral growth, the boundaries of moral concern must be continually broadened, and that democratic institutions must be established to hold leaders (be they business, government, or religious) accountable on an ongoing and permanent basis to the stakeholders affected by their decisions and policies. All of this holds both inside the various Jewish communities and beyond.

Irving Greenberg came to his conclusion through his own encounter with the Holocaust. Unlike theologians and philosophers who have tried to subsume the enormity of the Shoah into preexisting categories, Greenberg now understands that there are no fixed categories or a single story belonging to a single family or religion that can do justice to the enormity of this particular historical event. In the end, it is not a thing to be understood or grasped. "The insistence that all narratives are grounded in specific groups (and their authority is conditioned by that factor) is an attempt to set needed limits on valid truths. No matter how distinguished or powerful systems/narratives/truths are, they must be taught their limitations and their brokenness" (2006, p. 222). He adds just two paragraphs later that this is true not only for man-made systems but even "for divinely revealed systems" (p. 222). Others have reached similar postmodern conclusions, not necessarily through an encounter with the Holocaust, but through other difficult paths and arduous wonderings.

Greenberg's encounter with the Shoah has not left him a pessimist, relativist, or a cynic. In fact, it is precisely through embracing limitations, pluralism, accountability to the other, and imagination that Greenberg sees the possibility of renewal. It is only by awakening to new relational modes that he sees the hope for reimagining the centrality of human responsibility in human affairs (see especially Greenberg's *For the Sake of Heaven and Earth: The New Encounter between Judaism and Christianity,* 2004). Tellingly the single most important example of ethical progress he provides in his essay is the Christian response to the Shoah:

One of the most remarkable religious developments of our time is...the re-visioning of the relationship of Christianity and Judaism. A poisonous, millennia-long history of hatred and degradation has been built on the premise that Judaism as a religion was finished and that Christianity had replaced it in the divine and human economy. Yet, within fifty years after the Holocaust, in some of the main Western Christian churches...this tradition has been seriously challenged, if not yet completely reversed. (2006, p. 224)

It is with this powerful and carefully selected example that Greenberg reminds his coreligionists that the "moral purification of the Jewish religion" is fully contingent upon our own similar recognition of brokenness.

Kol Yisrael Arevim Zeh Bazeh—All Israel is Responsible for One Another

The optimistic case for the future of Jewish ethics begins with the recognition that ethics, Jewish or otherwise, provides no guarantee of future progress. There are simultaneously regressive and progressive tendencies in Jewish life. There are forces trying to pull us backward into the past (*yeridat hadorot*), and there other forces pushing us forward, on into the future (naïve messianism). Jewish ethics is about our own ability to balance these forces against one another to create the energy to live meaningful lives in the present moment. In striving to live an ethical life, we are like the captain of a yacht playing off the power of the wind against the opposite power of the keel to keep the boat moving in a straight line.

When we begin to take ownership and responsibility for Jewish ethics, as we must in a postmodern age, rather than viewing it merely as a set of rules existing out there and imposed upon us, we come to see that ethics is most fundamentally about reflecting upon and harnessing our current desires as biological and finite creatures, as individuals with private goals and aspirations, as members of the Jewish people, and as members of the human community. In doing Jewish ethics today, we start by critically examining ourselves: our knowledge, memory, emotions, beliefs, hopes, and desires. We ask ourselves a set of difficult but highly practical questions:

Which activities are most the meaningful to me?

Do I achieve the identity I aspire to best by increasing my wealth, helping others, studying, consuming, meditating, doing good work, striving for self-fulfillment or happiness, loving my family, being true to my history and heritage, improving my golf game, building up my neighborhood, acquiring a particular kind of reputation, creating a better future for myself and my children, surfing the internet, visiting the sick, buying fancy gadgets, etc.?

Are my own desires—upon reflection and dialogue—truly desirable?

Is there any way to lessen the felt gap between means and ends?

How do I begin to weave my choices and actions into a single life with purpose, substance, and direction?

How do I integrate my life into the life of my community or communities?

The kind of pervasive, self-reflective attitude I am talking about here is not the product of a single mind working things out by him or herself at a fixed point in time, but rather the self-reflective attitude is accomplished in continuous dialogue with the members of one's family, communities, country, and beyond. We do not rely only upon rational discourse but upon intellect, emotions, intuition, imagination, and creativity,

For better and for worse, we challenge one another and learn from one another. As Irving Greenberg noted and as I have cited above, "the alternate response is perceived not as an enemy but as the complementary position, or as the corrective movement, or as the challenge that tests and purifies one's own position" Knowledge, beliefs, desires, and emotions are shared and tested in the company of others. One is responsible and accountable not only to one's self, but to all of those people affected by one's decisions and actions.

Kol Yisrael arevim zeh bazeh—all Israel is responsible for one another. It is through these ongoing, imperfect, and broken dialogues that inherited ethical norms are confirmed or disconfirmed, and new norms begin to emerge and evolve. Further, it is through these dialogues that individual and community identities are formed and altered.

The optimistic case for the future of Jewish ethics is not based on certainty nor does it provide any guarantees or promises. The optimistic case hinges on our ability to work together and use all of the resources at our disposal, including all of those elements that constitute the inherited ethical infrastructure, to describe and invent a possible and plausible path of real growth and development. It is a path attractive enough that it compels us to move forward, not by an outside force or by magic, but by the meaningful and substantive life it provides for those who take the risk and choose to traverse it.

HYPERNORMS

Philosophers and applied ethicists today speak of two types of ethical norms. There are the everyday, taken for granted *local norms* through which we normally live our lives in our own communities, and then there are the *hypernorms* (see especially Donaldson and Dunfee, 1999). Ed Hartman defines local norms as follows:

> We can think of a norm as a piece of practical knowledge. It tells us how to do things right. A [local] norm usually serves a common purpose of the sort that a community, a company, a team, or almost any collective has. Where these shared purposes relate to important interests and concerns and help solve important local problems, we think of the associated norms as ethical norms. The most significant ethical norms serve purposes whose achievement is a necessary condition of our living together on satisfactory terms. (2009, p. 708)

By contrast, hypernorms—great principles based on settled understandings of deep moral values—are those norms that cut across local communities and are shared by almost everyone, everywhere. These hypernorms include strictures against killing, torture, humiliation, and inflicting unnecessary pain on others. They may also include certain basic human rights such as freedom of speech and religion.

The significance of hypernorms is that the legitimacy of any given local norm can be challenged through invoking a hypernorm. Hartman explains the process this way:

> We determine the legitimacy of a local ethical norm by applying one or more hypernorms...which set limits on the range of local norms that are morally acceptable. Theologians, philosophers, and wise people generally agree that, for example, no majority is justified in treating members of a minority group harshly or having a contemptuous attitude toward them just because they are minorities. (2009, p. 707)

In practice, however, it is highly unlikely that someone will be able to immediately alter the behavior of a local community—acting in the name of a local norm—merely by invoking a hypernorm and asking pointed questions. For example, Ed Hartman notes:

> Nepotism will not go away because people begin to notice that it violates a hypernorm. It will appropriately fall out of use when conditions in certain developing countries change sufficiently that it ceases to be the best way to deal with all sorts of issues involved in employment—those related to the society and to the particular company. (2009, p. 711)

Similarly, a religious community that has for centuries been teaching its young boys to read and write, but not its young girls, will probably not be too impressed by the invocation of a hypernorm concerning gender equality, whether the claim is made by a fellow insider or an outsider. Nevertheless, once the issue is raised, over time, it is possible that leaders and others will come to see *on their own* that such a discriminatory practice, while once a sensible allocation of scarce resources in the community, is no longer in the interests of the local community—*as the community itself defines those interests*. In other words, in light of other practices and claims, traditionalists may come to frame their own educational problem in new and more productive and meaningful ways, alternatives more consistent with the core teachings of their own tradition.

Hypernorms do not work like trump cards or clubs to bully one's opponents into submission. Nevertheless, they do serve an important function in ethical practice. Consider the case of extreme low wages in developing countries. An ethicist certainly might raise legitimate questions about this practice, based on the existence of a hypernorm stating that it is unethical to compensate employees an amount below a "living wage." However, before any conclusions are reached, it is necessary to look at the facts on the ground. A possible and plausible answer to such a question is that given the particular circumstances, at this company, in this country, at this point in time, there is no way we can raise wages. Such an answer, sensitive to the particular context in which a hypernorm has been invoked, may be true or false and further investigation is usually needed. The existence of hypernorms helps to jumpstart real conversations. It puts new issues on the agenda, reframes old ones, and begins to institutionalize some form of minimal accountability. It does not predetermine solutions in any given case.

Moral progress is fitful and slow. It does not always occur when and where we would like it. Often leaders and spokespersons of local communities will continue to defend outdated norms and customs despite the fact that the original reasons for the disputed practices no longer hold. Hartman elaborates more fully:

> Some may have an emotional investment in the old norms and find new ones repugnant. Today, in societies in which men do not hunt, women do not gather, and most hard physical labor is done by machines—societies, that is, in which gender differences do not matter as much as they used to do—there are still many men and women who consider it unnatural for women to be managers and professionals, and even more who would think it odd that the husband should stay home with the kids. This is a case in which norms that used to serve a purpose have become part of what it means to be a man or a woman, with the result that abandoning them would be deeply painful for some. It does not follow that traditional societies are able to justify their views about women's status. (2009, p. 712)

In responding to hypernorms, leaders and others may begin to realize that they really do not have any good reasons to support the old customs after all. "'What reason do we have, come to think of it, for treating women so differently?' As we know, people have not found it easy to answer that question; but once it is in play, things are more likely to change. It increases the probability that the next question will be not, 'Why should I let a woman tell me what to do?' but instead, 'Exactly what is wrong with a woman being a manager?'" (Hartman, 2009, p. 714).

At the heart of contemporary ethics are those various and ongoing dialogues between advocates for local ethical norms (and the status quo justified by such norms) and advocates for hypernorms (and the progressive demands implied by such hypernorms). Ethical progress is inherent in the process of promoting, institutionalizing, and sustaining such dialogues, where all participants are accountable to one another, even when there are strong differences of opinion and trust is low.

JEWISH HYPERNORMS

Imagine Jewish hypernorms: a set of ethical norms shared by the entire Jewish people, grounded in the local norms of the various individual Jewish communities, but cutting across them and binding them together as one. Such Jewish hypernorms are derived from great *Jewish* principles based on settled understandings of deep moral values—and are shared by almost everyone, everywhere *who identifies himself or herself as a member of the Jewish people.* These are the ideals and aspirations articulated by rabbis, theologians, philosophers, and wise Jewish people generally.

Many Jewish hypernorms will be recognized beyond the Jewish people as universal hypernorms, but many, no doubt, will not. The unique Jewish hypernorms, intermediary norms located somewhere between the thick local norms of specific communities and the thin universal norms, serve as standards or ensigns around which the Jewish people gather and communicate with one another. The Jewish hypernorms are not stated as specific rules of behavior nor are they meant to be used as tools for one community to chastise another. The purpose of Jewish hypernorms is to provide a useful description and summary to date of those deeply-engrained Jewish habits of thought and Jewish values currently shared by nearly all members of the Jewish people.

In light of Irving Greenberg's critique discussed above, it should be stipulated that any articulation of a set of Jewish hypernorms is experimental and tentative, at best. Recall Greenberg's insistence that "we learn from the Shoah that *all* human-implicated Absolutes must be reduced, made partial, in order to make them sources of life and not death" (2006, p. 218). John Dewey, a founder of American Pragmatism, anticipating Greenberg's uncertainty, described the role of moral principles in decision-making as follows:

> They are hypotheses to be worked out in practice, and to be rejected, corrected and expanded as they fail or succeed in giving our present experience the guidance it requires. We may call [moral principles] programs of action, but since they are to be used in making our future acts less blind, more directed, they are flexible. Intelligence is not something possessed once for all. It is in constant process of forming, and its retention requires constant alertness in observing consequences, and open-minded will to learn and courage in readjustment..." (as quoted in Guinlock, 1994, p. 133).

Jewish hypernorms, despite widespread and nearly universal agreement, therefore, are not absolute directives, set in stone once and for all. Hypernorms, Jewish or otherwise, like Dewey's moral principles, are "to be worked out in practice" and adjusted in light of history and experience. Jewish hypernorms are the best hypotheses about Jewish ethics that the Jewish people can put forward at any given point in its history. And, while the hypernorms are used as a set of criteria to evaluate specific norms of behavior within individual Jewish communities, the hypernorms themselves are always subject to critique and reconstruction. In ethics, as in science, there are no final formulae to follow. Even in a tradition like the Jewish tradition, with its long history and seemingly infinitely varied experiences, life constantly has its surprises, and there is always room for human innovation, improvisation, and imagination in ethics. Even as we talk about the possibility of Jewish hypernorms, as I believe we must, it is imperative that we do not lose sight of the degree of freedom each one of us possesses simply by dint of our humanity. Jewish hypernorms are neither the result of pure discovery of what already exists out there nor are they the result of pure invention, but there are always traces of both discovery and invention in the process of articulating Jewish hypernorms.

Proposing a list of such Jewish hypernorms is a first step toward institutionalizing Jewish accountability, perhaps the single most important element in promoting ethical progress and growth. Since everyone who identifies as being a Jew agrees with the Jewish hypernorms, everyone can be held responsible to answer to them in a meaningful way. As with universal hypernorms, Jewish hypernorms are not offered as a panacea, but as a systematic way of thinking and talking about Jewish ethics. Jewish hypernorms offer a formal mechanism for the Jewish people, as a whole, to begin to challenge the local norms of specific Jewish communities and to allow those Jewish communities to respond to these challenges. They are always invoked as conversation starters and never as conversation stoppers.

PLAUSIBLE CANDIDATES

I offer the following list of Jewish hypernorms, not as exhaustive, definitive, or final, but as reasonable and plausible candidates to begin a conversation.

1. Holocaust as a touchstone for Jewish Ethics

First, following Rabbi Irving Greenberg's articulation cited above, I suggest that his notion of the Shoah as a touchstone to Jewish theology and morality can serve as a Jewish hypernorm. Any claim any one of us makes concerning Jewish ethics and Jewish morality must make sense in light of the enormity of this event. Greenberg himself draws many conclusions from this proposal, and as I have already stated above, I believe that such a notion would raise questions about specific beliefs, pronouncements, and actions made in the name of *yeridat hadorot* (the decline of the generations) and naïve messianism. Such questions and answers might lead to more subtle understandings of these concepts (their "moment truths" may be revealed as Greenberg might put it) or even their complete rejection.

2. "Thou shalt have no other gods before Me"

Similarly, Greenberg's insistence on our inability to grasp the entire truth, our brokenness, as he calls it, might usefully be couched in the more familiar language of the Jewish prohibition of idolatry. "Thou shalt have no other gods before Me. Thou shalt not make unto thee a graven image, nor any manner of likeness" (Exodus 20:3–4). Such a prohibition, understood in its broadest terms, along the lines of Maimonides, and much later, Will Herberg, is an excellent candidate for a Jewish hypernorm. According to Maimonides, "The essential commandment against idolatry prohibits worshipping any one of all the creations—not an angel nor a sphere nor a star nor one of the four elements ("fire", "water", "spirit" or "earth") nor any one of all the beings created out of them" (Maimonides, Laws of Idolatry 2:1). Herberg in a similar spirit, using contemporary language wrote:

> To grasp the full scope and significance of this principle it is necessary to understand the essential meaning of idolatry. Idolatry is not simply the worship of sticks and stones, or it would obviously have no relevance to our times. Idolatry is the absolutization of the relative; it is absolute devotion paid to anything short of the Absolute. The object of idolatrous worship may be, and in fact generally is, some good; but since it is not God, it is necessarily a good that is only partial and relative. [Herberg, 1959, pp. 93–94, emphasis in original]

The prohibition against turning the relative into the absolute is almost certainly acceptable to religious Jews, be they Orthodox, Conservative, Reform, or Reconstructionist. And, since it requires no positive theological assumptions or beliefs, it is also an ideal to which secular Jews can aspire, as well.

3. *Kol Yisrael arevim zeh bazeh*

As a third candidate, I also return to a concept already cited in this chapter and that is *kol Yisrael arevim zeh bazeh*—all Israel is responsible for one another. This principle is widely promoted and seemingly accepted by Orthodox, Conservative, and Reform Jews as a quick search on the internet reveals, and it is also a principle that secular Jews, especially those living in Israel, can wholeheartedly endorse. To the extent that the entire Jewish people embrace this notion, it implies, at least, a minimum acceptance of toleration of significant differences and some kind of an endorsement of pluralism. If we are all identical to one another, there is hardly a need to specify explicitly that all Israel is responsible for one another. Of course, I am responsible for those who are exactly like me (this goes without saying). The moral ideal and aspiration here makes sense and has teeth only to the extent that each one of us is seen as unique and special and that of the different communities that together make up the Jewish people *each* possesses a degree of legitimacy and are *all* carriers of a part of the truth of the Jewish people. As the *midrash* reminds us there "are seventy faces to the Torah" (*Bamidbar Rabbah* 13:15).

The meaning of this concept is surely contested, but it is a useful idea to consciously have in mind as we discuss and debate conversion issues, intermarriage, interdenominational concerns, the relationship between Ashkenazi and Sephardic Jews in Israel, the status of new immigrants in Israel, and American Jewry and its relationship to Israel. None of these issues will be solved by simply invoking a single hypernorm, but if we think of these hypernorms as habits of thought and unique and special ways of inhabiting the Jewish world, the concept of *kol Yisrael arevim zeh bazeh* might become the default principle by which all of us together think through these issues. Rather than framing each new problem and issue as a question about who gets what and how much, as our instincts automatically demand, we might begin to hold ourselves responsible, as a people, to a loftier conception of what is right and what is wrong in any given case.

4. Sabbath Consciousness

The notion of a "Sabbath consciousness" takes us beyond the realm of the purely ritual (although it does arguably require ritual practice, religious or otherwise, to ground it) into the realm of the ethical. Rabbi David Hartman, a contemporary Israeli rabbi, elaborates on the Jewish Sabbath and its implications for contemporary life. He writes:

> *Halakhah* [Jewish law] prohibits my plucking a flower from my garden or doing with it as I please. At sunset the flower becomes a "thou" with a right to existence

irrespective of its instrumental value for me. I stand silently before nature as before a fellow creature and not as before an object of my control. By forcing us to experience the meaning of being creatures of God, the Sabbath aims at healing the human grandiosity of technological arrogance. (1999, p. 78)

Commenting on David Hartman's position, Harvard philosopher, Michael J. Sandel notes, "the obligation to keep the Sabbath serves to check our drive to dominion" (2005, p. 206).

Rabbi Abraham Joshua Heschel has written eloquently on the Sabbath consciousness in his famous little book, *The Sabbath*. He wrote:

The Sabbath as experienced by man cannot survive in exile, a lonely stranger among the days of profanity. It needs the companionship of all other days. All days of the week must be spiritually consistent with the Day of Days. All our life should be a pilgrimage to the seventh day; the thought and appreciation of what this day may bring to us should be ever present in our minds. For the Sabbath is the counterpoint of living; the melody sustained throughout all agitations and vicissitudes which menace our conscience; our awareness of God's presence in the world. (1951, p. 89).

The inclusion of Sabbath consciousness as a hypernorm necessarily raises ethical questions about the appropriate use of power and control, on the one hand, and acceptance and surrender, on the other hand.

From a Jewish perspective, technology has its positive uses—within limits. Given our finite knowledge and limited ability to predict the future, there are surely technological boundaries beyond which we should not trespass. Cloning, genetic engineering, using nuclear power, deep water oil drilling are all practices that raise potential dangers and clear risks of permanent changes to the human and natural environment. Often, in these kinds of cases, the kinds of risks we are talking about are neither quantifiable nor predictable in the usual ways. Surely, at some point in time, the burden of proof shifts from those who wish to stop, regulate, or at least slow down these technological breakthroughs to those who insist on continuously pushing the frontiers of technological advancement.

To gain control of the world of space is certainly one of our tasks. The danger begins when in gaining power in the realm of space we forfeit all aspirations in the realm of time. There is a realm of time where the goal is not to have but to be, not to own but to give, not to control but to share, not to subdue but to be in accord. Life goes wrong when the control of space, the acquisition of things of space, becomes our sole concern. (Heschel, 1951, p. 3)

This is the single best articulation of a Sabbath consciousness with which I am familiar. Viewing this as a Jewish hypernorm gives little or no explicit guidance on how to deal with specific issues as they arise. For this we need the input of scientists, politicians, and many others. A Sabbath consciousness does, however, demand that we learn how to hold scientists and researchers accountable for both the short term and the long term effects of their work, regardless of how interesting and creative it is. And, as Michael Sandel noted, it does serve to "check our drive to dominion."

Certainly not all Jews today hear God's commandment not to pluck a flower on the Sabbath. In proposing Sabbath consciousness as a Jewish hypernorm, I assume very little about Jewish ritual practice. What I do suggest, however, is that nearly everyone who identifies themselves as a Jew, religious or secular, today can hear the echo of Rabbi Heschel's claim that there is an important aspect of life where the goal is "not to control but to share, not to subdue but to be in accord." Those dialogues where this insight is taken for granted and shared by everyone enhance the case for ethical progress in the long run. At least that is the conceit here.

5. Kashrut Consciousness

Kashrut—"keeping kosher"—has been jettisoned as a ritual practice by the majority of Jews. Nevertheless, the notion of a kashrut consciousness, shared by all Jews everywhere, is not an impossible idea.

A Reform rabbi, writing to his congregation about the movement's new perspective on keeping kosher, explained the reason why his movement discarded the kosher laws in the nineteenth century. "Early Reform Rabbis feared that Jews who kept kosher would think that they had already done what God wants of them. Perhaps these kosher Jews would not feel the need to pursue the supreme Jewish imperative to strive for social justice." This concern, however, has now been overcome. Today, this rabbi writes:

> Keeping kosher may actually be a path to heightening our moral consciousness, rather than a hindrance to it. Those who observe the dietary laws may become more sensitive to animals. Some have argued that, if nobody ate meat, and we therefore did not feed so much of our grain to livestock, then there would easily be enough food for every man, woman and child on Earth. Others point out the environmental problems caused by raising animals for food. Many have suggested that veal be declared non-kosher, because of the essentially inhumane way in which calves are raised for consumption as veal. Based on these ideals, some Jews have adopted various forms of vegetarianism as a way of working toward messianic redemption, while also observing the fundamental principles of the Jewish dietary laws. (downloaded on July 29, 2010 from http://www.beth-elsa.org/be_s0119a.htm)

I would like to suggest that while a heightened sensitivity to the needs of animals is certainly at important part of kashrut consciousness, the concept is even more expansive than this.

Rabbi David Teutsch, a past president of the Reconstructionist Rabbinical College, has recently noted that an increased sensitivity to kashrut and kashrut observance serves to (1) strengthen identification with the Jewish people, (2) creates a sensitivity to the ethical issues surrounding food, and (3) helps to cultivate an attitude of gratitude and responsibility for the food we eat (Teutsch, 2000).

Rabbi Arthur Waskow, director of the Shalom Center, has been one of the strongest supporters of a renewed and dramatically expanded kashrut consciousness in Judaism. He has written eloquently about the link between the traditional concept of kashrut and the need to protect the environment:

> What can we learn by renewing the ancient [Torah] text? For shepherds and farmers, food was what they ate from the earth. For us, it is also coal, oil, electric power, paper, plastics, that we take from the earth. For shepherds and farmers, kashrut was the way of guiding their eating toward holiness. For us, eco-kashrut should do the same.
>
> We should ask: Is it eco-kosher to eat vegetables and fruit that have been grown by drenching the soil with insecticides? Is it eco-kosher to drink Shabbat Kiddush wine from non-biodegradable plastic cups? Is it eco-kosher to use 100 percent unrecycled office paper and newsprint in our homes, our synagogues, our community newspapers? Might it be eco-kosher to insist on 10 percent recycled paper this year, 30 percent in two years, and 80 percent in five years?
>
> Is it eco-kosher to destroy great forests, to ignore insulating our homes, synagogues, and nursing homes, to become addicted to automobiles so that we drunkenly pour carbon dioxide into the atmosphere, there to accelerate the heating of our globe?
>
> We can light a blaze to consume the earth. Or we can make a holy altar of our lives, to light up the spark of God in every human and in every species. (Waskow, 2010)

One does not necessarily have to agree with Waskow's expansive understanding of the implications of a kosher consciousness. In suggesting that kosher consciousness is a Jewish hypernorm, I am suggesting, more modestly, that in Judaism consumption has been traditionally understood as more than a matter of private conscience. Through the observance of the dietary laws the Jewish people have aspired to elevate consumption into a holy and meaningful activity, beyond fulfilling basic nutritional needs. From a Jewish perspective, *consumption has been and is today always considered a social activity*. This does not mean that we need to reduce consumption to subsistence levels as some extremists might argue, but it does mean that we should become more aware of both the costs and the benefits of consumption (for an extensive and rigorous discussion on this topic from the perspective of a social scientist see Csikszentmihalyi, 2000). Further, framing consumption as a social activity entails responsibility and accountability to all of those parties affected by one's consumption decisions.

Is Jewish ethical progress possible? The creation of a new kind of "kosher" certification is evidence that the answer to this question is an emphatic yes, at least on occasion. Here is how the newly established Magen Tzedek organization describes its mission:

> Founded on the principle that we are what we eat, Magen Tzedek is an ethical seal signifying that kosher food has been prepared with the highest degree of integrity. Products carrying the Magen Tzedek seal reflect the highest standard on a variety of important issues: employee wages and benefits, health and safety, animal welfare, corporate transparency and environmental impact.
>
> A concept that grows more relevant with every passing day, Magen Tzedek demonstrates that ritual and ethical commandments have an equal place at our tables. (downloaded on July 1, 2010 from http://magentzedek.org/)

The Magen Tzedek seal has not been designed to replace the traditional ritual kashrut certification, but it has been designed to extend kashrut consciousness beyond its historical borders. Interestingly, and importantly for the Jewish people as a whole, the Orthodox Union (OU), the largest kosher certifying agency in the world, is on the record as stating that it will allow its own OU symbol to appear alongside the newly created Magen Tzedek seal, despite its associations with the Conservative movement (Oppenheim, 2010).

Historically, the Reform movement has been concerned that more ritual observance means less ethical responsibility. There has been a reciprocal worry among more traditional Jews that an increased focus on ethical responsibility leads to less scrupulous ritual observance. The emergence of both a powerfully felt kashrut consciousness and Sabbath consciousness across the denominations (and potentially even among secular Jews) has demonstrated that, in fact, both of these propositions are false. Ritual observance can and does lead to a heightened sense of ethical awareness, and an increased sensitivity to ethical responsibility can and does lead to an increase in religious observance. Rabbi Morris Allen, program director for Magen Tzedek writes, "We need to be in a world where we can say that keeping kosher is the way in which I demonstrate not only a concern for my relationship to God and Torah but the Jewish concern for our relationship to the world in which we live." (downloaded on July 1, 2010 from http://rabbimorrisallen2.blogspot.com). Ritual and ethical language are not at war with one another, but ritual and ethical language can be and often are mutually reinforcing.

6. All Human Beings Are Created Equal in the Divine Image

A hypernorm is not like the piercing, intermittent light of a laser, cutting through hard metals, but it is like the diffuse, continuous light of the sun, warming our planet, a source of energy and life. "God created humankind in His own image, in the image of God he created them, male and female He created them" (Genesis 1:27). To this day, we continue to debate the meaning and significance of this verse in our daily lives.

In the Jewish tradition, one of the main *human values* understood to be inherent in this idea is the aspiration of *kavod habriyot* variously, translated as individual honor or human dignity. "The Hebrew word *kavod* is the most significant word in the Talmud to express the most desirable of relations of mutual respect for the dignity of one's fellow. It is employed in every aspect of that relationship, both for the respect which is due from the inferior to the superior, but also, and more significantly, for the concept of the respect and consideration which one should have for one's equal, for mankind as such" (downloaded on July 1, 2010 from www.Jewishvirtuallibrary.org).

Rabbi Jonathan Sacks argues that *kavod habriyot* is central to the Jewish concept of equality. He writes:

> Judaism represents a highly distinctive approach to the idea of equality, namely that it is best served not by equality of income or wealth, nor even of opportunity. Nor is it sufficient that we have equal standing before God at times of prayer, and before the law in cases of dispute. A society must insure equal dignity, the Hebrew phrase is *kavod habriyot,* human honor to each of its members. (2005, p. 39)

If Rabbi Sacks is correct, as I believe he is, it follows that those members of society who are at its margins, and who are viewed as second class citizens, have an ethical *right* to invoke *kavod habriyot* in order to awaken their society to insure that they are treated with equal dignity and honor. In turn, Jewish leaders, and the community at large, possess an obligation to respond to such a request. In many cases, perhaps even most, leaders and others may choose to simply ignore the marginalized group. The felt power of an authentic Jewish hypernorm like *kavod habriyot*, however, makes this strategy untenable and unlikely to work over time. Like the light of the sun, *kavod habriyot* energizes those on the periphery, wishing to gain a degree of respect to which by virtue of their humanity alone they are already entitled. Some Jewish leaders may explicitly defend the status quo by stating that those individuals making a claim in the name of *kavod habriyot* are simply mistaken for one reason or another. But, if reasons are provided, there is the possibility for a real dialogue, a give and take even among those who strongly disagree with one another, which will potentially clarify the issues at stake and lead to moral progress over time.

Of course, it is not just the existence of hypernorms that immediately resolves long-standing injustices. More likely, it is the human contacts and interactions made possible, in part, by the hypernorms that help to provoke new thinking and alternative frames. "At some point, as people meet each other and realize that the Other is a human being whose difference is nothing to fear, a critical mass, usually a healthy minority and not yet the majority, pushes through the change..." (Kula, 2010). Invoking hypernorms does not guarantee progress, but it does provide a plausible mechanism to jumpstart a conversation that may lead eventually to progress and development.

A timely example of this is has been the recent give and take between Orthodox Jewish gays and a group of Modern Orthodox Rabbis and educators. In December of 2009, a panel discussion on the experiences of being gay in the Orthodox community took place at Yeshiva University in New York City. The discussion was attended by about 700 people while more than a 100 were turned away at the door. Openly gay students and alumni from Yeshiva University took part in the conversation, which was moderated by Yeshiva University administrators. The focus of the evening was on personal stories and not on Jewish legal issues.

After the event, Rabbi Steven Greenberg an openly gay Orthodox Rabbi, ordained at Yeshiva University's Rabbinical Program, and a senior Teaching Fellow at the National Jewish Center for Learning and Leadership, stated that this was the first time that an Orthodox Jewish institution was willing to listen to the stories and difficulties faced by gay Orthodox Jews in a public forum. According to Rabbi Greenberg, the next step in the conversation is to discuss how the "*halacha* (Jewish law) can incorporate the reality of Jewish homosexuals" who wish to maintain and deepen their ties to the Jewish community and who want to continue to participate in Jewish ritual observances. Reactions to this event within the Orthodox community were mixed, with nuanced opinions and strong emotions felt and expressed by many.

People meet each other and come to see that the Other is a human being. Just about a half a year later, a group of about 60 Modern Orthodox Rabbis and educators have issued a "Statement of Principles on the Place of Jews with a Homosexual Orientation in Our Community." This statement is one of the most tolerant documents toward gays ever published in the Orthodox world. While reiterating the prohibition of homosexual acts, the principles state that Jewish law "does not prohibit orientation or feelings of same-sex attraction, and nothing in the Torah devalues the human beings who struggle with them." Further, the principles also note that "various homosexual acts" are categorized in Jewish law "with different degrees of severity and opprobrium."

The principles leave the decision to be open about one's sexual orientation to the individual and see no prohibition in publicly acknowledging one's homosexuality. Importantly, the document specifies in clear and unambiguous language that:

> Jews with homosexual orientations or same sex-attractions should be welcomed as full members of the synagogue and school community. As appropriate with regard to gender and lineage, they should participate and count ritually, be eligible for ritual synagogue honors, and generally be treated in the same fashion and under the same halakhic and hashkafic [philosophic] framework as any other member of the synagogue they join.

In addition, it is up to each synagogue, together with its rabbi, to determine whether or not "openly practicing homosexuals" should be accepted as members. Synagogue standards must be applied fairly and objectively to all "open violators of *halakha*." Although the document does not say so explicitly, this last phrase clearly implies that *if* a synagogue has non-Sabbath observant members *it must* allow for the possibility of openly practicing homosexuals to become members. Further, the principles do not rule out the possibility, under certain circumstances, of openly gay members leading religious services, even on the High Holidays.

In Modern Orthodox circles, this statement reflects a giant step forward. Obviously not all Modern Orthodox Rabbis have signed this document, and certainly few Orthodox rabbis to the right of Modern Orthodoxy have been willing to sign it. Nevertheless, a real dialogue has finally broken out in the Orthodox world in which rabbis, educators, lay leaders, and openly gay Orthodox Jews are participating fully.

Tellingly, the first of the 12 principles explicitly invokes a Jewish hypernorm. "All human beings are created in the image of God and deserve to be treated with dignity and respect (*kevod haberiyot*)." This principle can and is being used to evaluate the local norms of individual Jewish communities as a kind of yardstick. "Embarrassing, harassing or demeaning someone with a homosexual orientation or same-sex attraction is a violation of Torah prohibitions that embody the deepest values of Judaism." There is a new understanding of what toleration implies in the Modern Orthodox world. And, while it is clearly something new, it is, in the end, *merely* an application of a piece of ancient wisdom, deeply grounded in the Jewish tradition.

Do these principles go far enough? Or, are the principles themselves subject to *additional* interpretation? Have the rabbis and educators who have signed this document spoken once and for all? In light of a Jewish hypernorm, like the call for universal human dignity, it is impossible to answer these kinds of questions with certainty. Nevertheless, I believe that it is the case that *kavod habriyot* represents even more than a demand for mere toleration, as the specifics of these principles call for, although toleration is a necessary first step.

Rabbi Sacks insists that, according to Judaism, a society must insure *equal* dignity to each of its members. With this document, are we there yet? Let us use our moral imagination to feel what it might be like to be taught over and over again that your sexuality is deeply flawed through no fault of your own. Let us imagine what it is like to be told that your community will not recognize or accept the one personal relationship in your life that most defines who you are as a person. Imagine being told that you can be a member of a synagogue as long as there are already members of the synagogue who break the Sabbath, who do not keep kosher, or who violate the Torah in some other way. What does it feel like to be told that unless everyone in your synagogue accepts your sexual orientation you cannot lead religious services?

Beyond toleration is a pluralism that recognizes that everyone possess part of a larger truth. Beyond toleration is an acknowledgement by the majority that what it takes as self-evidently true and beyond doubt, may in fact be wrong.

The last paragraph of the statement of principles introduces three additional Jewish "qualities of being..." We aspire, we are told, to be merciful (*rahamanim*), modest (*bayshanim*), and to engage in acts of loving-kindness (*gomelei hasadim*). Mercy, modesty, and acts of loving-kindness are all human qualities that necessarily challenge us to take the next step beyond the status quo. These are the qualities of being that prod us on beyond toleration and lead us to embrace an even deeper level of *kavod habriyot,* where the distance between us and them is reduced still further not just by changing them but by changing ourselves, as well. This is not meant as a criticism of the statement of principles. The point is that this document, interpreted at its best, is designed not as a still-life of a final resting place, but as a dynamic set of principles to guide us along on a new path toward new relational modes.

AKIVA, YOU HAVE CONSOLED US!
AKIVA, YOU HAVE CONSOLED US!

The six hypernorms identified and discussed above are only some of the potential candidates. Other Jewish hypernorms might include such deep Jewish values as (1) providing universal education to all Jewish children, even those with severe learning disabilities and other kinds of problems ("teach them to your children, talking about them when you sit at home and when you walk along the road, when you lie down and when you get up" (Deuteronomy 11:19)), (2) seeking justice ("justice and only justice you shall pursue" [Deuteronomy 16:20]), (3) giving charity ("you shall freely open your hand to your brother, to your needy and poor in your land" (Deuteronomy 15:11)), and (4) repairing the world (*tikkun olam).*

To these last four, I will add only one more Jewish hypernorm, especially relevant here. It is based on the following story told in the Talmud about Rabbi Akiva's response to the destruction of Jerusalem and the holy Temple:

> It happened that Rabban Gamliel, Rabbi Elazar ben Azaria, Rabbi Joshua, and Rabbi Akiva went up to Jerusalem. When they reached Mt. Scopus, they tore their garments. When they reached the Temple Mount, they saw a fox emerging from the place of the Holy of Holies. The others started weeping; Rabbi Akiva laughed.
>
> Said they to him: "Why are you laughing?"
>
> Said he to them: "Why are you weeping?"
>
> Said they to him: "A place [so holy] that it is said of it, 'the stranger that approaches it shall die,' and now foxes traverse it, and we should not weep?"
>
> Said he to them: "That is why I laugh. For it is written, 'I shall have bear witness for Me faithful witnesses—Uriah the Priest and Zechariah the son of Jeberechiah.' Now what is the connection between Uriah and Zechariah? Uriah was [in the time of] the First Temple, and Zechariah was [in the time of] the Second Temple! But the Torah makes Zechariah's prophecy dependent upon Uriah's prophecy. With Uriah, it is written: 'Therefore, because of you, Zion shall be plowed as a field;' [Jerusalem shall become heaps, and the Temple Mount like the high places of a forest.] With Zechariah it is written, 'Old men and women shall yet sit in the streets of Jerusalem.'
>
> "As long as Uriah's prophecy had not been fulfilled, I feared that Zechariah's prophecy may not be fulfilled either. But now that Uriah's prophecy has been fulfilled, it is certain that Zechariah's prophecy will be fulfilled."
>
> With these words they replied to him: "Akiva, you have consoled us! Akiva, you have consoled us!" (Makkot 24b)

Rabbi Akiva is saddened by the sight of the destroyed Temple from Mt. Scopus. This is indicated in the story by the fact that he, too, tears his garment as the traditional Jewish sign of mourning requires. But, unlike his colleagues who started weeping upon seeing a fox emerging from the place of the Holy of Holies, Rabbi Akiva begins to laugh.

Events do not interpret themselves, and the meaning of a fox, of all animals, emerging from the Holy of Holies, of all places, at precisely this moment in time, is inherently ambiguous. Rabban Gamliel, Rabbi Elazar ben Azaria, and Rabbi Joshua choose to see the fox as a dark and negative omen. "'The stranger that approaches it shall die,' and now foxes traverse it, and we should not weep?" they rhetorically ask.

Rabbi Akiva, however, interprets the identical fox in positive terms. "Now that Uriah's prophecy has been fulfilled, it is certain that Zechariah's prophecy will be fulfilled." The path is now clear, according to Rabbi Akiva's understanding, for that future time when "old men and women shall yet sit in the streets of Jerusalem." Akiva's optimism is a faith grounded in the possibility of progress. I hear his laughter upon seeing the sly fox, not as a belly laugh, but as wry, wise, and subtle expression of confidence in a better future.

It is as if Rabbi Akiva is letting his friends (and us) in on a profound secret. The contemporary situation, regardless of when we live and what we may be reading about in the newspapers, is always precarious and uncertain. Rabbi Akiva may have been the first to teach us—but certainly not the last—a new potential hypernorm. As Jews we must make the conscious choice to approach our world with a touch of sadness, a sense of humor, an eye for irony, and a deep faith in the possibility of progress.

It is with this faith in mind that I can look at my children, students, and the next generation with a straight face and tell them that although I lack Rabbi Akiva's supreme confidence in the certainty of his prediction, I do not for a moment think that this is a world where the Abramoffs, Madoffs, Troppers, Kassins, Elons, and Rubashkins, will have the last word. These *are* the best of times and these *are* the worst of times. It is our collective choice, as it has always been, what we decide to make of them.

NOTE

1. "On January 13, [2009] the New York State Board of Regents approved the application for the Hebrew Language Academy Charter School, a school that would teach the Hebrew language and aspects of Jewish culture, largely with public funds. Michael Steinhardt, a former hedge fund manager who has championed a number of high-profile Jewish causes, funded the application." (Weiss, 2009).

REFERENCES

Buber, Martin, *I and Thou* (New York: Charles Scribner's Sons, 1958).
Csikszentmihalyi, Mihaly, "The Costs and Benefits of Consuming," *Journal of Consumer Research*, 2000, Vol. 27, pp. 267–272.
Donaldson, Thomas, and Dunfee, Thomas, *Ties That Bind: A Social Contracts Approach to Business Ethics* (Boston: Harvard Business School Press, 1999).
Glover, Jonathan, *Humanity: A Moral History of the Twentieth Century* (New Haven: Yale University Press, 1999).
Greenberg, Irving, *For the Sake of Heaven and Earth: The New Encounter between Judaism and Christianity* (Philadelphia: The Jewish Publication Society, 2004).
Greenberg, Irving, "Theology After the Shoah: The Transformation of the Core Paradigm," *Modern Judaism*, 2006, Vol. 26, No 3, pp. 213–239.

Guinlock, James, Editor, *The Moral Writings of John Dewey* (Amherst, NY: Prometheus Books, 1994).

Hartman, David, *A Heart of Many Rooms: Celebrating the Many Voices within Judaism* (Woodstock, VT, Jewish Lights Publishing, 1999).

Hartman, Edwin, "Principles and Hypernorms," Journal *of Business Ethics*, 2009, Vol. 88, pp. 707–716.

Herberg, Will, *Judaism and Modern Man* (Philadelphia: Jewish Publication Society, 1959).

Heschel, Abraham Joshua, *The Sabbath: Its Meaning for Modern Man* (New York: Farrar, Straus and Giroux, 1951).

Kellner, Menachem, *Maimonides on the "Decline of the Generations" and the Nature of Rabbinic Authority* (Albany: State University of New York: 1996).

Kula, Irwin, "Leviticus loses: The Inevitability of Equal Rights for Homosexuals," downloaded on July 1, 2010 from www.huffingtonpost.com.

Lamm, Norman, *Torah Umadda: The Encounter of Religious Learning and Wordly Knowledge in the Jewish Tradition* (Northvale, NJ: Jason Aronson Inc., 1990).

Moscowitz, Shaindel, "The Role of the Home," downloaded on July 20, 2010 from http://www.breslev.co.il/articles/family/children_and_education/the_role_of_the_home.aspx?id=12646&language=english.

Nussbaum, Martha, "On Moral Progress: A Response to Rorty," *The University of Chicago Law Review,* 200x, Vol. 74, pp. 939–960.

Oppenheim, Rivka, "Ethical Kosher Seal Nearing Marketplace for Conservative Jews," *The Jewish Week* (May 27, 2010).

Rorty, Richard, "Is Philosophy Relevant to Applied Ethics?" *Business Ethics Quarterly*, 2006, Vol. 16, No. 3, pp. 369–380.

Sacks, Jonathan, *To Heal a Fractured World: The Ethics of Responsibility* (New York: Schocken Books, 2005).

Sandel, Michael J. *Public Philosophy: Essays on Morality and Politics* (Cambridge: Harvard University Press, 2005).

Teutsch, David A. *A Guide to Jewish Practice: Introduction, Attitudes, Values and Beliefs, Kashrut: The Jewish Dietary Laws* (Wyncote, PA: RRC Press, 2000).

Walzer, Michael, *Spheres of Justice: A Defense of Pluralism and Equality* (New York: Basic Books, 1983).

Walzer, Michael, *Exodus and Revolution* (New York: Basic Books, 1985).

Walzer, Michael, *Interpretation and Social Criticism (*Cambridge, MA: Harvard University Press, 1987).

Walzer, Michael, *Moral Argument at Home and Abroad* (Notre Dame: University of Notre Dame Press, 1994).

Waskow, Arthur O., "Eco-Kashrut: Environmental Standards for What and How We Eat," downloaded on July 1, 2010 from myjewishlearning.com/practices/Ritual/Kashrut_Dietary_Laws

Weiss, Anthony, "N.Y. Okays Public School With Hebrew Focus: Philanthropists Lay Plans for National Charter Network," *Jewish Daily Forward* (January 23, 2009).

Index

Aaron, 5–6, 39, 48, 56
Abba Sikrah, 59
Abbaye, 74
Abraham, xi, xii, 23, 73, 121, 141–142
Abramoff, Jack, 14, 163, 165, 167–168, 176, 198
Abtalion, 141
accountability, 21, 38, 74, 79, 113, 158–159, 180, 184, 186, 192
Ackerman, Bruce, 144, 145
Adam and Eve, 27, 161
Adler, Rachel, 11, 24
Agriproccesors, 71, 76–79, 88, 119, 125–130, 132–134, 164
Agudas Yisroel, 88
Akiva, 8, 43, 53, 171–172, 196–198
Allen, Rabbi Morris, 129, 192
Allen, Woody, 4, 167
Alstott, Anne, 144, 145
Amalek, 49
Amir, Yigal, 75–76, 117
Amos, 44
Annie Hall, 4
anti-Semitism, 110–112, 165, 173
Ariel, Rabbi Yisrael, 20
Aron, Lewis, 24

Badaracco, Joseph, 4, 24
Bal, Mieke, 11, 24
Bar Illan University, 34
Bar Kochba, 43
Bateson, Gregory, 161
Bathsheba, 102

Ben & Jerry's, 157
Ben Azzai, 8, 10
Ben Haim, Rabbi Eliahu, 109, 112, 164
Benhabib, Selya, 99, 103
Berger, Michael, 167
Berkowitz, Rabbi Eliezer, 28, 46, 71, 73
Bibi, Rabbi David, 112–113
Birnbaum, Philip, 12, 14, 24, 54, 65, 160, 161
Bloom, Stephen, 127
Boaz, 12–14
Boesky, Ivan, 14
Bonder, Rabbi Nilton, 6, 8, 19, 24, 120, 135, 149, 155, 159, 161
Boulding, Kenneth, 156, 161
Boyarin, Daniel, 11, 24
Brecht, Bertolt, 28
Buber, Martin, xiv, 97, 103, 153, 159, 179, 198
Buchholz, Rogene, 100, 103

Caillois, Roger, 161
Callahan, David, 93, 103
capital punishment, 43, 155
Caro, Rabbi Yosef, 170
Carse, James, 92, 98–100, 103, 152, 157, 159, 161
Carter, Stephen, 137, 145
Cattle Buyers Weekly, 127
Centrist Orthodoxy, 69–71
chaos, xii, 124
chesed (kindness), 14, 141–142

Chofetz Chayim, 85, 89
Choose life, 18, 40, 45
choseness, 29, 35
Cohen, Hermann, 123
compromise, xiii, 47–65, 75, 105, 117, 120, 133, 137
Consumption tax, 144
covenantal leadership, 57
Csikszentmihalyi, Mihaly, 150, 161, 192, 198

deeds of lovingkindness, 59–61
Defining moment, 59
democracy, 4, 75–76, 8587, 117, 137–139, 144, 173
Dennett, Daniel, 106, 116, 117
Derech eretz, 72
Dersowitz, Alan, xiv
Des Moines Register, 129
Dewey, John, 32, 46, 101, 103, 134, 135, 185, 186
dialogue, xii, xiii, 1, 4, 11, 16, 17, 21–23, 28, 30, 33, 34, 41, 43, 57, 63, 64, 72, 74, 75, 79, 80, 85–88, 92, 93, 98, 99, 101, 102, 105–107, 110, 112, 115, 116, 121, 132, 150, 155, 166, 179, 182, 185, 190, 193, 195
Dickens, Charles, 115
Dickinson, Emily, 22
Donaldson, Thomas, 183, 198
Dunfee, Thomas, 183, 198
Dunlap, Al, 123
Dwek, Rabbi Isaac, 109, 114
Dwek, Solomon, 109, 113, 114

Ecclesiastes, 149, 160
eco-kashrut, 191
Eigen, Michael, 8, 24, 34, 42, 44, 45, 46
Eight levels of charity, 143
Elon, Mordechai, 164–165, 167, 168, 176, 198
Emerson, Ralph Waldo, 10, 93, 103
Emperor's Club VIP, 95
Empire, 129
emunah (faith), 18
Esau, 15
Esbjorn-Hargens, Sean, 150, 156, 162
Eternal Jewish Family, 164
ethics and play, xiv, 2–5, 149–161
Ezekiel, 51

Feuerstein, Aaron, 123–125, 133, 135
financial fraud, 76, 128, 164
Fish, Mordechai, 164
Flax, Jane, 157, 161
Forbes Magazine, 125
foreign workers, 7, 128, 132, 139
forgiveness, 3, 48, 64, 100, 179
Forward, 128, 130, 133
Frank, Robert, 144, 145
Freud, Sigmund, 94
Friedlander, Dr. Lester, 128
Friedman, Rabbi Moshe Manis, 42–43
Fromm, Eric, 9

Garrison, Jim, 101, 103, 120, 134, 135
gay rights, 70, 74, 173
Ghent, Emmanuel, 10, 24, 37–38, 46
Glover, Jonathan, 174, 198
Goldin, Judah, 62, 142
Gordon, Gwen, 150, 156, 162
Gorenberg, Gershim, 115, 117
Goya, Fransico, 105, 117
Green, Arthur, 55
Greenberg, Blu, 11, 24
Greenberg, Rabbi Irving, 28, 45, 46, 177–182, 185, 187, 198
Greenberg, Rabbi Stephen, 194
Grossman, David, 17, 24

Halakhah (Jewish Law), 64, 67–69, 71–76, 78, 188, 195
Harlop, Rabbi Yaacov Moshe, 50–52, 56, 61–62
Hartman, Ed, 183–185, 199

Hartman, Rabbi David, 36–37, 45, 46, 73, 75, 82, 117, 135, 139–140, 145, 188–189, 199
healthcare, 74, 142, 173
Hebrew Language Academy Charter School, 198
Hebrew National, 129
Hechser Tzedek, 129
Herberg, Will, 187, 199
Herman Miller, 157
Herzfeld, Rabbi Shmuel, 129
Heschel, Rabbi Abraham Joshua, 53, 65, 72, 82, 103, 189–190, 199
Hillel, xvii, 58, 96, 119, 121, 140–141
Hofstadter, Douglas, 54, 65
Holocaust *(Shoah)*, 174, 177–178, 180–181, 187
Hosea, 59
human rights, 173, 183
hypernorms, 182–198

identity, 7, 15, 16–17, 19, 32, 38, 51, 106, 154, 179, 181
income inequality, 138, 142
inside information, 15
Isaac, 15
Isaacs, William, 98
Isaiah, 44

Jacob, 15, 176, 178
Jacobs, Rabbi Louis, 53, 65
James, William, 32, 163
Jensen and Meckling, 2, 24, 25
Jerusalem Post, 75, 117, 138
Jewish Press, 111, 116
Jewish Principles and Ethical Guidelines (JPEG), 76–79
Job, 52–53, 141–142
Jubilee, 138–139, 144

Kagan, Rabbi Israel Meir HaCohen, 85
Kakun, Yitzhak, 110
Kant, Immanuel, 93
kashrut, 71, 76–79, 128, 130, 190–192

Kassin, Rabbi Saul, 109, 112, 164–165, 167–168, 176
Kavod Habriyot (human dignity), 193, 195–196
Kegan, Robert, 98, 103, 156, 162
Kellner, Menachem, 167–168, 170–172
Kessef Mishnah, 178
K'hal Adath Jehurum, 129
King David, 12, 13, 42, 102, 169
King, Martin Luther, 103
Korah, 5–7
Kristeva, Julia, 120, 135
Kula, Rabbi Irwin, 8, 16, 25, 54, 65, 121, 135, 194, 199

Lahey, 156, 162
Lahey, Lisa Laskow, 156, 162
Lamm, Rabbi Norman, 34, 45, 46, 141, 143, 145, 170, 172, 199
lashon hara (slander), xiii, 85–89
Lebowitz, Nechama, 139
Lekh lekha (go forth), 23
Lerner, Michael, 144, 145
Levine, Aaron, 103, 144, 145
Lichtenstein, Rabbi Aharon, 67–82
lifnim mishurat hadin (beyond the letter of the law), 67–69, 73–74
Lincoln, Abraham, 95–96, 102
Long Island Jewish Star, 112
loving the stranger, xiii, 11, 14, 45, 119–121, 123, 125, 133–134, 173
Luzzato, Rabbi Chaim, 167–168, 170–171, 174

Madoff, Bernard, xiv-xvii, 3, 14, 163, 165, 167, 168, 176, 198
Magen Tzedek, 192
Maharal, 168
Maimonides, xi, 32, 35, 36, 37, 40, 45, 53, 64, 65, 67, 113, 122, 143–144, 170–171, 174–175, 178, 187
Malden Mills, 123–124, 133
March, James, 152–153, 157–162

Margalit, Avishai, 47–49, 52, 58, 61–63, 65
Marra, Ralph J., 109
Meir, Rabbi Asher, 79
Mercaz HaRav yeshiva, 50
Mesillat Yesharim (Path of the Just), 167
Messiah or messianism, 13–14, 29, 30, 42–45, 62, 171–172, 174, 178, 181, 187, 190
Micah, 44
Mishnah Torah, 178
MIT, xiv
Mitchell, Stephen, 8–10, 17, 24, 25, 96, 103
mitzvot, 36, 68, 70, 139
Modern Orthodoxy, 71–72, 74, 78
money laundering, xiii, 76, 105, 108–110, 117, 164
moral capital, 44, 96, 113, 166
moral imagination, 105, 134, 173, 180, 196
moser (traitor or informant), 113, 117
Moses, 5, 6, 7, 18, 19, 35, 39, 40, 49, 55–58, 67, 78, 171–172

Naamah, 29–30, 45
Nachmanovich, Stephen, 7, 25
Nachson ben Aminadab, 18–20
Nadab and Abihu, 39–40
Nahmanides, 28, 45
Nahum, Rabbi Edmund, 109, 112, 164
Naomi, 12–13
Nathan, 102
National Council of Young Israel, 134
National Jewish Center for Learning and Leadership, 194
Nehring, Cristina, 9, 25
nepotism, 183
Netziv, 114
New York State Board of Regents, 198
New York Times, 35, 88, 95, 127, 130, 131
Ninth of Av, 31–33
nostalgia, 29, 31–32, 41, 43–45

Nussbaum, Martha, 173, 199

Orand, Shannon, 164
Orthodox Union, 77–78, 88, 128–129, 131, 192
Ouderkirk, Father Floyd Paul, 133

Passover, 60, 142, 175
Persico, Carmine, 163
PETA, 127–128, 130–131
Pharaoh, 18, 19, 121
Phillips, Adam, 1, 11, 13–15, 18, 22–23, 25
Piaget, Jean, 9, 153
Pinchas, 48–53, 56
Plaskow, Judith, 11, 25
pluralism, 17, 75, 117, 137, 179–180, 188, 196
Polartec Fleece, 123
Ponzi Scheme, 2
Popper, Nathaniel, 126–127
Porritt, 157, 162
Postville, Iowa, 76, 126–127, 129

Quinn, Robert, 101, 103

Rabban Gamliel, 197
Rabban Shimon ben Gamliel, 140
Rabbi Bunam, 97
Rabbi Elazar ben Azariah, 197
Rabbi Eliezer ben Azariah, 72
Rabbi Hanina ben Dosa, 167
Rabbi Joshua, 197
Rabbi Mordecai, 97–98
Rabbi Yannai, 94–95
Rabbi Yehuda, 18
Rabbi Yochanan ben Zakkai, 43, 58–62, 64
Rabbincal Council of America, 71, 88, 129, 166
Rabin, Yitzhak, 75–76, 117
racism, 36, 173
Rackman, Rabbi Emanuel, 34, 46, 72, 82
Raful, Rabbi Ezra, 128

Rashi, 15, 41, 140, 170
rational model (of decision-making), 2, 158, 160
Reconsturctionist Rabbincal College, 191
Repentance, xi, 48, 64, 179
Riskin, Rabbi Shlomo, 57, 65, 135
Rollin, Dr. Bernard, 128
Rorty, Richard, 92, 103, 154–155, 162, 173, 199
Rosen, Rabbi David, 128
Rosenthal, Sandra, 100, 103
Ross, Tamar, 11, 25
Roth, Philip, 41, 46
Rothenberg, Naftali, 40, 46
Rubashkin, Aaron, 76, 125–126, 131–132
Rubashkin, Moshe, 126, 130
Rubashkin, Shalom, 76, 126–134, 164
Ruth, 12–14

Sabbath conciousness, 139, 188–190, 192
Sabbatical laws, 139–140
Sack, Rabbi Jonathan, 119, 122, 135, 193, 196, 199
Sacred messiness, 16, 89, 121
Safran, Rabbi Avi, 130
Samson and Delilah, 30
Samuel, 7, 13, 49–53, 56, 102
Samuel, 7, 13, 49–53, 56, 102
Sandel, Michael J., 189–190, 199
Sarasvathy, Saras, 125, 135
Saul, 13, 49–51
Schwartz, Lavel, 164
sexual abuse, 71, 87, 174
Shabbatai Zevi, 44
Shakespeare, Wiliam, 27
Shalom Center, 191
Sharansky, Natan, 16–18, 22, 25
Shema Prayer, 8, 86
Shemaya, 141
Shir Ha-Shirim, 52–53
Shulkhan Aruch, 170
Singer, Peter, 92

slavery, 19, 173
Soloveitchik, Rabbi Joseph, 29–31, 38, 46, 64
Spitzer, Eliot, 14, 91, 94–97, 102
Springstein, Bruce, 32
Stakeholder Society, 144
Starr, Karen, 11, 25, 38, 46, 116, 117
Steinhardt, Michael, 198
strange loop, 54
Strenger, Carolo, 107–108, 110–111, 114–115, 117
Submission, 29, 37–40, 43–45, 100, 184
sustainability, 86, 143, 157–158
Sutton-Smith, 161, 162
Swift, Jonathan, 23

Tamar, 30
Taylor, Mark, 16, 54
Telushkin, Joseph, 94, 104
Temple Institute, 20–21
Teutsch, Rabbi David, 191, 199
The Body Shop, 157
Thoreau, Henry David, 102
Tianmen Square, 103
tikkun olam, 169, 196
Time Magazine, 123
Titmus, Richard, 22
tochacha(moral rebuke), 85
Tom's of Maine, 157
Torbert, Bill, 154, 162
Transformation, xi, 10, 38, 150
triple-bottom line, 79, 157
Troppper, Rabbi Leib, 164–165, 167, 168, 176, 198
Twersky, Isadore, 141, 144
tzedakah(charity), 143–144

Unger, Roberto Mangabeira, 119, 120, 135
Uri L'zedek, 129
Uriah, 102
Uriah the Priest, 197
Uriah the Priest, 197
utility maximization, 2, 24, 25

utopia or utopianism, 29, 163, 178

Voltaire, 33

walk humbly before God, 45
Wall Street, xiv, 94
Walzer, Michael, 21, 25, 91, 104, 153, 162, 174–176, 199
Waskow, Rabbi Arthur, 191, 199
wealth inequalities, xiii, 86, 137
Weinreb, Rabbi Zvi, 128
Winnicott, D.W., 150, 162
Women of the wall, 36
Wurzburger, Rabbi Walter, 37, 46, 72, 82, 141, 143, 145

Yale University, 99
Yavneh, 43, 59–61
Yehuda Halevi, 37
yeridat hadorot (decline of the generations), 167–170, 172, 175, 178, 181, 187
Yeshiva University, 34, 88, 130, 164, 172, 174, 194
You shall be holy, 16, 54
Youtube, 87

Zechariah, 197
Zelophehad, daughters of, 56
Zornberg, Aviva, ix, 2–5, 7, 12, 13, 15, 16, 17, 23, 25, 134, 135